# Democracy
AND
# Deliberation

# Democracy

## AND

# Deliberation

**DENNIS DAVIS**

BComm LLB (UCT) MPhil (Cantab)
Judge of the High Court of South Africa
Honorary Professor of Law in the University of Cape Town

PUBLISHED BY

**JUTA & CO, LTD**

**1999**

First published 1999


Juta & Co, Ltd 1999
PO Box 14373, Kenwyn 7790

Cover design by Joy Wrench


Typesetting by THE DESIGN HOUSE


ISBN 0 7021 5141 6


Printed and bound in the Republic of South Africa
by The Rustica Press, Ndabeni, Western Cape
D7710

# PREFACE

The nature and role of law has been at the top of the South African jurisprudential hit parade for a long time. During the darkest periods of apartheid, vigorous debate took place over the role of law in a repressive state and whether
there was any room for progressive lawyering in such a context.

After the normalization of political activity in 1990, these debates continued,
albeit within the context of the role of a bill of rights as an instrument for transformation. This book was born out of these intense debates, to some of which I
was privileged to have been a minor participant. A number of the chapters in this
book began life as articles in law journals, although in each case they have been
extensively rewritten to respond to my immediate concern — the smug complacency
and impoverished legal imagination of the legal community and the tenacity of
the hold of that distinctive brand of formalism that fuelled legal scholarship for
the past century.

Viewed in this context, this little work is only a first movement, as it were,
of what I intend will be a larger opus on constitutional law. I had many discussions with Etienne Mureinik, far and away the finest academic public lawyer this
country has produced, about writing a more ambitious work. Without Etienne's
creativity, I have had to scale down both the ambition of this work and that of
the larger project. None the less, I hope that this book will make a small contribution to the debate about the direction of law and the need for transformation
in our legal thinking.

Over the years I have incurred many intellectual debts. For almost the entire
period during which this work was written I was at the Centre for Applied Legal
Studies, University of the Witwatersrand, where I was privileged to work with
some of the finest legal minds this country has produced: John Dugard, Edwin
Cameron, Halton Cheadle, Fink Haysom, Paul Benjamin, Gilbert Marcus, Carole
Lewis, Martin Brassey and Etienne Mureinik were all at Wits when I arrived there
— has there ever been a more talented group of lawyers in one institution in this
country (or beyond)? Later, others joined, including Cathi Albertyn, Stuart Woolman,
John Klaaren, Matthew Chaskalson, Alfred Cockrell and Beth Goldblatt. The many
vigorous debates with these colleagues and friends have influenced much of what
appears in this publication.

The bulk of the writing took place while I was on sabbatical leave. I was fortunate to have been a visiting fellow at University College, London, and able to use the extensive research facilities available to me there. Dean Dawn Oliver and Jeffrey Jowell were most helpful during my stay. Back at the University of Cape Town, Mike Blackman, Danie Visser and Hugh Corder ensured the kind of collegial academic environment that stimulates open debate. The work of Anton Fagan and Denise Meyerson provoked my ideas and confirmed how fortunate I have been, at both Wits and UCT, to surrounded by creative scholars.

Throughout this period of writing I have been unconditionally supported by my family. Claudette has taught me so much about implementing the idea of community within our family; Liat and Joshua about the tension between according to each a district zone of freedom without breaching the concept of equality.

Simon Sephton and Lindsay Norman of Juta have put up with both my delays and the poor quality of my typing without ever appearing to be grumpy. I am very grateful for having had such support from my publisher.

**D M Davis**
*Cape Town, August 1999*

# CONTENTS

# TABLE OF CASES

# INTRODUCTION

*'It is necessary to emphasise that "institution-building" rather than "nation-building" should take precedence in a multi-ethnic society. If institutions that can cope with mediating the conflicts and tensions that arise out of cultural pluralism cannot be strengthened, then no amount of symbolic exhortation will overcome them.'* [1]
*'Where is the song before it is sung?'* [2]

The past ten years have been the constitutional decade, with first a range of eastern European states establishing liberal democratic constitutional regimes and then, in 1994, something that had surely seemed impossible at the commencement of this decade, namely the writing of a democratic constitution for South Africa.

It is beyond the scope of this work to document the history of the constitution-making process, but some reference to the formulation of the Bill of Rights is necessary.

## THE CONSTITUTION-MAKING PROCESS

It seems astonishing that, less than a decade before South Africa held its first free elections, the two main participants in the negotiation process that led up to these elections, the National Party (NP) and the African National Congress (ANC), were both opponents of an entrenched constitution with a bill of rights, although there were signs of interest from the ANC as the Eighties ran their course. [3]

Given the history of the country, it seems remarkable also that it took only slightly more than four years from F W de Klerk's mould-breaking speech in February 1990 until the democratic state was ushered into existence. During that period, however, the road to democracy was subjected to a number of stages, each fraught, many unsuccessful. The Groote Schuur talks, the D F Malan Minute, the Convention for a Democratic South Africa (CODESA) all came and went, until a 'record of understanding' was reached in 1993 and the Multi-party Negotiating Process was born.

---

1   Heribert Adam, Frederik van Zyl Slabbert and Kogila Moodley *Comrades in Business* (1997) at 103.

2   Quoted by Isaiah Berlin 'My Intellectual Path' 1998 *New York Review of Books* (14 May) at 56.

3   In 1988, Albie Sachs produced a lengthy pamphlet analysing the role of a bill of rights for South Africa. Later the ANC published an important set of constitutional guidelines. Sachs' early work was later published in *Protecting Human Rights* (1990).

Its origin was hardly propitious in that the parties could not even agree on a name for the institution. But they had agreed on more important matters, including an interim five-year government of national unity in which all the parties who polled over 5 percent of the total vote cast would be represented proportionally in the cabinet. A Transitional Executive Council (TEC) representing all the negotiating parties would be constituted to oversee the first government prior to the elections. This would ensure fair conditions for all parties in the run-up to the elections. During the five-year term of the interim government, a fully elected Parliament doubling up as a Constitutional Assembly (CA) would write the 'permanent' Constitution which would be based on a set of principles that had been agreed at CODESA before the latter collapsed.

In order to facilitate the process a number of technical advisers were drawn into the process. They were nominated by the participating parties but they were mandated to act as impartial technicians and not negotiators.[4] When the negotiations recommenced in 1993, four main pieces of legislation were urgently required, namely an interim Constitution, a Transitional Executive Council Act, and two pieces of legislation to create the necessary election machinery. There would also be legislation to regulate broadcasting. Two further teams of technicians were appointed, one to consider the need to abolish apartheid legislation and the other to protect those rights which were necessary to conduct free political activity and therefore hold a free election. There was far less clarity as to the content of these two pieces of legislation. To this extent the technicians, who were overwhelmingly drawn from the legal profession, had significant discretion. When it tabled its first report before the negotiating council, the committee on fundamental rights listed some 30 rights which it then classified into three groups: those essential for free elections; those that were desirable, and a third group of optional rights. Taken together, their list represented a comprehensive bill of rights. In the compilation of this list the technical committee drew from a range of comparative precedent as well as the ANC's constitutional guidelines and the reports of the South African Law Commission dealing with 'human and group rights'. However, a careful examination of the committee's report reveals the influence of another document, the Charter for Social Justice, which had been produced by a group of academics from

---

4  Some did advise political parties and hence did have a partial influence, although the practice was
   hardly confined to any one party.

the Western Cape.[5] This was hardly surprising, in that a major author of that work had been Hugh Corder, who was a member of the technical committee, while another, Lourens du Plessis, was also a prominent academic from the Western Cape.[6]

The significance of the Social Charter was twofold: its partial replication in the first report meant that the possibility of a comprehensive bill of rights rather than a transitional document to facilitate free elections had been formally put before the negotiators. In addition, the model followed by the Social Charter became important. The authors of the Social Charter had been hugely influenced by the work of a Canadian academic, David Beatty, who had been spending part of a sabbatical in Cape Town. With almost evangelical zeal, Beatty had argued in favour of a model of balancing the output of the democratic process with constitution-ally entrenched rights as the Canadian courts had interpreted their Charter of Rights and Freedoms in *R v Oakes*.[7] When the first report was tabled—at this stage it was only a classification and prioritization of rights—the major parties react-ed quite differently. The ANC was not in favour of a comprehensive bill of rights. Its constitutional and legal team had drafted a Transition to Democracy Bill in 1992 which contained a number of rights, including freedom from racial and sex-ual discrimination; freedom of expression, thought, conscience, belief and asso-ciation; the right to privacy, particularly the right against arbitrary search and seizure; the right not to be detained without trial; the right to collective bargaining, and the right to respect for dignity. As detailed as this list was, the ANC said that 'the final bill of rights should be adopted by the Constitutional Assembly as part of the final constitution'.[8] The ambivalence of its position was reflected in the rec-ommendation that any existing or future legislation contrary to these rights should be void.[9] In short, the ANC was not against entrenched rights at this stage, but it appeared to favour a mini-bill of rights, leaving the major construction of the document to the final process.

---

5  H Corder et al *A Charter for Social Justice: A Contribution to the South African Bill of Rights Debate* (1992).

6  Du Plessis and Corder subsequently wrote a book dealing with this process — *Understanding South Africa's Bill of Rights* (Juta, 1994) — from which some of this account has been drawn. I have also relied upon my own recollections as a participant in the process, as well as the archived CODESA documents.

7  26 DLR (4th) 200. See also 'David Beatty Talking Heads and the Supremes'. *The Canadian Production of Constitutional Review* (1990).

8  Report to the Negotiating Council 12 May 1993.

9  Ibid.

The NP seized upon this ambiguity. It wanted a written instrument to constrain a majority party in Parliament, which it knew it could not be after 1994. Hence in its submission it argued that an interim bill of rights should not differ substantially from a final bill as 'human rights are not interim or final in nature but universal and inherent'.[10] When those who had spent a lifetime destroying human rights suddenly arrive at this conclusion, it is a safe bet that the ambivalent quality of rights has suddenly been perceived!

Once the comprehensive list of rights had been tabled, the NP were able to push ahead with what, on the surface, was a coherent argument; far more so than the ANC's halfway house. From this point the complete list of rights drawn from the Social Charter became the very source of the interim document. Again, it is important to emphasize that the Social Charter was less important to the agreement on a comprehensive bill of rights and more so to the model which was adopted. Once there had been agreement on a two-stage process, which necessitated the compilation of an interim constitution, the only question which remained in respect of a bill of rights turned on its range, scope and content. It was here that the technicians had an influence and, as a result, South Africa obtained a comprehensive instrument, the foundations of which had been derived from the Canadian Charter of Rights and Freedoms. Upon these foundations, however, was built a comprehensive structure that, in significant part, was the outcome of delicate negotiations. The controversy raged not only during the process but for a long time thereafter as to the meaning of the agreements.

For the purposes of this work one illustration of considerable importance must suffice. There had been considerable debate about the scope of the bill of rights and, in particular, whether it should apply to private relationships. Eventually a compromise was reached. Du Plessis and Corder suggested that the compromise expunged an earlier proposal to give the courts a discretion to extend the application of the chapter to private persons but to provide for a 'seepage' clause (s 35).[11] Halton Cheadle, who was a member of the ad hoc committee on the bill of rights,[12] has argued that the effect of the compromise was to remove the

---

10   Submission to the Negotiating Council by the Minister of Justice M J Coetzee 19 May 1993.

11   Du Plessis and Corder at 110–16.

12   This committee was formed at a late stage in the process when the importance of the work of the technical committee was grasped. Cheadle and Penuell Maduna represented the ANC, Sheila Camerer the NP and Tony Leon the DP.

scope from private relationships and to make all private law the subject of the strictures of the bill.[13]

When it came to writing the final Constitution, the die had been partly cast. In terms of the agreements that had been struck during the negotiations in the predemocratic phase, the final Constitution had to comply with 34 principles. In terms of s 71(2) of the interim Constitution the final text would be of no force and effect unless the Constitutional Court had certified that all the provisions of the new text complied with these 34 principles.[14]

The extensive, ambitious nature of the interim Bill of Rights effectively guaranteed that the final document would be overwritten final Constitution differs from its interim predecessor but these often add to the complexity of the instrument. There is a comprehensive set of socio-economic rights in the 1996 version, the commitment to dignity has been strengthened and the limitation clause has clearly been fashioned upon the approach to the limitation clause set out by Chaskalson P in *S v Makwanyane*.[15] In significant respects the final document reflects the product of the first two years of democracy. Thus s 35(1)*(f)* of the final Constitution purported to alter the interim position with regard to bail and place the onus upon the arrested person to make a case for bail, whereas the interim Constitution had granted a person a right to bail unless the interests of justice require otherwise. The clause dealing with just administrative action includes a provision that national legislation must be introduced to give effect to this right and such legislation must, inter alia, promote an efficient administration—a provision which was inserted in order to be able to qualify the extensive right under the interim Constitution and which had placed a heavy burden on the administration, much to the anguish of those in government.[16]

---

13  Halton Cheadle in D M Davis et al *Fundamental Rights in the New Constitution* (Juta, 1997) at 30–1.

14  In a way these principles were similiar in role to UN Security Council Resolution 435 which was foundational to the drafting of the Namibian constitution. For the outcome of this process in South Africa see *Ex Parte Chairperson of the Constitutional Assembly: In re Certification of the Constitution of the Republic of South Africa* 1996 (4) SA 744 (CC).

15  1995 (3) SA 391 (CC) at para 104, where he set out his understanding of s 33(1) of the interim Constitution.

16  These concerns were articulated during the debates of the Theme Committee on the Bill of Rights during the 1995 deliberations. The position regarding bail rapidly descended into chaos. Courts were uncertain as to the meaning of s 35(1)*(f)* and, whatever the intention of the drafters, uncertainty was the only outcome. The Constitutional Court has recently handed down a judgment which purports to settle the matter. See *Dlamini v S; Dladla & others v S; S v Joubert; S v Schietekat* (unreported, Constitutional Court, CCT 21/98).

The content of the property clause was the subject of fierce debate. It was clear that such a clause was necessary in that, without it, certification was unlikely. The compromise was reached between negotiators from the Democratic Party (DP) and, less vocally or energetically, the NP, who wished to strengthen the protection of property, and sections within the ANC and the Pan-Africanist Congress (PAC), who were anxious not to constrain the imperative of land reform. Likewise, there were serious debates between traditional leaders who wished for constitutional protection of their customs and traditions and those, mainly women, who desired an equality trump. Notwithstanding these debates, this matter was never resolved and its outcome depends on the development of equality jurisprudence. The output of the court also had an effect. As noted above, the issue of the scope of the bill of rights had been a controversial one. It was, however, settled by the Constitutional Court[17] shortly before the final Constitution was settled by the parties in the Constitutional Assembly. The extended scope of the final text had always been on the agenda, but the narrowly couched judgment of the Constitutional Court fuelled anxieties that private power would be left immune from constitutional scrutiny and hence the judgment contributed to the acceptance of an extremely wide scope as contained in the application clause in the final Constitution, the formulation of which came extremely late in the day.

So much for a summary view of the origins of the Bill of Rights, now known as Chapter 2 of the final Constitution. This book is an attempt to raise questions about its role in the shaping of democracy, and the interpretation of the key values that underlie the entire text. Even this truncated summary of the history serves to reflect on a process of fierce debate and contest which has made the means to achieving a coherent interpretation all the more challenging.

## CONSTITUTIONALISM

Constitutionalism does not come without its own problems. As Habermas has observed, many of the traditional concepts of constitutional democracy, such as sovereignty, citizenship and representation which have depended for their meaning upon the idea of a homogeneous nation state made up of individuals with an equal stake in it, have been found seriously wanting during the 1990s.[18]

---

17   *Du Plessis v De Klerk* 1996 (3) SA 850 (CC).

18   Jurgen Habermas 'Citizenship and national identity: Some relections on the future of Europe' 1992 (12) *Praxis International* 1.

It is perhaps *the* great miracle of the South African transition that the new constitutional enterprise, even four turbulent years into the new order, promises the possibility of nationwide recognition of citizenship and representation.[19] Bearing in mind the divisive, apartheid past in which the rupturing qualities of racism dominated the unifying element of common humanity, the following passage from Habermas' recent book on law is particularly pertinent:

> *'What grounds the legitimacy of rules that can be changed at any time by the political lawgiver? This question becomes especially acute in pluralistic societies in which comprehensive world-views and collectively binding ethics have disintegrated, societies in which the surviving post-traditional morality of conscience no longer supplies a substitute for the natural law that was once grounded in religion or metaphysics.'*[20]

The Constitution which ushered in the democratic South Africa laid down the goal of the new society as a new order in which all South Africans will be entitled to a common South African citizenship in a sovereign and democratic constitutional state.[21] It sought, in short, to establish a legitimate constitutional state out of the wreckage of a bitterly divided past. In one act South African law was required to come to grips with the difficulties of constitutionalism and thereby to make meaning of this new promise of unity. In other words, not only did the new Constitution envisage empowering the majority but it wished to do so within constraints to be defined by courts.

The most influential contemporary attempt to reconcile the democratic 'will

---

19  That is not to claim that the call to ethnic nationalism is no longer a threat in South Africa. It would be foolish to ignore the development of a project of exclusive nationalism in which identification with certain values will purchase an admission ticket to true representation in the new South Africa. Failure to acquire such a ticket is accompanied by the sign 'right of admission reserved to loyal and democratic, loving South Africans'! Michael Ignatieff *Blood and Belonging; Journeys into the New Nationalism* (1993) distinguishes between ethnic and civic nationalism as follows: 'The only reliable antidote to ethnic nationalism turns out to be civic nationalism, because the only guarantee that ethnic groups will live side by side is shared loyalty to a state strong enough, equitable enough to command their obedience. A struggle is going on ... between those who still believe the nation should be home to all, and that race, colour religion and creed should be no bar to belonging, and those who want their nation to be home only to their own. It's the battle between the civic and ethnic nation' (at185). It is truly difficult to accept this distinction in that nationalism per se presupposes the other who is inevitably excluded from the nationalist enterprise, howsoever called. However, in South Africa it would appear that an inclusivist project is about to do battle with a competing exclusivism. Suffice to say in a book devoted to other questions, more progressive politics will remain in the memory.

20  Jurgen Habermas postscript to 'Between Facts and Norms' in M Deflem (ed) *Habermas, Modernity and Law* (1996) at 136.

21  Preamble to the Republic of South Africa Constitution, Act 200 of 1993.

of the people' with constitutionalism is that of John Rawls as contained in two major works, *A Theory of Justice* and *Political Liberalism* in which the possibility of attaining common ground on a set of principles that can serve as the bedrock of the Constitution is carefully examined. Habermas appears to follow a similar path to that of Rawls, save that in his case he disapproves of the idea of the 'just institution' which flows from Rawls' search for an overlapping consensus. Within the context of a deeply divided past, Habermas' approach, with less reliance on substantive values, provides perhaps a more fruitful start.[22]

Habermas rests his justification for the rule of the constitution in promoting democracy on a proceduralist basis. The constitution is not justified on the basis of its being based on a set of values to which all the citizenry can agree but on the idea that a constitution facilitates deliberation, which in turn is the very stuff of the democratic enterprise. As he argues:

> 'The democratic process bears the entire burden of legitimation. It must simultaneously secure the private and public autonomy of legal subjects. For individual private rights cannot even be adequately formulated, let alone politically implemented, if those affected have not first engaged in public discussions to clarify which features are relevant in typical cases as alike or different and then mobilised communicative power for the consideration of their newly interpreted needs.'[23]

In the constitutional state, the political and legal institutions function as translators of public opinion and deliberation into the concrete matter of legal rules and adjudicative outcomes. A legal system cannot lift itself into the arena of legitimacy unless its content flows from public debate and deliberation.[24] The relationship between human rights and democratic process which therefore gives rise to a legitimate system is described by Habermas as follows:

> 'The requirement of legally institutionalising self-legislation can be fulfilled only with the help of a code that simultaneously implies the guarantee of actionable individual liberties. By the same token, the equal distribution of these liberties … can I turn only be satisfied by a democratic procedure that grounds the supposition that the outcomes of political opinion and will-formation are reasonable.'[25]

---

22  I examine Rawls in ch 2, where an attempt is made to justify this submission.

23  Habermas at 137.

24  For this reason Habermas concludes that this 'proceduralist view is just as incompatible with the platonistic idea that positive law can draw its legitimacy from a higher law as it is with the empiricist denial of any legitimacy beyond the contingency of legislative decisions' (at 137–8).

25  Habermas at 142.

With the demise of the grand narrative and 'collectively binding ethics' Habermas argues that 'constitutional patriotism becomes the replacement for natural law and nationalistic and ethnic ties. In other words, the history and traditions of a political community are mediated through the patriotism of the constitution. The constitution thus becomes the cement which holds the society together. It does not constitute a grand moral narrative in that there is no single set of substantive commitments that must flow from each constitutional instrument. However, the insistence on the central principle of deliberation amongst the citizenry presupposes a framework of individual rights which grants private autonomy in order to allow each citizen the ability to exercise equal rights of political participation. Simultaneously, the existence of rights to personal autonomy ensures the conditions of public autonomy in which the process of deliberation takes place.[26] In this Habermas appears to be placing a progressive spin on the civic nationalism of Michael Ignatieff and arguably on the guiding spirit of the South African Constitution with its vision of an open democracy based on human dignity, freedom and equality. Habermas distinguishes constitutional patriotism from the love of nation. Whereas nationalism seeks to promote national identity into the normative principle of social integration, constitutional patriotism promotes the principle of deliberative democratic participation. Within this latter framework a democratic multiculturalism is possible. As Habermas writes:

*'In the public process of transmitting a culture we decide which of our traditions we want to continue and which we do not. The debate on this rages all the more intensely the less we can rely on a triumphal national history, on the unbroken normality of what has come to prevail, and the more clearly we become conscious of the ambivalence of every tradition.'*[27]

---

26  In this way Habermas attempts to negotiate between the Scylla of liberal individualism in which the protection of private autonomy is the entire justification for the constitutional enterprise and the Charybdis of collectivism in which the concern for public welfare ignores the legitimate claims of individual negative rights and hence the private sphere.

27  Habermas as cited in Martin J Matustik *Post-national Identity* (1993) at 23. In similar fashion Habermas has written more recently that '[b]uilt into the self understanding of the national state there is a tension between the universalism of an egalitarian legal community and the particularism of a cultural community joined by origin and fate. This tension can be resolved on the condition that the constitutional principles of human rights and democracy give priority to a cosmopolitan understanding of the nation as a nation of citizens over an ethnocentric interpretation of the nation as a prepolitical entity': 'The European nation state — Its achievements and its limitations. On the past and future of sovereignty and citizenship' 1996 *Ratio Juris* 125 at 131.

The ethnic nationalism of apartheid has certainly raised the potential for ethnic/racial mobilization in the future. In a society with such a divisive history and an even more skewed distribution of wealth, ethnic nationalism has an almost irresistible political appeal in that it promotes a feeling of belonging while simultaneously creating a climate of closure in which exclusive power and monopoly over resources can be obtained.[28] The deliberative themes of the Constitution are the antidote to these poisons inherited from the past. Through the practical implementation of the principles contained in the constitutional text, the possibility of institutions and procedures to mediate the conflicts and tensions that arise within this pluralistic context arises. Viewed thus, the Constitution gives 'priority to a cosmopolitan understanding of the nation as a nation of citizens over and against an ethnocentric interpretation of the nation as a prepolitical entity'.[29]

Habermas' emphasis upon deliberation does not imply that the rights that sustain deliberation are themselves removed from political debate and hence contestation. These rights are given content by the legislature and the judiciary and hence their content, far from being fixed in stone, shifts with changes in society and its views.[30]

It is this idea of contest that lies at the heart of my objection to the application of the theories of Rawls and Dworkin to the interpretation of a constitution. Rawls' reason and Dworkin's integrity sit uneasily in a heterogeneous society in which many seek the crown of the philosopher king and hence the inevitability of the right answer depends from which segment of the community one comes. At the risk of being accused

---

28  See in this connection Adam et al at 121–5.

29  Habermas 'The European nation state —Its achievements and its limitations. On the past and future of sovereignty and citizenship' in G Balakrishnan (ed) *Mapping the Nation* (1996) 281 at 287. Habermas's emphasis on the ideal speech situation does mean that as the consequence of the non-coercive deliberative process involves acceptance of a position which is contrary to the starting point of a party, the possibility of exclusion arises, not only of such a participant but also of those who foresaw such possibility and hence refused to participate. The source of such apprehension lies in adherence to an ultimately universalistic theory. As will, one hopes, become apparent, the argument of this work is that there is no such valid theory. By contrast, constitutionalism is about deliberative contest in which different outcomes will ebb and flow through a long run of cases. On this point see David Sciulli *Theory of Societal Constitutionalism: Foundations of a Non-Marxist Critical Theory* (1992).

30  This marks a significant difference between Habermas and J H Ely *Democracy and Distrust* (1980), whose justification for judicial review seeks to draw a line between the procedural and substantive provisions of the constitution. See the penetrating attack on Ely by L H Tribe 'The puzzling persistence of process-based constitutional theories' (1980) 89 *Yale Law Journal* 1063. For Habermas the limits of private autonomy should be demarcated in a manner which enables private persons to qualify as citizens able to participate meaningfully in the politics of their society. To this extent procedure and substance meet.

of being a post-structuralist dabbler, I believe the idea of the 'constitutive outside' can be usefully employed in this connection. The constitution of identity is based on the exclusion of the 'other', be it black, white, man, woman, for example. The very purpose of a constitution is to open the possibility, after decades of apartheid closure, of denying mastery of the foundation of society to any one. On the face of it Rawls and Dworkin do precisely the opposite, that is, they appeal to a concept of an 'overlapping concensus' that coincidentally resolves the Western philosophical dispute between the individualism of Mill and the argument in favour of equal respect of Kant. The very essence of the constitution should be to promote a society in which this process (as with all others) should be subject to debate, scrutiny and hence justification. If this is indeed the object of the Rawlsian enterprise, then there can be no inevitability in the nature of the overlapping concensus; hence uncontested reason gives way to politics. The former is the way of exclusion, the latter the way of politics.

To the vast disappointment of all too many South African academic lawyers, no doubt, politics and law might not be divided by some conceptual Chinese wall. It is to this issue that we must now turn.

## CONSTITUTIONAL LAW: POLITICS BY OTHER MEANS[31]

That the judiciary shapes public opinion is hardly a revolutionary proposition for a South African audience. The imbrication of the judiciary in the reproduction of apartheid over many decades has been superbly documented and analysed in a number of different works.[32] In particular, the record reveals a judiciary which, at the very least to the white population, was seen as impartial and independent. By placing the status of the judiciary behind apartheid rule, whether the case turned on the erosion of yet another common-law freedom or the assessment of the opposition to apartheid by means of the oft-employed political trial, the outcome would cause people's views either to change or to be confirmed.[33]

---

31  I have been influenced considerably in the analysis of this question by Duncan Kennedy *A Critique of Adjudication (fin de siècle)* (1997).

32  See in particular C J R Dugard *Human Rights and the South African Legal Order* (Juta, 1978); Hugh Corder *Judges at Work* (Juta, 1984); David Dyzenhaus *Hard Cases in Wicked Legal Systems: South African Law in the Perspective of Legal Philosophy* (Juta, 1991).

33  There has been little empirical work which has tested popular attitudes to the judiciary but it would, I consider, be a fairly uncontroversial proposition to state that white South Africa had considerable confidence in the judiciary.

Now that South Africa has moved into a constitutional era, the question, asked in other comparative legal contexts, becomes pertinent, namely whether the judicial intervention into the legislative arena is an undemocratic exercise. Laurence Tribe has defined the problem thus:

> 'Whether imposed by unelected judges or by elected officials conscientious and daring enough to defy popular will in order to do what they believe the Constitution requires, choices to ignore the majority's inclinations in the name of a higher source of law invariably raise questions of legitimacy in a nation that traces power to the people's will.' [34]

For this reason, much of the literature which attempts to justify the institution of judicial review within the context of a democratic society turns on the argument that majority rule is not itself democracy in that, if a majority intrudes on political rights or excludes opposition groups, it violates democratic norms. In other words, if 'the majoritarian process is defective from the standpoint of deliberative democracy itself, the case for judicial control becomes stronger'.[35]

The question about democracy and judicial review and the response concerning deliberation is necessitated by the assumption that in some way judicial review is actually undemocratic in that a small group of unaccountable men and—sadly but all too often—a far smaller group of women (similarly unaccountable) can and do subvert the output of the democratically elected representatives of 'we the people'. In itself the proposition is far too simplistic for, as Kennedy argues, there is no vacuum-packed, hermetically sealed terrain in which the will of the people is formed without 'some contamination' by a variety of sources of authority in society, including the media, religion, other professions, other arms of government. In other words, the question is not simply a dichotomy between the pure, uncontaminated exercise of 'we the people' and the power of an unrepresentative institution termed 'the judiciary'.

The fallacy of this dichotomy is illustrated by exploring the consequences of a replacement of judicial by legislative review. Accordingly, when a statute is challenged, a party disgruntled with the decision of the court can appeal to the legislature, which would have to decide, in effect, that its previous product was unconstitutional. Given that judicial review of the constitutionality of legislation is no more, the reviewing body, namely the legislature, would be free to ignore the previous

---

34  Laurence H Tribe *American Constitutional Law* (1988) at 10.
35  Cass R Sunstein *Legal Reasoning and Political Conflict* (1996) at 180. See also Ronald Dworkin 'Equality, Democracy and Constitution' (1990) 28 *Alberta Law Review* 325.

body of constitutional jurisprudence but would be required to apply their own judgement to the interpretive dispute. Hence the change in system results in the members of the legislature rather than the judiciary binding the freedom of the people according to the former's assessment of the meaning and purpose of the Constitution.

For this reason, a constitutional enterprise involves the mediation of 'the People's' assessment of foundational values of the society through another body, in this case the legislature or the judiciary. Naturally, there is the difference in that the judiciary are unelected, although this is not inevitably the case. Accordingly, it is not sufficient a distinction to deflect from the main point, namely that once a constitutional system of government operates, the inevitability of mediation must be accepted.[36] As the only alternative model which could sensibly attack the undemocratic nature of review, namely a political programme based on popular mobilization, is not on the agenda, certainly not on that of the critics who most often raise this issue, that alternative does not need to be canvassed.

The argument which is put forward for consideration in this work is that a constitutional enterprise represents a distinct form of politics in which opposing positions of the population are reflected in the disputes that are the very essence of constitutional litigation. The judiciary reflects these opposing world views and in turn the output of the judiciary affects the nature and direction of popular consciousness, and indeed the cementing of a constitutional patriotism.[37]

As Kennedy notes,[38] since the bourgeois revolutions of the 18th and 19th centuries, disempowered groups have couched their struggles in terms of the very same rights and freedoms as possessed by the 'citizens' of the society. Rights struggles have been struggles for a reconstitution of the rule system to broaden the concept of citizenship to include these groups. In essence, that is what occurs in constitutional struggle. The battle is about the reconstitution of society. Hanna Pitkin reminds us, 'our constitution is more something we do than something we make; we (re)shape it all the time through our collective activity. Our constitution is … our activity: a stranger learns its principles by watching our conduct.'[39]

---

36  I would argue that the same conclusion holds even where there is no bill of rights in that the institution of representative government presupposes the act of mediation.

37  For the origin of these submissions see Kennedy op cit Ch 12.

38  This point emerges from the discussion in Kennedy op cit Ch 15.

39  Hanna Fenichel Pitkin 'The Idea of a Constitution' (1987) 37 *Journal of Legal Education* 167 at 168.

The judiciary is therefore part of the political arena of society. By virtue of the fact that it is engaged in the meaning of a text, the nature of this form of politics is, of course, very different from that carried out elsewhere to society. But while texts constrain, they do not determine mechanistically. The interpretation of a constitutional provision and the further act of application to a set of facts is the outcome of argument, of competing or differing political projects or visions, of the influence and impact of contending ideological argument.[40]

It is within this context that this work has attempted to analyse some of the key themes of the Constitution as well as competing attempts to set out interpretive frameworks. These debates are taking place in a context which, but a few years ago, would have seemed inconceivable in a society burdened by the savagery of the Botha regime. The year 1994 heralded more than the end of 300 years of white rule and of further descent into the heart of Botha's darkness; it represented the establishment of a new *Grundnorm* and with it a legal revolution. Not only was every law to be brought under the authority of the new Constitution with its promise of the creation of an open and democratic society based on freedom and equality but, the parsimony of the majority of the Constitutional Court in *Du Plessis'* case notwithstanding, every court was enjoined to audit every law, whether sourced in legislation or the common law, to ensure compliance with the spirit, purport and objects of the Constitution.[41]

Within this context, this work attempts to examine the response of the legal community to these dramatic developments, in particular the judiciary and the academic community.

## HAS IT SIMPLY BEEN JURISPRUDENTIAL BUSINESS AS USUAL?

*'While we must always be conscious of the values underlying the Constitution, it is nonetheless our task to interpret a written instrument. I am well aware of the fallacy*

---

40  There was a major dispute as to the scope of the 1993 Constitution and in particular as to whether it applied to disputes involving private parties, ie where the state was not involved. In *Du Plessis v De Klerk* 1996 (3) SA 850 (CC) the majority of the court came down in favour of the narrower, vertical approach. For a detailed critique of this decision see Stuart Woolman and Dennis Davis 'The last laugh; *Du Plessis v De Klerk*, classical liberalism, creole liberalism and the application of fundamental rights under the interim and the final constitution' 1996 (12) *SAJHR* 361.

41  Section 35(3) of the 1993 Constitution; s 39(2) of the 1996 Constitution.

*of supposing the general language must have a single "objective" meaning. Nor is it easy not to avoid the influence of one's personal intellectual and moral preconceptions. But it cannot be too strongly stressed that the constitution does not mean whatever we might wish it to mean.*

*… If the language used by the lawgiver is ignored in **favour of a general resort to** "values" the result is not interpretation but divination' (emphasis added).*[42]

Thus spoke the Constitutional Court in its first judgment. This expression of the 'proper' interpretive approach by Kentridge AJ set a tone for the way the court went about its constitutional business. On one level Kentridge AJ's dictum can be employed to support much of the interpretive approach advocated in this work. But the words chosen by Kentridge AJ to set out his interpretive approach leave the reader (at least this one) with a nagging doubt that there is a clear distinction to be drawn between *the words and the judge's opinion.*[43]

This doubt grows stronger when the question of substantive reasoning is considered. The record of the judiciary until 1994 could, with significant exceptions, safely be classified as representative of a formalistic legal approach.[44] But the Constitution demands an engagement with substantive values in that by its very nature a constitution demands not only an enquiry into the pedigree of the applicable rule but also the substantive content thereof, so that to be valid the legal rule must not only comply with a valid source but with certain substantive values.[45] In assessing the first year of the court Alfred Cockrell concludes that in the engagement with sub-

---

42  *S v Zuma* 1995 (2) SA 642 (CC) at paras 17–18. See also Sachs J in *S v Makwanyane* 1995 (3) SA 391 (CC) at para 349: 'We are not called upon to decide between these positions. They are essentially emotional, moral and pragmatic in character and will no doubt occupy the attention of the Constitutional Assembly. Our function is to interpret the text of the Constitution as it stands. Accordingly, whatever our personal views on this fraught subject might be, *our response must be a purely legal one.*'

43  It is, of course, arguable that Kentridge AJ was, in effect, distinguishing between giving the meaning to the text which the judge believes best reflects the 'right result' and giving effect to the text in a manner which gives the words of the text the best meaning which she considers can be attached to the words themselves. If the latter was what was intended by the court (which, after all, signed on to this opinion), it is regrettable that no judicial clarification has been made in subsequent cases.

44  Apart from the works cited in n 14, see also Hugh Corder (ed) *Essays in Law and Social Practice* (1988), especially Ch 1.

45  For a detailed analysis of this distinction see P S Atiyah and Robert S Summers *Form and Substance in Anglo-American Law: A Comparative Study of Legal Reasoning, Legal Theory and Legal Institutions* (1987).

stantive values 'the record has been a patchy one ... in some respects (the) court has shown an unwillingness fully to embrace the substantive vision'.[46]

In certain of the judgments, there is a clear acknowledgement of the importance of substantive reasoning, particularly in a series of cases dealing with equality.[47] However, as will be argued later in this work, the court's recognition of the country's racist history and therefore the need to ground the future society upon the principle of equality never receives a clear conceptual engagement, an omission which is shown to best (or worst) effect in the exclusive concentration on the anti-discriminatory provision and the concomitant elision over the general equality provision, s 9(1),[48] which provides that everyone is equal before the law and has the right to equal protection and benefit before the law'. In the equality case under review, this provision is treated as if it were a header rather than a section with any independent jurisprudential weight.

That has not been the only difficulty with the court's jurisprudential record. We still await a coherent approach to the limitation test, in terms not only of the interpretation of the applicable section but also the substantive justification for limiting constitutionally entrenched rights. The vague laundry list approach to the limitation initiated by Chaskalson P in *S v Makwanyane*[49] has been followed in subsequent judgments;[50] alas, the list has been unwisely followed by the drafters of the 1996 text. This vague approach means that, some four years into the constitutional enterprise, we have little understanding of how a limitation test should function, particularly in its role of rewriting legislative and constitutional democracy.

---

46  Alfred Cockrell 'Rainbow Jurisprudence' (1996) 12 *SAJHR* at 10. Cockrell's superb study provides a fine example of the kind of scholarship needed in the constitutional era but which, as will be argued below, has been slow in forthcoming.

47  See in particular *President of the Republic of South Africa & another v Hugo* 1997 (4) SA 1 (CC) and *Prinsloo v Van der Linde* 1997 (3) SA 1012 (CC).

48  For the purposes of these cases the court was required to canvass the interim Constitution, the section being s 8 (1), which provides that every person shall have the right to equality before the law and to equal protection of the law.

49  1995 (3) SA 391 (CC).

50  See, for example, in *S v Lawrence; S v Negal; S v Solberg* 1997 (4) SA 1176 (CC) at para 166. The judgments of Justices Sachs and O'Regan in this case are particularly significant. Sachs J is prepared to limit rights by means of a generous reading of a government claim; O'Regan J insists upon clear evidence as to why the limiting law serves its (proclaimed) purpose. The recent judgment in the *New National Party v The Government of the Republic of South Africa* (unreported, Constitutional Court, CCT 9/98) raises further doubt about the advocated approach and particularly whether the deference of Sachs J in *Lawrence* is to be the adopted approach. See also *Dladla & others v S* (note 16).

While some clear and elevating engagement with these substantive and historical questions has been produced,[51] there has also been a clear neo-liberal strand in certain judgments, perhaps none more so than those delivered by Kentridge AJ and Ackermann J in *Du Plessis v De Klerk*,[52] where the concept of a nightwatchman state exerts considerable influence over judgments dealing with the issue as to the scope of the Bill of Rights. In both judgments there was an emphasis on the purpose of the Bill of Rights being to protect the individual against legislative and executive action[53], without any engagement with the question of power in general and the private power which, as Madala J reminded his collegues, lay together with state power at the heart of the discriminatory society that the Constitution was designed to transform.[54]

A related point concerns the reference to foreign authority. From the handing down of its judgment in *Makwanyane's* case,[55] it became clear that a compendious use of comparative authority would become part of the style of the judgments handed down by members of the court.[56] This has obviously influenced certain counsel to follow suit, a practice that has not met with unanimous judicial approval. Thus Kriegler J commented that

> *'far too often one sees citation by counsel of, for instance, an American judgment in support of a proposition relating to our constitution, without any attempt to explain why it is said to be in point. Comparative study is always useful, particularly where courts in exemplary jurisdiction have grappled with universal issues confronting us. ... But that is a far cry from blithe adoption of alien concepts or inappropriate precedents.'*[57]

This judicial observation is obviously borne of the frustration of reading argument weighed down with comparative authority organized in terms of the scatter gun

---

51  See the judgments by Kriegler J (in which Didcott J concurred) and Mahomed DP in *Du Plessis v De Klerk* 1996 (3) SA 850 (CC) as well as a number of judgments in *S v Makwanyane (supra)* and that of O'Regan J in *Bernstein & others v Bester & other NO* 1996 (2) SA 751 (CC).

52  1996 (3) SA 850 (CC).

53  See, for example, Kentridge AJ at para 45. See also Ackermann J's use of Isaiah Berlin in *Ferreira v Levin NO; Vryenhoek v Powell NO* 1996 (1) SA 984 (CC) at para 52ff.

54  *Du Plessis v De Klerk* at paras 162–3.

55  1995 (3) SA 391 (CC).

56  Ackermann and Sachs JJ are the most enthusiastic advocates of this approach, although Chaskalson P, O'Regan J and Kentridge AJ have peppered their judgments with considerable comparative authority.

57  *Bernstein & others v Bester & others NNO (supra)* at para 133.

approach.[58] While not suggesting that the court has engaged in the 'blithe adoption of alien concepts' all too often, there is a clear indication as to how comparative authority is employed. The traditional South African approach to comparative law—namely screeds of description of the applicable position in other countries without any substantive engagement as to the possible principled basis for the application of such material to South African law, is evident in a number of judgments.[59]

A related issue concerns the use that is made of such comparative authority. Thus Karl Klare[60] refers to the way in which Kentridge and Ackermann JJ cite with approval two criticisms of the decision of the United States Supreme Court in *Shelley v Kraemer*[61] in order to lend support to their conclusions in *Du Plessis v De Klerk*.[62] The articles by Louis Henkin and Herbert Wechsler[63] were both highly critical of the decision in *Shelley v Kraemer* and, as Klare argues, the cumulative effect of the two judgments is to leave the mistaken impression that a scholarly consensus existed in so far as *Shelley v Kraemer* was concerned, whereas the decision had both early

---

58  The role of counsel in helping to shape constitutional jurisprudence is an important issue, but, of necessity, it must fall outside the scope of this enquiry. It is perhaps fair to note that with the sole exception of a few distinguished practitioners from the Bar (and then almost exclusively from Johannesburg and Cape Town) the legal profession has not revealed itself capable or willing to assist in the development of constitutional jurisprudence.

59  A good example of an exhaustive summation of the comparative position, arguably extending way beyond the need to resolve the issue before the court is the court's judgment in *Fose v Minister of Safety and Security* 1997 (3) SA 786 (CC). The judgment represents an impressively researched 'Cook's tour' of the position in a multitude of countries relating to constitutional damages; but having exhausted the reader, the conclusion is contained in a lengthy paragraph (55) in which the position of the United States is linked to the problem confronting the court. But save for one sentence referring to Canada one is left none the wiser as to the purpose of the earlier exercise. Kentridge AJ's judgment in *S v Coetzee* 1997 (1) SACR 379 (CC). In *S v Lawrence; S v Negal; S v Solberg* 1997 (4) SA 1176 (CC)  Sachs J begins by warning against the comparative 'Cook's tour' method when he writes: 'our solutions to these problems (ie freedom-of-religion questions) and difficulties will, of course, be found not in the complex and often contradictory North American jurisprudence on the subject' (para141). The warning notwithstanding, the same temptation then proves too much. See paras 157 et seq.

60  Karl E Klare 'Legal culture and the problem of constitutional application in the United States' (unpublished paper delivered at a conference hosted by CALS, July 1997).

61  334 US 1 (1948).

62  1996 (3) SA 850 (CC).

63  Louis Henkin '*Shelley v Kraemer*: Notes for a Revised Opinion' (1962) 110 *University of Pennsylvania Law Review* 473; Herbert Wechsler 'Towards neutral principles of constitutional law' (1959) 73 *Harvard Law Review* 1.

and more contemporary defenders.[64] Doubtless it will be suggested that lawyers invariably use authority to bolster their position, an accusation of which I, during the course of this work, will doubtless also be accused. But this serves only to confirm the point, namely that the court has used comparative authority as one would expect from judges, namely to bolster their particular opinion and to lend it the intellectual and jurisprudential gravitas that such a contested conclusion requires.

So where does that leave an assessment of the court? Alfred Cockrell concluded his incisive analysis of the first year of the court's record thus:

> 'My argument has been that the significance of Chapter 3 of the constitution lies in the manner in which it provokes a shift from the formal vision of law to a substantive vision of law ... the Constitutional Court has struggled fully to internalise the substantive vision of law ... the unwillingness of the Constitutional Court fully to take on board substantive reasons has on occasion manifested itself in wishy-washy statements of rainbow jurisprudence.'[65]

Three years later, the judgments have generally become less voluminous and (although this is relative) in certain areas such as equality the court has begun to engage with foundational values and to invoke the history of the country into the interpretive matrix. In this process, the issue of constitutional choice has become more apparent, but the essence of the criticism remains. The court has not yet developed a coherent substantive vision of the Constitution—or, if it has, it sure is not telling the rest of the country. Its style therefore still follows pre-constitutional formalism, certain judgments excepted, and, perhaps for this reason more than any other, our law has not yet undertaken the jurisprudential transformation required with the introduction of the new Constitution.[66]

But the court is not the only institution that is challenged by the Constitution.

---

64 See, for example, Louis H Pollak 'Racial discrimination and judicial integrity: A reply to Professor Wechsler' (1959) 108 *University of Pennsylvania Law Review;* Derrick A Bell '*Brown v Board of Education* and the Interest–Convergence Dilemma' (1980) 93 *Harvard Law Review* 518, an article which, given its critical race perspective, has clear relevance to the South African context.

65 Cockrell at 37.

66 As these issues are not material to my purpose I have omitted from analysis the impressive way in which the court dealt with the question of constitutional certification and its clearly independent line of decisions on the positive side, as well as the restrictive approach to access to the court on the negative side. This latter practice has been most disappointing and stands in clear opposition to a constitutional enterprise designed to transform our society and thereby introduce a resilient human rights practice. This parsimonious approach to access is illustrated in a number of decisions, including *Nel v Le Roux NO & others* 1996 (3) SA 562 (CC) at para 26 and *Luitingh v Minister of Defence* 1996 (2) SA 909 (CC).

For this reason this work devotes a chapter to the nature of academic output in the belief that the academic community bears a substantial burden if our law is to become congruent with the spirit, purport and objects of the Constitution. Indeed, the 1996 Constitution contains a major innovation in respect of the horizontal application of the Constitution,[67] which passes a radical challenge to legal scholarship.

South African law has long been dominated by private law. Public law was very much of secondary importance, notwithstanding the influential role played by some public lawyers, particularly John Dugard, Tony Mathews and Barend van Niekerk.[68] The Constitution provides the opportunity to expand public-law scholarship, but perhaps more importantly to follow the Constitution in examining the validity of the public/private divide.

While there has been a significant increase in academic contributions to constitutional law, there has been little indication, assessed by the nature of private-law scholarship or the repositioning of law faculties, to break down barriers between public and private law where these prove inappropriate to the spirit of the new constitutional era.[69]

In order to show the magnitude of the problem facing an academic community within the context of a legal revolution, I have attempted to dissect a collection of essays which purport to be a history of private law, written after the advent of the Constitution. An analysis of the application provisions of the Constitution provides a context in terms of which the essential argument of this book can be understood, namely that 1994 represented both a profound moment for the legal system as a whole, not simply constitutional law, in that the entire body of law

---

67  Section 8 of Act 108 of 1996.

68  Only Dugard was exclusively a public lawyer but the other two made such significant contributions to this field that it would surely be churlish to classify them in any other way.

69  At a recent colloquium on legal education in the United Kingdom Anthony Bradley observed that 'British university law schools are undergoing a radical change in the nature of legal research and scholarship. Whilst they were once dominated by pure doctrinal analysis the new generation of legal scholars are either abandoning doctrinal work or infusing it with techniques and approaches drawn from the humanities and the social sciences. Law schools will be able to take a direct and full part in the intellectual debates that go on in the humanities and social sciences thus breaking the isolation that has hitherto characterised its position' (Abstracts for 2nd Theory in Legal Education Colloquium, 21 January 1998). Bradley then observes that the effect of these developments is a questioning of the notion of legal coherence but suggests that coherence should never be at the expense of the truth. The dominant South African position has always been to worry about coherence and consider truth to be a question to be explored by the philosophy department down the road!

came under the scrutiny of fundamental values and an awesome challenge, that is to contribute to the fundamental question about the scope of laws' potential to help heal our country. What is sadly the case is that the challenge is all too often being ignored in the rush to ensure that it remains 'business as usual'.

Arguably, the most important contribution which the Constitution promises to make to a new society is the introduction of a culture of justification. All exercise of power must be justified in terms of the constitution. But so must our claims to valid interpretation and our proclaimed models within which law is analysed. This small work is a contribution to the explanation of the selfish nature of the culture of justification.

# DEMOCRACY & INTEGRITY

In the most cited article in the first four years of the new Constitution,[1] Etienne Mureinik wrote: 'If the new Constitution is a bridge away from a culture of authority, it is clear what it must be a bridge to. It must lead to a culture of justification — a culture in which every exercise of power is expected to be justified.'[2] Applied to any of the socio-economic rights guaranteed in the Constitution, Mureinik argued that if government failed to deliver basic goods and services as set out in the Constitution, it should be called upon to justify its failure, an onus which it might fail to discharge if it argued that scarce resources constrained delivery in circumstances where it had spent lavishly on unnecessary luxuries, such as a monument, or even nuclear submarines.[3]

Justification requires standards in terms of which the disputed conduct can and must be judged. Accordingly, the formulation of such standards becomes the key to the constitutional project. In turn this entails recourse to the text of the Constitution which raises the controversy of the best way in which to read the text.[4]

This chapter is concerned essentially with arguments about legal interpretation. In searching for an interpretative yardstick, my purpose is to examine the two approaches, drawn from Oxford-orientated positivism and Rawlsian inspired political philosophy, which have been offered as *the* solution to the understanding of the South African Constitution.

In engaging with this task I need to make two introductory comments. First, as Derrida reminds us, no idea or semantic order is powerful enough to constitute itself without some violence or force. However, the more powerful the idea, the less violence will be required to inscribe and maintain itself and conversely with a less powerful inscription. As Derrida observes, the attempted inscription of a powerless idea, apartheid, required excessive and, inevitably, insufficient violence.[5]

---

1   'A Bridge to Where? Introducing the Interim Bill of Rights' (1994) 10 *SAJHR* at 31.

2   At 32.

3   Sections 26 and 27 of the Republic of South Africa Constitution, Act 108 of 1996 contain a range of commitments to the provision of socio-economic rights.

4   As the most creative South African public lawyer, Mureinik would have held clear views on this subject. Sadly, he was never to make the definitive contribution to a debate which is beginning to take shape within the context of our own constitutional enterprise.

5   Jacques Derrida in Derrida and Tlili (eds) *For Nelson Mandela* (1987) at 18.

Without having to purchase the ambiguities of the presence and absence of politics which has characterized post-structuralism, it is important to consider that which various interpretive frameworks exclude. As I argue later in this work, the Constitution appears to promise inclusion of all that was so violently excluded by South African law. My argument is that the Constitution holds out the hope of a transformative constitutional jurisprudence, one which seeks to alter fundamentally the country's political, social and legal institutions so as to promote an open participatory form of democracy. The preferred models of interpretation fail this promise, so the chapter puts up another framework in an attempt to develop a meaning of the Constitution that justifies the desire to move away from the imposed culture under apartheid.

## THE NEW SAVIOUR OF SOUTH AFRICAN POSITIVISM

As a country which until 1994 experienced only the constitutional model of Westminster, it is not surprising that the literal approach to a legal text, even to a constitution, would still have some resonance in South Africa. As Galgut AJA said in *Government of the Republic of Bophuthatswana v Segale*:[6]

> 'The task of the Courts is to ascertain from the words of the statute in the context thereof what the intention of the Legislature is. If the wording of the statute is clear and unambiguous they state what that intention is. It is not for the Courts to invent fancied ambiguities and usurp the functions of the Legislature.'

In its first judgment the Constitutional Court rejected this approach but then proceeded to muddy the waters by arguing in favour of a generous approach to constitutional interpretation which might well overlap with a purposive approach.[7] This confusion has been seized upon by textualists who urge a return to a reading informed by ordinary language.

The most thoughtful contribution to this approach within the South African context has been made by Anton Fagan.[8] In essence Fagan's argument turns on

---

6   1990 (1) SA 434 (BA) at 448G.

7   See Kentridge AJ in *S v Zuma* 1995 (2) SA 642 (CC).

8   A Fagan 'In defence of the obvious — Ordinary language and the identification of constitutional rules' (1995) 11 *SAJHR* 545. Fagan draws heavily on Raz's *The Morality of Freedom* (1986). As I understand Raz, a rule has authority, it provides a person with a reason for compliance. The rule contains reasons for its existence. Hence, if a person complies with a rule because of the reasons

two fundamental propositions, namely, (1) the source of constitutional rules is the constitutional text and (2) to determine what constitutional rules are created by the constitutional text we have to do no more than give the text its ordinary meaning.

These propositions stand in sharp contrast to Dworkin's idea of integrity as well as to the purposivists, who make the idea of constitutional rules dependent in part, at least, on moral considerations. For Fagan constitutional rules are to be identified by social fact; in this case the ordinary meaning of the words employed in the text.[9]

Drawing on the work of Joseph Raz,[10] Fagan distinguishes between conformity and compliance in the interpretative process. 'Conform' is used in this context to describe a situation where I act in the appropriate way but not for the appropriate reason. By contrast, 'comply' defines the situation where I act in the indicated manner and for the appropriate reason. Thus if a court does not comply with a moral reason directly, it can still achieve better conformity if it follows the constitutional rules rather than its own moral position. In other words, the moral position inherent in the rules provides a better guide to moral reasoning than the 'fallible assessment of the court'.

---

therefor as opposed to the rule itself, the consequence in Raz's view is that either the rule or the reasons for holding it to be binding should be counted, but not both. To do otherwise is to be guilty of 'double counting' (at 58). Thus the court should apply the authoritative rule because it has authority rather than because of the morality which the court considers provides the reason for the existence of such rule. As I hope to make clear in this chapter, the division between the moral or political justification and the rule is not constructed on the basis of Chinese walls but rather as permeable membranes.

9   Dworkin's idea of integrity is best developed in his work *Law's Empire* (1986). More recently he has published *Freedom's Law. The Moral Reading of the American Constitution* (1996). In this later work he describes his proposal as a moral reading of the Constitution and says: 'The moral reading proposes that we all — judges, lawyers, citizens — interpret and apply these abstract clauses on the understanding that they invoke moral principles about political decency and justice' (at 2). The purposivist approach is well set out by Peter Hogg 'Interpreting the Charter of Rights ' (1990) 28 *Osgoode Hall Law Journal* 817 at 819. Within the South African context see D M Davis et al *Fundamental Rights in the New Constitution* (1997) at 11ff.

10   I find Fagan's reference to Raz in the constitutional context somewhat puzzling. In the work *Morality of Freedom* on which Fagan draws Raz writes at a very early stage of the work that 'there is no value-neutral definition of liberty ... any assessment of degrees of liberty depends on the importance of various actions for the protection or promotion of values other than freedom.' Now, if freedom/liberty is such a value-laden term, neither any dictionary nor any plaintive appeal to ordinary conceptions is going to unlock its meaning. I would have thought, therefore, that this approach by Raz would have acted as a caution to the approach so enthusiastically advocated by Fagan.

Within the South African context Fagan argues that the Constitutional Assembly had the ability to make the rules it wanted to make. It had this ability in so far as it held the belief that it could predict how a court would identify constitutional rules; that is the Constitutional Assembly employed the use of a written text to fashion constitutional rules and in the knowledge of ordinary linguistic convention it had knowledge of how constitutional rules would be identified. Owing therefore, to the linguistic nature of the Assembly's rule-making act, the court has a reason to identify constitutional rules by giving the text its ordinary meaning. Fagan distinguishes this approach from that of the original intentionalists in that for the latter the only intention relevant is the intention of the Constitutional Assembly to make a rule rather than another by its enactment of a particular clause in the constitutional text. In so far as interpretation is concerned, no other intention is relevant. Hence if the Constitutional Assembly intended to protect free speech, the possible further intention which is not contained in the text, such as for example that the clause should not protect pornography, would be irrelevant to the interpretative process.[11]

Fagan's argument finds its ultimate justification in the following passage:

> 'The way in which we identify constitutional rules must not render unintelligible our constitutional practice. A key feature of that practice is the general acceptance of the idea that the court should make constitutional decisions on the basis of constitutional rules. Rule-based decision-making by the court is generally believed to be justified. This does not make sense, unless it is at least possible that the court does better by following the rules than by following its own moral judgement. It must be possible, therefore, that the constitutional rules reflect moral reasons more closely than does the court's own judgement. It must be possible that the constitutional rules substitute, for the fallible assessment of the court, a more reliable guide to moral reasons.'[12]

We thus arrive at the purpose behind the call to ordinary language. The moral reasons which underpin our Constitution can best be found in a reliance on the plain meaning of the words employed by those who drafted the original text. Only in this way can our constitutional practice become coherent and intelligible. The alternative is to allow judges to rely upon their personal moral convictions in the

---

11  Although the advocates of original intent do emphasize the importance of the original intention of the 'founding fathers', the essence of the argument of theorists such as Bork in *The Tempting of America: The Political Seduction of the Law* (1989) turns on the importance of original intent as reflected in the text — precisely the point made by Fagan.

12  Fagan at 559.

interpretation of the constitutional text. This argument is not a million miles removed from that of Bork and Posner as summarized best, perhaps, in Posner's statement that 'the moment we openly avow the need for judicial choice it follows that we argue in effect "that the Constitution is what we want it to be"'.[13]

The concerns that judges should not run moral riot and that the constitutional enterprise should fit within the political model of democracy are both understandable anxieties and important political considerations, and are not in any way undermined by the use by conservative advocates of the ordinary language argument within the United States. However, there are far too many questionable assumptions adopted in the argument to convert this approach into a sustainable theoretical framework.

At the most basic level the argument is based on a theory of language which admits of no ambiguity or difficulty of application in a penumbral case. It was precisely the latter problem that forced Hart to rely on the core/penumbra distinction to preserve the certainty of interpretative result in the core case whilst conceding that the judge would rely on discretion in the rarer, penumbral case. In itself the concession that ordinary language might run out points to a deeper problem, namely the sustainability of the doctrine of semantic autonomy which is essential to the line of argument developed by Fagan. By semantic autonomy I mean the ability of words, phrases and sentences to carry meaning which is independent of the communicative intentions of both user and interpreter of these words and symbols.[14] If there is a concession to the problems of language, it represents but a fleeting doubt in the mind of its protaginists. The theory of dependent reasons is then invoked. Such reasons are said to flow directly from the employment of ordinary meaning to make sense of the text. From this reading dependent reasons, that is reasons that are dependent upon the meaning given to the text by the initial employment of ordinary language. Only from such a reading of the text can one glean reasons which are dependent upon the text. Thus, were a constitution to guarantee a right to dignity, a court must decide whether a common-law rule of defamation is unconstitutional. A judge would then turn to the reasons which are justified by the right to dignity. This would lead to the right to reputation. If this is justified by the right to reputation the common-law rule of defamation is constitutional,

---

13  R Posner (1986) 84 *Michigan Law Review* 551.

14  See in particular F Schauer *Playing by the Rules: A Philosophical Investigation of Rule-Based Decision Making in Law and in Life* (1991) at 55ff.

a result which is then in accordance with the text and its guarantee of the right to dignity.

In this manner we are assured that there is no need to begin by examining the reasons that will justify the reading of the text.[15] It never ceases to amaze how elaborate 'nonsense on stilts' can be developed by an intellectual sleight of hand. The concept of dependent reasons emerges from the text which is read in unproblematic fashion from the ordinary meaning as employed by the drafters. In this way penumbral cases can be disposed of without any deviation from the commitment to the unproblematic nature of language.

How is this supposed to operate within the context of the Bill of Rights? Take, for example, the provision that everyone has the right to life. Does this include the foetus, does it entail an obligation on the part of the state to promote the quality of life of the citizenry[16] and how does a court decide the vexed question of euthanasia? What was the Constitutional Court to do about the death penalty in circumstances where the drafters deliberately left the matter open for decision by the court, owing to the inability of the political parties to agree on a solution to this controversial issue? How does semantic autonomy help to resolve these, even if such a concept of language was viable? How does one know the ordinary meaning of the text in order to develop the dependant reasons with which to come to a justifiable conclusion?

The ordinary language enterprise slides over these problems because its own purpose is to present all law, including the new constitutional enterprise as a static, abstract system of rules which have an existence independent of the manner in which law is created, interpreted and applied. Leaving aside controversies about statutory interpretation which of necessity must fall outside the scope of this chapter, the examples cited are designed to show that constitutional interpretation is inextricably involved in a process of the creation of the concrete from

---

15  A Fagan 'The limits of legal theory' (unpublished paper, 1999).

16  See, for example, the decision of the Indian Supreme Court in *Olga Tellis v Bombay Municipal Corporation* 1987 LRC 351. Frank Michaelman in 'Constitutional authorship, Solomonic solutions, and the unoriginalist mode of constitutional interpretation' 1998 *Acta Juridica* 208 notes that the Constitutional Court was aware of the way in which the drafters at Kempton Park had required a 'Solomonic solution' to the constitutionality of the death penalty. Of this Michaelman writes in a devastating riposte to the Fagan approach: ' [F]or the court to follow the instruction of drafters even if expressed in good faith, to the best of its ability, cannot mean for the justices to supress — to the contrary, it must mean for them to consult and take into account — their considered judgments as to which decision on this matter is the one that is best or right or fitting for the South Africa for which the Constitution as a whole purports to speak' (at 221).

the abstract values which are the very stuff of the text. Dworkin puts it thus with his customary clarity:

> *'Though I think that the moral judgement required to apply the more abstract moral principles of the Constitution is constricted by history and precedent, in virtue of the commands of legal integrity, it is plainly not pre-empted by that history. Fresh questions of moral principle … inevitably remain.'*[17]

Fagan concludes his analysis by suggesting that

> *'in sum, for our constitutional practice to make sense, it cannot be the case that constitutional rules are to be identified by reference to moral considerations. Dworkin, the purposivists and the pure natural lawyer have got it wrong'.*[18]

Mercifully, legal debate is not won by hopeful assertion alone! The essence of the constitution is a set of abstract moral principles which point towards the bridge which Mureinik considered could transport South Africa towards a democratic future. The foundational values of freedom, equality and dignity refuse to be railroaded into a scheme of authoritarian closure. Significantly, the drafters recognized this when in s 39(1) they provided that, when interpreting the Bill of Rights, 'a court … must promote the values that underlie an open and democratic society based on human dignity, equality and freedom'.

Some readers will no doubt be asking why I have been so nasty to that nice Dr Fagan and his attempt to import the even nicer Prof Raz into the country's jurisprudential economy. The answer lies in the issue of authority. For me, this form of recourse to ordinary language is about closure of debate and deliberation. Over time it will support an attempt to squeeze the political life out of the Constitution in order that the text adds legitimacy to the conception of the nation that the new rulers wish to mandate.

As was written more than two hundred years ago of another constitutional enterprise, 'the very attempt to make perpetual constitutions, is the assumption of the right to control the opinions of future generations; and to legislate for those over whom we have as little authority as we have over a nation in Asia'.[19]

The very argument of this chapter is that the Constitution is not only about the past, not only about some epigrammatic claim to be the autobiography of the nation

---

17  Ronald Dworkin 'Fidelity as Integrity' (1997) 65 *Fordham Law Review* 1249 at 1255.

18  Fagan at 559.

19  N Webster 'On Bills of Rights' (1987) cited by J Rosenfeld 'Freedom and time' 1998 *Acta Juridica* 291 at 298.

(whatever that may mean). It concerns the deliberations of the present and the constant political process of prefiguring the future. To say that this is what the nation meant when it wrote the text (if that was at all possible, which, in any event, my argument about the nature of language would deny) is to promote a particular national conception that can only ensure exclusion and the untimely death of deliberation.

## RAWLS ON SAFARI

Since the publication of John Rawls' *A Theory of Justice* in 1971, political philosophy has significantly influenced the shape of constitutional theory. It is thus not surprising that the appearance of a new book by Rawls, namely *Political Liberalism*, in 1993 would have a considerable impact upon constitutional debate.

In *Political Liberalism*, Rawls poses the fundamental concern of the book thus: how is it possible that there may exist over time a stable and just society of free and equal citizens profoundly divided by reasonable though incompatible religious philosophical and moral doctrines? Expressed somewhat differently, how might it be possible that deeply opposed though reasonably comprehensive doctrines may live together and all affirm the political conception of a particular constitutional regime.[20] In short, Rawls is concerned to find some premise that the citizenry can accept for the purposes of establishing a *modus operandi* by which to resolve disagreement. In this way all citizens can agree on certain basic principles, the acceptance of which will render legitimate the exercise of political power which can be justified in terms thereof.[21]

Recently, Denise Meyerson[22] has sought to apply Rawls' search for an overlapping consensus to the South African Constitution, particularly the phrase 'open and democratic society based on human dignity, equality and freedom' as contained in the general limitation clause (s 36(1)), the phrase with which Fagan's ordinary language theory so abysmally fails to come to terms.

---

20  *Political Liberalism* (1993) at xviii.

21  *Political Liberalism* at 16–17.

22  Denise Meyerson 'Reading the Constitution through the Lens of Philosophy' (inaugural lecture delivered at the University of Cape Town 1997). Meyerson's intervention is most timely in that, Rawls' influence on constitutional law notwithstanding, the formalistic nature of South African legal education has resulted in precious little creative use of political philosophy in South African legal scholarship. A notable exception was Etienne Mureinik, who was almost solely responsible for introducing the work of Ronald Dworkin into local legal debate.

Meyerson commences her analysis with an expression of the same concern that fuelled Rawls' *Political Liberalism*, namely that the phrase 'open and democratic society based on human dignity, equality and freedom' contains a clutch of inherently contested concepts which are 'capable of being differently interpreted from judge to judge. If so, interpretation of the Bill of Rights becomes a highly subjective and uncertain matter.'[23]

For this reason Meyerson's objective is to discover an approach to the interpretation of the phrase which will avoid 'the serious problems' of subjectivity and uncertainty.[24]

This requires a search for some formulation of a legitimate rationale for state action in limiting a constitutionally entrenched right. By 'legitimate' I mean a process of justification that can be endorsed by the entire body of citizens as an understandable exercise of political power. The solution is to be found in Rawls' use of public reasons.

Although disputants in a debate that occurs in the public domain may never be able to agree on the arguments employed by the other side, they will be forced to concede that their opponents' arguments possess some weight if they appeal to considerations that are commonly acknowledged to have relevance, that is 'presently accepted general beliefs and forms of reason found in common sense and the methods and conclusions of science when these are not controversial'.[25] The nature of these methods can, perhaps, be best illustrated by the converse, namely private 'reasons' such as the religious belief of an adherent who seeks to justify a particular path towards salvation. The explanation that will be given by a religious advocate will at root be based upon a system of truth claims that cannot be demonstrated or proved by the employment of commonly recognized methods of reason.

Applied to s 36(1), this distinction between public and private reason means that the state is required to justify action which infringes upon a constitutionally

---

23  Meyerson at 1.

24  Meyerson raises an important further difficulty with the wording of s 36(1), namely the paradox of protecting rights of equality, freedom and dignity (see ss 9, 12 and 10) and allowing these rights to be limited on the basis of a justification grounded on the same values. I have not dealt with this objection to s 36(1) as it is not necessary to the argument being developed in this chapter.

25  Rawls *Political Liberalism* at 224. Thomas Nagel said something similar which helps to clarify the point, namely 'one should treat humanity never merely as a means, but always also as an end … it implies that if you force someone to serve an end that he cannot be given adequate reason to share, you are treating him as a mere means — even if the end is his own good, as you see it but he doesn't': *Equality and Partiality* (1991) at 159.

entrenched right in terms of a public set of reasons, namely reasons 'which are guaranteed to carry weight with all reasonable people' — which accordingly prevents the state from pursuing a parochial course of action that favours one set of disputants in a controversy over a conception of the good.[26]

But one may ask, at this stage of her argument, is it then at all possible for the state to act pursuant to s 36(1) without infringing the central framework of the argument? The answer is once more to be found in Rawls, this time in his conception of 'needs as citizens'. According to Meyerson, these needs include bodily integrity, personal security, freedom from interference in central areas of life such as the family and religious belief, freedom from discrimination, rights of participation in the exercise of political power, a right to reputation, rights to health and 'some' education, and a minimum standard of welfare and income.[27]

It is as well to recall Meyerson's objective before examining the coherence of the argument. It is to develop a jurisprudence around the limitation test which is neither subjective nor uncertain[28] and consequently the state can be permitted by the courts to restrict a constitutionally entrenched right only on the basis of a justification that is couched in 'neutral terms' or to which reasonable citizens would attribute some force.[29] How successfully does such an approach meet its proclaimed objectives?

Observe the concluding claim: the state is obliged to justify a limitation in neutral terms or terms which all reasonable citizens would accord some force. Are these the same? I would suggest not. To substantiate this claim I propose to employ an example used by Meyerson to support her argument, namely the decision of the United States Supreme Court in *First National Bank of Boston v Bellotti*.[30]

A Massachusetts statute prohibited certain categories of company from spending their funds in order to communicate their opinion about any subject of a referendum

---

26 Meyerson at 5 and 9. Meyerson uses Rawls in this connection to mean one of the many holistic views about what, in the final analysis, gives life meaning.

27 Meyerson at 10. This list is effectively that which flows from Rawls' egalitarian difference principle as set out in *A Theory of Justice* (1971), particularly at 178ff. Significantly, this list is similar to the list of rights contained in ss 26 and 27 of the Constitution.

28 I assume that the approach should not be restricted to the limitation clause and that the same line of argument would be applicable by a Rawlsian to the interpretation of the substantive clauses of the Bill of Rights.

29 Meyerson at 15.

30 435 US 765 (1978).

which did not materially affect the business of the company. The legislation also deemed the taxation of individuals to be a subject which did not materially affect the business of any company. The court held that the state could only infringe the rights of expression of such companies if it was able to prove that the law was both necessary and sufficiently narrowly couched to serve a compelling state interest. The court did not question the basis of the state's interest in so preventing companies from exercising undue influence upon the outcome of a referendum but found that the legislation simply assumed that such corporate expenditure would distort the political process in question.[31]

Meyerson suggests, on her interpretation of s 36(1), that similar legislation would pass constitutional muster in that 'the legitimacy of government depends, in part, on citizens having a roughly equal opportunity to influence the outcome of political decisions, and therefore on the roughly equal worth of freedom of expression in the political context to everyone, regardless of social or economic position'.[32]

To put the matter beyond any doubt it is necessary to state immediately that I agree with the conclusion at which Meyerson has arrived. I do so because I consider that there is a legitimate and compelling justification for the state to be concerned with the exercise of private power in the public domain. Differential access to resources can have a major influence on the outcome of a political process and can render the right to freedom of expression no more than a grand illusion for the majority of the population. As one American commentator on the *Bellotti* case has argued, constitutional protection for corporate speech 'could significantly reduce the regulatory power of government over an institution whose existence is uniquely a function of government authorisation, whose power and wealth often far exceed those of the government that created it, and that has long been a subject of pervasive government regulation'.[33]

My agreement with these views is sourced in the argument that equality is as important a value as liberty, presumably an opinion that can be classified as 'social democratic'.[34] That, however, is not an uncontested position. An opponent

---

31   At 786.

32   Meyerson at 15.

33   W Brudney 'Business corporations and stockholders' rights under the First Amendment ' (1981) 91 *Yale Law Journal* 235 at 236.

34   I am reluctant to engage in definitional combat about the meaning of a social democrat. Suffice it to state for the purposes of my argument that, however defined, a social democrat will be concerned with the unfettered exercise of market power, the need to concern oneself with the

might respond in a number of different ways. She could say that, while the justification is one to which some reasonable citizens may accord some force, it is hardly neutral. She could find support in the monumental treatise of Laurence Tribe, who, notwithstanding a book that is clearly sympathetic to the politics behind Meyerson's position, writes of the *Bellotti* decision as follows:

> *'while the view that corporate speech is constitutionally protected remains controversial it is difficult to reject the principle … that first amendment analysis must focus on the speech itself and not on the speaker, and that speaker-based restrictions on speech itself and not only on the speaker may amount to impermissible censorship of the flow of ideas and information regarding the relevant set of listeners even if the speakers subject to restriction cannot complain that their rights as speakers have been violated'.*[35]

The claim to neutrality proves to be somewhat illusory. Perhaps the reason lies in the more modest scope of reason employed by Rawls' intellectual *paterfamilias*, Kant, who wrote as follows:

> *'To employ one's own reason means simply to ask oneself, whenever one is urged to accept something, whether one finds it possible to transform the reason for accepting it or the rule which follows from what is accepted, into a universal principle governing the use of one's reason.'*[36]

The concept of reason is stretched exceedingly far by Meyerson in order to meet her purpose. As the contest about the ultimate purpose of the Constitution hots up, one finds that the concept of a universally accepted outcome of reason gives way to a peek at the fundamental aspirations of the Constitution, aspirations which themselves are the subject of contested interpretations. In short, as the debate around *Bellotti's* case reveals, contested views about the reading of the text cannot be resolved by the claim of a neutral justification. Significantly, Meyerson's

---

capricious use not only of political but also economic power and the need to give tangible effect to the principle of equality. Within the South African context these concerns assume vital importance for the new democratic enterprise. As Heribert Adam, F van Zyl Slabbert and Kogila Moodley note in their recent book *Comrades in Business* (1997) at 3–4, South Africa has one of the highest gini-coefficients in the world at 0.62, indicating a greater gap between rich and poor than is experienced, for example, in South Korea, Thailand, Singapore, Malaysia and Indonesia. Adam et al therefore conclude: 'The struggle to abolish apartheid pales in comparison with the task to address apartheid's material and psychological legacies' (at 4).

35  Laurence H Tribe *American Constitutional Law* (1988) at 796.

36  Cited by Nora O'Neil in Andrew Heath, Barbara Herman and Christine M Korsgaad (eds) *Reclaiming the History of Ethics. Essays for John Rawls* (1997) 170 at 173. Significantly for my purpose, O'Neil suggests that this passage reflects accurately the scope of Kant's ambit of the concept of reason.

list of uncontested rights, which in themselves recall the ultimate content of the societal vision contained in *A Theory of Justice*, serves to remind us of Rawls' own observation about his earlier book, namely that the well-ordered society as set out in this work entails the endorsement by the citizenry of a comprehensive philosophical doctrine — a general view of what is of value in human life.[37] That comprehensive philosophical view represents a conception of the basic institutions in democratic society.[38] Read in this light, Meyerson has put up a compelling argument in favour of a particular reading of the Constitution. It does not, however, prevent other such readings from being chosen, and accordingly can hardly be said to meet the overall claim to eradicate subjectivity and uncertainty. How do we decide whether to prefer Meyerson's conception of our constitutional commitments over that of Ackermann J in *Ferreira v Levin NO; Vryenhoek v Powell NO*,[39] where a negative concept of liberty appears to mean closure for the egalitarian objectives of an alternative approach? Meyerson's use of Rawls might appear to be unproblematic in so far as many of the applications of the limitation process are concerned, but it runs into heavy water when issues relating to substantive commitments of the Constitution are concerned.[40]

In a debate with Rawls, Jurgen Habermas has pinpointed the great dilemma of liberalism in this context, namely that while human rights cannot be imposed externally on the public in its exercise of autonomy, that very autonomy cannot legitimately violate those rights by the laws it enacts. According to Habermas, Rawls' concept of political liberalism forces the political to give way to the liberal, that is, to *a priori* liberal values. As he writes, the public

*'cannot re-ignite the radical democratic embers of the original position in the civic life of their society, far from their perspective all of the essential discourses of legitimation*

---

37  *Political Liberalism* at 13.

38  See John Rawls 'Kantian Constructivism in Moral Philosophy' (1980) 88 *Journal of Philosophy* 515 at 518.

39  1996 (1) SA 984 (CC). In his judgment at 30–3 Ackermann J appears to take an extremely critical view of government interference in the private ordering of social affairs on the basis, inter alia, that it will have adverse consequences for the economic wealth of the nation. See also the judgments of Kentridge AJ and Ackermann J in *Du Plessis v De Klerk* 1996 (3) SA 850 (CC).

40  Perhaps the problem relates to the Kantian approach to reasoning from which the Rawlsian analysis derives its pedigree. As O'Neil observes, the reflexive process of reasoning offers only an absence of an arbitrary starting point or an arbitrary conclusion (at 174). Applied to the range of problems thrown up by constitutional law, the absence of arbitrariness is simply not sufficient to offer assistance in puzzling out the extent of the substantive vision offered by the Constitution.

*have already taken place within the theory; and they find the results of the theory already sedimented in the constitution. Because the citizens cannot conceive of the constitution as a project, the public use of reason does not have the significance of a present exercise of political autonomy but merely promotes the non-violent preservation of political stability.'*[41]

Whereas Rawls insists that the individual rights 'are originary' in the sense that it is there that we begin,'[42] the fact is that we begin there only if we buy into the very set of truth claims that Rawls' overlapping consensus is trying to make us forget. In the final analysis Rawls' theory is a liberal one — nothing necessarily wrong with that save that he had set out to develop a theory that could accommodate profoundly different truth claims within the framework of political pluralism.

Rawls' is not the only theoretical enterprise that promises not only to assist in the building of a jurisprudence to create a culture of justification but to act as a bridge from an apartheid past towards a society that forges a workable unity between equality and freedom.[43] Accordingly, we turn to another influential source for the possibility of a more satisfactory answer.

## WOULD HERCULES PERSUADE THE JUDICIAL SERVICES COMMISSION ?[44]

Dworkin suggests that when lawyers dispute the *constitutional hard questions* (such as should government be able to curtail the speech of corporates), the dispute turns,

---

41 Jurgen Habermas 'Reconciliation through the public use of reason; Remarks on John Rawls' *Political Liberalism*' (1995) 92 *Journal of Philosophy* 109 at 128.

42 J Rawls 'Reply to Habermas' (1995) 92 *Journal of Philosophy* 133 at 165.

43 The concept of a bridge was derived from the interim Constitution. What a pity that a Canadian expert was given such free reign to introduce his concept of plain language, thereby squeezing the poetic life out of the final Constitution and therefore omitting many of the clearer transformative pointers from the text. None the less, the text, with its emphasis on foundational values, still represents a bridge.

44 The purpose of this section is to examine significant South African writing on the issue of constitutional interpretation. In so far as the work of Ronald Dworkin is concerned, Etienne Mureinik made a singular contribution in applying Dworkin to South Africa. See in particular his superbly crafted essay 'Dworkin and apartheid' in Hugh Corder (ed) *Essays in Law and Social Practice* (1988). Tragically, South Africa has been deprived of similar work within the context of the new constitutional enterprise, but an examination of the overall point of the text as a means of obtaining an overall interpretive framework would doubtless have been his starting point. As he said at the outset in his article 'A bridge To Where?' (1996) 10 *SAJHR* 31: 'If this bridge is successfully to span the open sewer of

in essence, on the 'best constructive interpretation' of that society's legal practice.[45] The task of the interpretator, and hence the judge, is to find the best possible interpretation of the text; that is, she must make of the text the best that it can be. In doing so, the judge rejects the originalist premise in that she searches for what the framers intended to say rather than what they 'expected the language to say'.[46]

For Dworkin the judge is 'not on her own' in this enterprise. Two important restraints limit the latitude that this approach grants to judges. First, constitutional interpretation must commence with an enquiry as to what the drafters said but in this the judge is governed by 'the principles they laid down — not by any information we might have about how they themselves would have interpreted those principles or applied them in concrete cases'.[47] Second, the reading is limited by constitutional integrity in that judges may not introduce their own moral convictions into the reading. Rather they must ensure that their reading is consistent in principle 'with the structural design of the Constitution as a whole' as well as the dominant line of past constitutional interpretation by the judiciary.[48]

Hercules J, Dworkin's model judge, inevitably ensures that he fits his ruling with pre-existing legal material while simultaneously ensuring that his judgment can be justified by the guiding principles, that is those that make the most sense of the Constitution by putting the text in its best possible light.[49]

The principle of integrity is illustrated in its practical operation in Dworkin's approach to the constitutional controversy surrounding abortion. For Dworkin the most difficult constitutional issue in this controversy is whether the state can decide not only what rights and interests people have and how they should be enforced and protected but whether human life is inherently valuable and, if so,

---

violent and contentious transition, those who are entrusted with its upkeep will need to understand very clearly what it is a bridge from, and what a bridge to.' For this reason, in particular, I sketch the basis of Dworkinian theory and the potential problems inherent in it.

45  *Law's Empire* (1986) at 224.

46  Dworkin *Freedom's Law* (1996) at 13.

47  *Freedom's Law* at 10.

48  Ibid. In *Law's Empire* at 228 Dworkin has compared this process to that of the writing of a chain novel, in which each author/judge writes a chapter/judgment that ensures the sense and coherence of the whole story.

49  Cass Sunstein *Legal Reasoning and Political Conflict* (1996) at 200 correctly, in my view, observes that Dworkin is not entirely clear on the balance of the relationship between fit and best possible light. In short, it is not clear to what extent fit is to be sacrificed for the sake of a conclusion that sustains a better moral theory of the text.

how it should best be protected.[50] To decide this question a court has to engage with two traditions which sometimes compete, namely religious and personal freedom and the responsibility of government to protect the 'public moral space' in which the citizenry must live.[51]

Confronted with this dilemma, Hercules J and his sister judges turn to the principle of integrity. This requires a return to the structure of the Constitution. The most basic premise of the Constitution is an unbending commitment to the dignity of the human being. Inherent in this commitment is the principle that all people have a moral right to confront and to answer for themselves the most fundamental questions which touch the meaning and value of their own lives. Thus the principle that runs like a thread through the Constitution promotes a community in which no faction thereof is deemed to possess such superiority of wisdom or religious insight that it can decide the most personal questions for other members of that community.

Applied to the issue of abortion, the Constitution recognizes a woman's right to procreative autonomy such that the state does not have the power simply to forbid a decision exercised pursuant to such a right. Assuming that the court is also satisfied on the question of fit[52] the court must now decide the abortion case in the light of the general principles discovered from a coherent reading of the abstract clauses of the Constitution and they must respect these principles even where their application will result in controversy or unpopularity.

This conclusion leads immediately to an even more fundamental question, that is, the relationship between majoritarian democracy and the constitutional society.[53] The majoritarian argument suggests that the laws and policies of a society should be those which, in the final analysis, are approved by the majority of the citizens. If political equals disagree on moral issues the greater, rather than the lesser, number

---

50  *Freedom's Law* at 94.

51  Ibid.

52  Dworkin argues that the commitment to fit is met in that the conclusion in favour of procreative autonomy fits with earlier privacy decisions of the court such as that in *Grisswold v Connecticut* 381 US 479 (1965).

53  At the time of writing, the issue of abortion has not arrived at the door of our courts and, although the South African text is vastly more favourable to a pro-choice argument than its United States counterpart (see s 12(2)), the issue is clearly a controversial one. At this time, however, it is the decision in *S v Makwanyane* 1995 (3) SA 391 (CC), which declared the death penalty to be unconstitutional, that has brought this relationship into sharp focus.

should rule.[54] Accordingly, something of significance is lost whenever a political decision is taken which does not reflect the will of the majority. But as indicated by the use of the word 'equals', the majoritarian premise cannot go unqualified. All the members of the community must be 'moral' members. In short, each member must have a part in any collective process, a stake in it and independence from it.[55] By 'part' is meant that each individual must have an opportunity of influencing the decision, that is, of making a difference in a collective decision. 'Stake' concerns a commitment of equal concern for the interests of all the members of the community, meaning that 'a person is not a member unless he is treated as a member by others, which means that they treat the consequences of any collective decision for his life as equally significant a reason for or against that decision as are comparable consequences for the life of anyone else'.[56] Independence is concerned with moral autonomy, with the protection of the individual from the community adopting coercive or hidden means to shape the moral, spiritual and ethical convictions of individual members.[57]

In this manner, Dworkin builds upon the work of Ely in seeking a democratic justification for judicial review.[58] Whereas Ely had argued that review which protected certain constitutionally disabling provisions that prevent the restriction of free speech, or the conduct of free elections, were functionally structural to the existence of democracy in that these provisions improved the ability of politics to reveal the will of the majority, Dworkin suggests that there is a far greater range of provisions essential to democracy defined not within the statistical mode of

---

54   See, for example, Robert Dahl *Democracy and its Critics* (1989).

55   *Freedom's Law* at 24. Dworkin has developed these concepts in 'Equality, Democracy and Constitution' (1990) 28 *Alberta Law Review* at 324.

56   *Freedom's Law* at 25.

57   Dworkin justifies this principle thus: 'citizens of an integrated community must be encouraged to see moral and ethical judgement as their own responsibility rather than the responsibility of the collective unit; otherwise they will form not a democracy but a monolithic tyranny': (1990) 28 *Alberta Law Review* at 340.

58   J H Ely *Democracy and Distrust* (1980). Ely's conception of judicial review can be summarized thus: 'the general theory is one that binds judicial review under the Constitution's open-ended provisions by insisting that it can apparently concern itself only with questions of participation and not with the substantive merits of the political choice under attack' (at 181). In other words, the Constitution leaves the discovery and selection of substantive values almost entirely to the political process, for it is overwhelmingly concerned on the one hand with procedural fairness and the resolution of individual disputes, and on the other with what might capaciously be designated process writ large — with ensuring broad participation in the processes and distributions of government' (at 87).

majoritarianism but rather in terms of collective agency.[59] The task of interpretation is to promote this conception of democracy which not only enriches the democratic enterprise but makes the most sense of the constitution.[60]

Dworkin offers two major contributions to the search for sound constitutional analysis by grounding his theory in the process of interpretation and by making out a compelling case for an alternative conception of democracy to that of the majoritarian model. It is in the first aspect that Dworkin is at his most controversial. Although he comes closer to an answer in *Freedom's Law*, Dworkin never really clarifies whether Hercules is more than a thought experiment and hence representative of an ideal for the reality of judging.[61]

This distinction is important for, if we are dealing with an ideal reading as advocated by one theorist, however distinguished he might be, the possibility must exist that there are alternative, possibly competing, readings of the same text. Assuming a plurality of interpretative possibilities, Dworkin needs to provide independent criteria or reasons why his advocated approach to interpretation makes of the text the best it can be. One searches in vain for such a justification. He concedes that 'there is room for disagreement about the right way to restate these abstract moral principles'[62] but cautions that judges 'may not read their own moral convictions into the Constitution. They may not read the abstract moral clauses as expressing any particular moral judgement, no matter how much that judgement appeals to them.'[63] In short, '[t]he moral reading asks them to find the best conception of constitutional principles — the best understanding of what equal moral status for men and women really requires, for example — that fits the broad story of America's historical record'.[64]

---

59  For Dworkin, statistical democracy is when the group performs like a bunch of individuals and the only group function is to count the views of the individuals concerned. Collective action becomes communal when it cannot be so reduced to a statistical function of the action of disparate individuals but represents a distinct, collective agency, in this case 'the people'. 'The people are distinct from the individual members thereof just as an orchestra's performance is not simply the sum of individual performances': *Freedom's Law* at 20.

60  Dworkin (1990) 28 *Alberta Law Review* at 344.

61  In *Freedom's Law*, Dworkin sets out a detailed methodology for a moral reading of the constitution, that is, that 'we all — judges, lawyers, citizens — interpret and apply these abstract clauses on the understanding that they invoke moral principles about political decency and justice' (at 2). On the surface this appears as a description of the interpretative process, but upon more careful analysis it seems as if Dworkin sets out an aspirational framework.

62  *Freedom's Law* at 7.

63  *Freedom's Law* at 10.

64  *Freedom's Law* at 11.

The best reading depends on a moral and historical reading. The best is assessed by first setting out a particular political vision which, it is claimed, is immanent in the text and then, having established this conception, the historical record is rewritten in this image and all competing moral arguments are dismissed as not being in the accordance with the historical record, so defined. In this manner Dworkin is able to justify the veracity of his political programme by calling up the weightiest of authority, namely the Constitution.[65]

Interpretation is a contested business. To interpret a text in a particular way is effectively to limit the text, for if it means A it does not mean B.[66] This point is well illustrated by the criticism of Fagan against any interpretative theory other than his own. As a formalist Fagan would claim that his interpretation is constrained by pre-existing limits and hence he is making an apolitical decision. By contrast, the so-called purposivists and Dworkinian approach to interpretation is, in his view, a relatively unconstrained exercise in subjectivity. The ordinary language advocate therefore limits the constitutional meanings that can be found to whatever is meant by the ordinary language of the text.

The same complaint can be made of Dworkin, for the very basis of his argument is that there exists a single methodology of correct constitutional interpretation. In effect, Dworkin prescribes to judges what the 'right' approach to the text must be, notwithstanding ambiguity, uncertainty or silence of the text. Law has an immanent truth which Hercules, the ultimate philosopher-king, is able to discern and apply to arrive at the correct answer. That the advocated methodology requires a fit with social consensus and legal history which may be disputed in the United States is clearly problematic, but such problems pale into insignificance when applied to a society such as South Africa with inherent social conflict rather than consensus and a legal history, which, even absent the apartheid cancer, is contested. In such circumstances

---

65  Dworkin denies that his moral reading is either a liberal or a conservative charter but remarkably in his constitutional reading conservative judgements always appear to be penumbral to the overall core of constitutional jurisprudence. Significantly, Dworkin suggests that in recent decades conservative judges have ruled less executive action and fewer statutes to be unconstitutional than their liberal colleagues because 'conservative political principles for the most part either favoured or did not strongly favour the measures that could reasonably be challenged on constitutional grounds in those decades' (at 3). So political positions are influential when it comes to describing judicial performance as opposed to persuading judges how to decide a constitutional case or to evaluate its result.

66  For a most useful discussion on this issue see Margaret Davies *Delimiting the Law: Postmodernism and the Politics of Law* (1996), particularly Ch 2.

any attempt to develop a 'true' description of the law or *the* interpretative theory, such as Dworkin's conception of integrity, is closure by another name.[67]

## CONTEST AND INTEGRITY

> *'It is nonetheless our task to interpret a written instrument. I am well aware of the fallacy of supposing that general language must have a single "objective" meaning. Nor is it easy to avoid the influence of one's personal intellectual and moral preconceptions. But it cannot be too strongly stressed that the constitution does not mean whatever we might wish it to mean.'*[68]

It is understandable, although faced with a new *Grundnorm*, that South African lawyers would retreat to that which they know best, namely a view of law that is a static structure of timeless principles and doctrines which have an independence from the law applying and enforcing community and which accordingly relies on mechanistic processes of interpretation — or eschew any possibility that the law might be subjective, uncertain or occasionally incoherent. After all, to argue in any other way is not to argue at all like a proper lawyer!

Our new constitutional dispensation introduced a promise of a culture of justification. Legislative and executive performance must be justified in terms of the Constitution and failure by the state to fulfil its constitutional commitments, best summarized in terms of s 7(2) of the Constitution, must be similarly explained.[69] However, the text's meaning does not simply spring towards the reader in a neat, uncreased and uncontroversial manner. After all, the proclaimed purpose is the establishment of an open democracy based on freedom, human dignity and equality — hardly uncontested values.

My argument has been directed to those who seek to discover the one correct approach that either by having access to *The Oxford English Dictionary* or by the conflation of reasoned exchange with the inevitability of a social demo-

---

67  As Davies notes: '[B]y emphasising the singular nature of the object, and not recognising that the maintenance of a singular vision simply eliminates all other possibilities, mainstream legal thought proceeds by appropriating or erasing the other, and by maintaining the (hierarchical) differend at the centre of its practice': *Delimiting the Law* at 63.

68  Kenridge AJ in S v Makwanyane 1995 (3) SA 391 (CC) at para 17.

69  Section 7(2) provides that the state must respect, protect, promote and fulfil the rights in the Bill of Rights. This clearly reinforces a range of obligations imposed on the state such as are contained in ss 9, 24, 26, 27, 28, 30 and 31.

cratic alternative, however attractive that might suddenly appear to be in the context of the prevailing ideology of a market-orientated globalization. My argument is that there is no single meaning within the text and that the limits to meaning are not only imposed by the language chosen to be contained in the text but also in terms of legal and linguistic conventions, themselves informed by politics. Constitutional law is politics by a different means but it remains a form of politics.

In discussing the idea of a constitution, Hanna Pitkin ascribes two meanings to the word, namely the characteristic way of life, the national character of a people, their ethos or fundamental — nature, that is, a summation of 'who we the people are' — and, secondly, not as a noun but as a verb which points in the direction of where 'we the people can go' or what 'we can do', or 'an aspect of the human capacity to act, to innovate to break the causal chain of process and launch something unprecedented'.[70] In respect of the latter Pitkin says:

> '[c]onstitutions are made, not found. They do not fall miraculously from the sky or grow naturally on the vine; they are human creations, products of convention, choice the specific history of a particular people, and (almost always) a political struggle in which some win and others lose.'[71]

Our Constitution represents an instrument which can help move us from where and indeed who we are. That is not to suggest that our history is not of vital importance to our constitutional enterprise, for it is only in the full knowledge of our history that we begin to be enabled to plot the future direction. As O'Regan J said in *Prinsloo v Van der Linde* when dealing with the interpretation of the equality clause, 'given the history of this country we are of the view that "discrimination" has acquired a particular pejorative meaning relating to the unequal treatment of people based on attributes and characteristics attaching to them. We are emerging from a period of our history during which the humanity of the majority of the inhabitants of this country was denied.'[72] The history of apartheid is essential to the understanding of the word 'discrimination' and on the basis of this analysis the court in *Prinsloo* defines discrimination in terms of a denial of recognition of inherent dignity.[73]

---

70  Hanna Fenichel Pitkin 'The Idea of a Constitution' 1987 (37) *Journal of Legal Education* 167 at 168.

71  Ibid.

72  1997 (3) SA 1012 (CC) at para 31.

73  See paras 31–32.

But the Constitution is about movement away from that history, about the 'constituting' of a new society, one that lasts, 'which, in human affairs, inevitably means something that will enlist and be carried forward by others'.[74] Within the context of constitutional interpretation that involves a process of creation of a new legal and political framework. That process of creation does not exist in a vacuum but within the context of the text which is rooted in a particular history. To an extent, Kentridge AJ is correct to remind us that there is a text and that it constrains the outcome, although the court's own performance reveals how pliable this constraint is in practice.

Take the example of *S v Makwanyane*. As Frank Michaelman has written of the judgment of Chaskalson P:

> *'If ... you look at Chaskalson P's dealings with the "proportionality" test under the limitation clause, and most especially at his assignments of relative values to various of the rights enumerated in the bill of rights, and of the relative weights to retribution and deterrence as considerations in the constitutional theory of punishment ... you may come to believe, not that the argument has taken leave of the text (for that would not be true) but that judicially held beliefs about what makes a constitution a good one, or a good one for South Africa, have inevitably infiltrated and coloured the text that is undergoing interpretation.'*[75]

This approach by the court in *Makwanyane* is not abnormal; rather it reflects the very essence of constitutional adjudication. The authority of the text cannot simply depend on the legitimacy bestowed on the Constitution by Kempton Park for all time. The content of that text and the later one fashioned by the Constitutional Assembly will be contested by competing visions of how these texts seek to reconstitute our society. In this process there is no certainty nor is there a chance of squeezing the possibility of politics out of the adjudication process.

We therefore arrive at the key difference between the argument of this chapter and the approaches adopted by the positivists and the Rawlsians. The positivists locate their explanation of law in Hobbesian authority, meaning that political power rather than moral truth lies at the heart of law and hence must be followed as the guide to the process of constitutional interpretation. The Rawlsians are concerned about the effect of political authority, even that of a democratic assembly, in undermining the very values they see as essential to a liberal democracy; hence the need

---

74  Pitkin at 168.

75  Michaelman at 222–3.

to infuse liberal values within the content of law, even that passed by a demo-cratic assembly, whether in the form of reasonable debate or principles of law to be guaranteed by Herculean interpretation. In contrast, I have argued that the fundamental principles of law do stand in contrast to the Hobbesian bleakness but the principles are not immutable. They are subject to debate, contest and change, the process being mediated through the political and cultural practices of the society in question.[76]

As an example of the validity of the essential proposition which underlies this chapter let us examine the conclusion reached by Michaelman in a paper designed to show 'that there is a lot of distance' between a judge 'consciously allow-ing his or her "reckonings" to influence the application of the constitutional text and the judge reading the constitution to mean what he or she might wish'.[77] He writes:

> '[T]he conclusion … was that judges best collaborate with the framers by exercising their own judgements as to "which proposed and contested reading or application best carries out the political project that is incompletely constituted by constitutional lan-guage and history", etc. The conclusion here is that sound, contemporary constitutional adjudication has to ratify the sense of the contemporary people at large that it's their constitution (not the judges) that their judicial officers are applying to their lives and affairs. There is an apparent tension between those two propositions, one that resonates the tension between the rule-of-law and the rule-of-the-people that structures and com-prises the regulative idea of constitutional democracy itself.'[78]

Michaelman suggests that the judiciary can succeed in resolving this tension and hence ratify the contemporary people's sense of the meaning and ambit of the text.[79] The argument of this paper is that such resolution is not objectively

---

76  As noted above, I have benefited enormously by Dyzenhaus's account of Heller. In particular, Heller argued that the constitutional state is an organization that makes the exercise of political power accountable to the citizenry by demanding justification for the exercise of such power. As Dyzenhaus writes, Heller 'does not equate the legitimacy of law with the instantiation of any particular set of moral values, although his thesis about the legitimacy of law does rest on a connection between law and morality. The moral value which he says law serves as is the collective value of self-government — of citizens deciding together on the terms of their common life' (at 253).

77  Michaelman at 209.

78  Michaelman at 231–2.

79  In another paper 'Do human rights need democratic legitimation?' (unpublished paper, 1996), Michaelman clarifies his conception of the role of the judiciary within this context, such that there is little dif-ference between our conclusions. In that paper he concludes that there is no possibility of deny-ing the impossibility of showing that laws by which the supposedly validating process is consti-tuted are objectively right are in every respect what they ought to be. The best we can achieve

possible. Agreed, the essence of constitutional adjudication is to read the abstract clauses of the text in terms of the constitutional reason of the living. In so doing, however, the judiciary is called to mediate between the text and the living 'people's conception of what the society should become. That task can never be performed as if the judges can repress their own conceptions of that ideal of reconstitution. To argue that it is achievable is but to perpetuate the myth of the apolitical nature of law.'[80]

The constitutional route chosen by South Africa in 1994 changed the legal terrain forever. It insisted on the transformation of our society away from one in which the central feature was the racism and sexism which divided people into a caring community based on freedom and equality and the inherent dignity of each member of an inclusive community. For those attempting to read the constitutional text, new challenges were posed. Writing admittedly within a different context, Rudolphe Gasche has argued that

> '[p]hilosophical concepts would be entirely homogeneous if they possessed a nucleus of meaning that they owed exclusively to themselves — if they were, in other words, conceptual atoms. Yet since concepts are produced within a discursive network of differences, they not only are what they are by virtue of other concepts, but they ... also, in a fundamental way, inscribe that otherness within themselves.'[81]

---

is that the set of fundamental laws is subject to a constant process of democratic re-evaluation. Thus the content of these laws which are so subject to examination is neither given nor immutable. The judiciary is, not about closure, nor, on this basis, can it be. For this reason the Michaelman approach lends decidedly distinguished support to my own conclusion.

80  See in this connection the compelling argument of Lourens du Plessis 'Legal Academics and the Open Community of Constitutional Interpreters' (1996) 12 *SAJHR* 214, who argues (at 220, 223), correctly in my view, that '[a]n open community of constitutional interpreters presupposes that language allows for more than one (equally) valid reading of the constitution. This encourages debate within the said community and banks on a pluralistic interplay of ideas to mould the eventual meaning of the text. ... The completed text posits, with authority, a starting point for interpretation and eventual application, but it invites, with equal authority, improvisation, thereby recognising its own inconclusiveness.' The concession that 'interpretative theory cannot dictate a single methodology of right interpretation' must be connected coherently to the solution proposed. See Jed Rubenfeld 'On Fidelity in Constitutional Law' (1997) 65 *Fordham Law Review* 1469. Rubenfeld's argument does constitute such an attempt. He correctly suggests that interpretation is not rewriting but that constitutional interpretation involves normative judgement 'beyond the letter of the law, and sometimes in defiance of the original intentions' (at 1487). Then we are told that the judge must look at the paradigm cases in which the underlying principles of the text and its purpose are to be found. Thereafter the role of normative judgement is to settle a principle which 'captures the provision's paradigm cases and that must, to be successful, offer itself as an account of what made this guarantee worthy of constitutional struggle' (at 1485).

81  R Gasche *The Tain of the Mirror. Derrida and the Philosophy of Reflection* (1986) at 128.

My argument against the uncritical application of Oxford positivism or Rawlsian or Dworkinian liberalism is that all these approaches seek to ground the Constitution on the basis that the concepts which are to be found in the text possess a conceptual homogeneity that forecloses on any conceptual contest. The other is not law and where it is conceded that the contrast between legal and moral reasoning is illusory and that the language used by the 'lawgiver' not only is written in moral principles but that judges are enjoined to apply moral reasoning to the text, standards are produced which are 'legally authoritative because they make the most moral sense'. Like Dworkin we therefore arrive, the moral maelstrom of the constitutional enterprise notwithstanding, at the right answer.[82]

This chapter should not be taken as an attempt to set out *the* meaning of the text; indeed, its very purpose is, by way of critique of the most interesting South African contributions to the constitutional debate, to point in the following direction: constitutionalism is about moral and political reasoning. When judges go about the business of constitutional adjudication, they are involved in a form of politics. The very material with which they work is not uncontested. Indeed, the meaning to be given to the content of the Constitution is part of a continuous process of construction. Meaning is shaped by a system of social, political and ideological relations within which it is formed, so that meaning is always in being and becoming. It is in the denial thereof that the Constitution becomes a means of exclusion, a mechanism to cast out the 'other', which was the very purpose of apartheid. Within the context of that history of the apartheid other and the promise of the antithesis of that 'other', namely *ubuntu*, an approach to the Constitution can be developed to establish an inclusivist society which acts self-reflexively in considering the consequences of interpretative exclusion.[83]

---

82　This is a brief summary of the justification outlined by Denise Meyerson *Rights Unlimited* (1997) at xxvi–xxvii for the application of the work of Rawls to the intepretative questions posed by the constitution. After completion of this text, I read David Dyzenhaus's most illuminating study on *Weimar Jurisprudence Legality and Legitimacy* (1997). In it he draws heavily on the work of Herman Heller to suggest a conclusion which leads those who tilt in favour of democracy (as opposed to liberalism) to concede that rights are needed to guarantee democratic participation, but that a democrat makes an issue out of the content of rights in that out of democratic debate a variety of different conceptions of the content of those very rights can emerge. Although the emphasis is on democracy, the content of the constitution is not frozen. In the context of a constitution which strives to be the fount of a democratic society, the idea of contest presupposed in the work of Heller provides much in the way of support for the argument set out above.

83　That is not to suggest that I am advocating an approach that anything goes so that the text is irrelevant and the judge simply concludes that her intuitive feeling gives rise to the best interpretation.

In short, within the context of our newly born constitutional venture, we need to acknowledge the poverty of our previous jurisprudential approach, which insisted that our system of law consist of a series of norms that transcended human interaction. The new era has ushered in the norm of justification. That in turn will involve differing reasons based on competing visions of the Constitution. Much of this work is devoted to putting forward a particular vision of the Constitution and its consequent challenges for our legal system. It therefore stands in contrast to the theories criticized in this chapter. That is the very point, for it is in this way that our Constitution will be contested and refashioned. It is in this context that our politics will be fought. Given our history of politics under apartheid, it is to be hoped that the new constitutional bridge has been made of sufficiently sturdy material.

---

his accusation is the favourite ploy of the positivists — either the text has a correct meaning or you are on your own in a world of complete discretion. In contrast, I acknowledge that we are involved in interpretative work; but the process is about competing interpretations and outcomes each of which requires justification. That the text gives indicators as to which justification is in keeping with the nature of the constitutional enterprise is, it is submitted, clear. That which is more in keeping with the community's conception of the constitutional society is likely to prevail. By acknowledging the contest, we leave open the possibility for deliberation, change and therefore politics.

# FREEDOM

## FREEDOM: ITS FIT IN AN EGALITARIAN SCHEME

In the previous chapter, I attempted to sketch a framework for the interpretation of the new Constitution. In the following two chapters, I want to put some flesh on this conceptual skeleton by means of an examination of the two fundamental values which must guide this interpretative process.

The 'People', acting through the Constitutional Assembly, may be the originators of all constitutional rules, but questions of interpretation and application are left to the judiciary in general and the 'People's' court — the Constitutional Court — in particular.

This division exists perhaps more comfortably in the realm of political theory than in the understanding of constitutional adjudication, where acts of interpretation cannot always be distinguished from acts of creation. As should be apparent from the argument developed in chapter 1, this distinction is beside the point, as the meanings of words are rarely ordinary, and constitutional phrases hardly spring from the page in a neat and orderly fashion. For this reason, the mystery of the words is discovered by a political theory that justifies the creative acts of the 'People'.

Judges grapple with the underlying theory to guide them as to the meaning of the text. Perhaps it was this obstacle, or a general attitude of philosophical caution, that influenced it to do so, but in its first four years of existence the Constitutional Court, although employing an impressive range of comparative authority in the compilation of its judgments, has made few attempts to develop a holistic jurisprudential framework within which to interpret the text. For this reason alone, the judgment of Ackermann J in *Ferreira v Levin NO; Vryenhoek v Powell NO*[1] has so much to commend it, for it represents arguably the boldest attempt by the court to engage with an underlying theory which informs the words of Chapter 3 of the Constitution. It is perhaps the text most worthy of analysis in that it also affords greater insight into the jurisprudential intentions of some members of the court. The concept of freedom (or liberty, as the concept is described in other

---

1   1996 (1) SA 984 (CC).

consititutional texts) is a contested one,[2] as I hope to demonstrate by using *Ferreira's* case as the key illustration.

The facts of the case were briefly as follows: s 417(2)*(b)* of the Companies Act 61 of 1973 provides that any person summoned for an examination into the affairs of a company being wound up as unable to pay its debts 'may be required to answer any question put to him at the examination, notwithstanding that the answer might tend to incriminate him, and any answer given to such question may thereafter be used in evidence against him'. In a referral to the Constitutional Court, the question of the constitutionality of this provision was raised in that it was argued that its effect was to compel a person summoned to a s 417 inquiry to testify and produce relevant documents even where such a person sought to invoke the privilege against self-incrimination. The applicants launched their attack on the basis that the provisions of s 417(2)*(b)* were inconsistent with an accused's right to a fair trial in terms of s 25(3) of the interim Constitution.

## STANDING

Ackermann J commenced his judgment with an investigation into the respondents' submission that the rights in terms of s 25(3) accrue to a person upon the commencement of a criminal trial and therefore do not apply to an examinee in a s 417 inquiry, for he or she is not at that time charged in terms of the criminal law; only the subsequent use of such answers at a criminal trial of an examinee would constitute a breach of s 25(3). Ackermann J put it thus:

> 'The real question … is whether an examinee who has previously been compelled under s 417(2)(b) to give answers which incriminate him may, at a subsequent criminal trial of the examinee, successfully attack the introduction of such incriminating answers on the basis that s 417(2)(b) conflicts with the unenumerated right against self incrimination in s 25(3).'[3]

If answered positively, a further question would then arise, namely whether the examinee may raise the issue of the constitutionality of s 417(2)*(b)* of the Act when the question is raised at the s 417 inquiry.

This submission required of Ackermann J that he examine the scope of the

---

2    See, in general, Quentin Skinner *Liberty before Liberalism* (1988).

3    Para 32.

*locus standi* provision in Chapter 3, s 7(4)*(b)*,which sets out those persons who are entitled to apply to a competent court of law for appropriate constitutional relief. They are:

(i)   a person acting in his or her own interest;

(ii)  an association acting in the interest of its members;

(iii) a person acting on behalf of another person who is not in a position to seek such relief in his or her own name;

(iv)  a person acting as a member of or in the interest of a group or class of persons;

(v)   a person acting in the public interest.

A person listed in s 7(4)*(b)* can apply to a court for relief if there has been an infringement of or threat to any of the rights entrenched in Chapter 3 (s 7(4)*(a)*). As Ackermann J observed:

> 'It is only when this condition is fulfilled that the persons referred to in para (b) "shall be entitled to apply to a competent court of law for appropriate relief". The crucial question is whether, when an examinee is compelled by s 417(2)(b) to answer a question which might tend to incriminate him or her, and the section further provides that "any answer given to such question may thereafter be used in evidence against him [or her]," a s 25(3) right to a fair criminal trial is being infringed or threatened with infringement.'[4]

Ackermann J held that the whole of s 7(4)*(b)* is qualified by subsec (4)*(a)*, which expressly renders the right to 'apply' to a competent court 'conditional upon' when an infringement of or threat to any right entrenched in this chapter is alleged.

For Ackermann J, subsec (4)*(a)* determines when the right to invoke the aid of the court arises; subsec (4)*(b)* determines by whom that right (when it accrues) may be exercised. Accordingly, Ackermann J held that an applicant can rely on s 25(3) of the Constitution only if he or she can show that there is an infringement of or a threat to a s 25(3) right, irrespective of whether the applicant is acting in his or her own interest or on behalf of another person who is not in a position to seek such relief in his or her own name, or even in the public interest.[5] For Ackermann J,

> 's 25(3) rights accrue, textually, only to "every accused person". They are rights which accrue, in the subjective sense, when a person becomes an "accused person" in a criminal prosecution. The examinee is not such an "accused person". It is a matter of pure spec-

---

4   Para 34.

5   Para 40.

*ulation whether the applicants will ever become accused persons. Even should they become accused persons, their rights against extra-curial self-incrimination ... are not automatically infringed when they become accused persons. It will depend on whether self-incriminating evidence given by the applicants at the s 417 inquiry is tendered in evidence against them. At that moment, for the first time, there is a threat to any s 25(3) right against extra-curial self-incrimination. The inescapable conclusion, therefore, is that s 417(2)(b) does not constitute an infringement or threat of infringement of any s 25(3) rights of the applicants, and that their attack on s 417(2)(b) on this basis can accordingly not succeed.'*[6]

This is a particularly parsimonious and restrictive view of standing within the constitutional context. In my view, O'Regan J is correct when she states '[t]here can be little doubt that s 7(4) provides for a generous and expanded approach to standing in the constitutional context'.[7] As she notes, the categories of persons who are granted standing to seek constitutional relief are far broader than those permitted under the common law. This is hardly surprising within the context of the constitutional enterprise, which seeks to ground all aspects of political, social and economic life within the framework of a constitutional democracy. To restrict the ability of the citizen to approach a court for constitutional relief, particularly on the basis of a strict construction of the standing requirements, curtails the possibility of constitutionalism before it has commenced.

The judgments of O'Regan J and Chaskalson P reflect this concern, notwithstanding different approaches to the problem. O'Regan J found on the evidence that the applicants had 'alleged neither a threat of prosecution in which compelled evidence could be led against them, nor an interest in an infringement or threatened infringement of the rights of other persons'. She held that the applicants did not have standing in terms of s 7(4)*(b)*(v): they had shown that they were acting genuinely in the public interest. Thus she decided that the applicants were not required to allege an infringement of or a threat to the right of a particular person. The applicants were simply required 'to allege that, objectively speaking, the challenged rule or conduct is in breach of a right enshrined in Chapter 3. This flows from the notion of acting in the public interest. The public will ordinarily have an interest in the infringement of rights generally, not particularly.[8]

---

6    Para 229.

7    Para 245.

8    See, in particular, paras 167–168.

Fortunately, five other judges concurred in the judgment of Chaskalson P, so that a measure of certainty has been achieved with regard to the interpretation of s 7(4). O'Regan J's approach to standing is not dissimilar to that of Ackermann J. Whereas the latter had found that the absence of a pending prosecution was fatal to the question, O'Regan J regarded this fact as fatal to a person who sought relief from the court in terms of s 7(4)*(b)*(i). Both judges appear to have interpreted the subparagraph as meaning that, if there was not a threat of a prosecution in which compelled evidence was to be led, or an interest of infringement, or a threatened infringement of the rights of other persons, no relief was available.

The differences between these two judgments is that O'Regan J sought to ground relief for the applicants in terms of s 7(4)*(b)*(v), on the basis that they were acting in the public interest. But in this case the applicants were not so motivated. They were acting in their own interest, since their self-motivation must surely have been inspired by the threat that a criminal prosecution could be launched against them in the light of evidence which they might be forced to provide at the s 417 inquiry. Chaskalson P found that, if s 25(3) of the Constitution conflicts with s 417(2)*(b)* of the Companies Act to the extent that the latter is invalid, '… it seems to me to be highly technical to say that a witness called to a s 417(2)*(b)* enquiry lacks standing to challenge the constitutionality of the section (para 163)'. Regarding s 7(4), Chaskalson P found that the section must be read in the light of ss 98(2)*(a)* and 101(3)*(a)*, which provide jurisdiction to deal with 'any alleged violation or threatened violation of any fundamental right entrenched in Chapter 3'. Section 7(4) provides that, 'where an infringement or threat of infringement of a constitutional right is alleged, any of the persons referred to in s 7(4)*(b)* will have standing to bring the matter to a competent court of law'. Section 7(4) applies this to s 98(2)*(a)* jurisdiction only if s 7(4) was read to apply to all of s 98(2); it would then be read as meaning 'where an infringement of or threat to any right entrenched in Chapter 3 is alleged the persons referred to in [para] *(b)* will have standing'.[9]

Chaskalson P therefore found that the applicants had standing in terms of s 7(4)*(b)*(i): they were acting in their own interests. All that the provision required was that

*'the person concerned should make the challenge in his or her own interest. It is for this Court to decide what is a sufficient interest in such circumstances. In my view, on the facts of the present case, the applicants have a sufficient interest to seek such a ruling.'*[10]

9   Para 168.
10   Para 169.

The court's approach to standing can be summarized thus: there is a parsimonious approach to the entire scope of s 7(4) adopted by Ackermann J, and a restrictive approach adopted by O'Regan J to standing by a person acting in his or her own interest. Having conceded the need for a generous interpretation of the principle of standing, O'Regan J was forced to find some other basis to grant relief to the applicants, albeit by following a circuitous route. A measure of consistency between the rhetoric of generosity and the practical application of the section can be found in the judgment of six judges. Kriegler J agreed with Ackermann J that s 25(3) was inapplicable, but based his conclusion on there having been an incorrect referral to the Constitutional Court. Mokgoro J also wrote a separate judgment, but on the issue of standing she concurred with Chaskalson P. Sachs J appeared to adopt a similar approach to standing to that taken by Ackermann J, but a reasonable reader might think otherwise.

Having engineered himself into considerable difficulty as a result of his analysis of standing, Ackermann J was forced to adopt an excessively generous interpretive approach to arrive at a favourable conclusion, a point acknowledged by Chaskalson P where he notes that, because of this finding of standing, 'Ackermann J was driven to base his judgment on s 11(1) of the Constitution and not on s 25(3).'[11]

Moving from parsimony to generosity without even the jurisprudential blink of an eyelid, Ackermann J found that the right to freedom in s 11(1) should be construed generously and extensively (at para 50).[12] Relying on this particular reading of Isaiah Berlin's two concepts of liberty, Ackermann J found that the word 'freedom' in terms of s 11(1) covers the area in which a person should be left to do what he or she desires without interference. In other words, s 11(1) is concerned to protect freedom in the negative sense. For this reason Ackermann J defined the right to freedom negatively as 'the right of individuals not to have "obstacles to possible choices and activities" placed in their way by ... the State'.[13]

Ackermann J recognized that Chapter 3 guaranteed a range of different freedoms, including those of privacy, religion, belief, opinion, expression, assembly, association, and residence. For this reason he concluded that s 11(1) constituted a residual right of freedom, to be applied when the specific guarantees failed to offer protection; furthermore, a residual concept of freedom, as a result of the

11  Para 169.

12  Para 50.

13  See, in particular, paras 54–57.

provisions of s 33(1), the limitation clause. In terms of proviso *(aa)* to s 33(1), a limitation on a right protected by s 11(1) can be constitutional only where the justification is proved to be both reasonable and necessary. The specified freedoms could be limited by reasonable means only.[14]

A further difficulty which confronted Ackermann J can be summarized thus: an extensive interpretation of freedom in this negative sense could lead the court to follow the *laissez-faire* jurisprudence pioneered by the United States Supreme Court in *Lochner v New York*,[15] which would justify decisions to set aside a range of welfare legislation on the grounds that their provisions offended negative freedom, that is, the protected sphere of individual autonomy.

Ackermann J based his conclusion on a reading of the entire document. Therefore the justification for this interpretive approach is grounded in the text: 'individual freedom is a core right in the panoply of human rights'[16] and '[freedom] is … the foundation of many of the other rights that are specifically entrenched'[17] and '[o]ne of the main objects of the Constitution is to eradicate such denial or restriction of freedom'.[18]

Thus the right to freedom in s 11(1) constitutes a residual right of an individual not to have obstacles to choices and activities placed in his or her way by the state.[19]

But is Ackermann J's justification compatible with the purpose of the section? He never attempts to reply to the telling point made by Mokgoro J that 'viewed within the context of the whole of s 11, "freedom" in s 11(1) undoubtedly points towards physical integrity and not a broad, all embracing right to freedom'.[20]

Ackermann J also fails to provide an adequate explanation of the existence of the necessity test for an unenumerated residual right of freedom whereas important enumerated rights, such as equality in s 8 or privacy in s 13, are protected only by the less onerous reasonable test. His reply is decidedly half-hearted:

*'I certainly disagree … that this is anomalous. Even if it were anomalous, I do not believe*

---

14  (1905) 198 US 45.
15  Para 47.
16  Para 48.
17  Para 51.
18  Para 69.
19  Para 210.
20  Para 58.

*that the anomaly assists this Court in construing the s 11(1) right to freedom. ... There may well be good reason why the limitation of a s 13 right is only subject to the "reasonable" test. It may be because of the natural tension between this right and the right to freedom, or for some other reason, about which it is unprofitable to speculate.'*[21]

The existence of a 'good' reason is not apparent to this reader of the judgment. It would surely have been to the profit of the judgment had there been some 'speculation' as to whether any adequate reason could be given, before concluding that a right which would otherwise fit within the scheme suggested by Mokgoro J should be given such an extensive interpretation.

Ackermann J was concerned about the consequences of his interpretation and the *Lochner* problem. He concludes: 'It is to me inconceivable that the broad sweep of labour legislation in the country could be struck down because of an argument that it infringed rights of contractual freedom protected by the Constitution.'[22]

He then suggests that '[a]s a general proposition it is difficult to see how labour and other social legislation would be struck down where such legislation easily passes constitutional scrutiny in countries such as the United States of America, Canada and Germany'.[23]

This is an exceptionally bold statement, particularly in the light of comparative precedent. The Canadian Supreme Court in *Lavigne v Ontario Public Service Employees Union*,[24] admittedly in an *obiter dictum*, stated that the right to freedom of association includes the right not to associate, which would entail a finding that closed-shop and union-shop arrangements breach the constitutional guarantee of freedom of association.

The United States Supreme Court in *Abood v Detroit Board of Education*[25] struck down a law compelling non-members to pay to a public employee's union a service fee equal in amount to union dues in those cases where ideological union expenditures were not directly related to collective bargaining. The majority decision did not uphold any right of a non-member to withhold contributions from the cost of communicative activities, so long as the activities were relevant to the union's operations as a representative of workers during the process of collective bargaining.

---

21  Para 65.

22  Para 66.

23  Para 66.

24  (1991) 81 DLR 545.

25  431 US 209 (1977). See, in general, Laurence H Tribe *American Constitutional Law* 2 ed (1988) at 805.

On the basis of this finding, and depending how far the notion of 'ideological expenditure' is developed, an agency-shop agreement as recognized in the Labour Relations Act 66 of 1995 may be vulnerable — a real possibility if the ideological content of Ackermann J's jurisprudence holds general sway.

The negative concept of freedom advocated by Berlin[26] is consistent with the approach which fired the jurisprudential outlook of the *Lavigne* and *Lochner* courts and, if followed, would clash fundamentally with the constitutional guarantee of equality and the balance of the social commitments analysed in chapter 2. There are a number of objections that can be raised against the manner in which Ackermann J employs Berlin. For my part, two are of the utmost importance. In the first place, as revealed in the quotation cited above, Berlin did not ignore the question of competing values. When he addressed the concept of liberty, Berlin was anxious to expose the corruption of the concept of positive liberty in which goals other than those defined by the affected person are implemented, defined in the main by rulers who purport to divine the true aspirations of every subject, notwithstanding what the individual might desire were he or she to be protected by the existence of negative freedom. However, the importance that he attached to negative freedom, particularly in his 'Two Concepts', should not serve to detract from the equally important argument against the conclusion that all political virtues can be harmonized by means of one over-arching principle. As he wrote:

> 'One freedom may abort another; one freedom may obstruct or fail to create conditions which make other freedoms, or freedom for many persons, positive; positive and negative freedom may collide; the freedom of the individual or the group may not be fully compatible with a full degree of participation in a common life, with its demands for cooperation, solidarity, fraternity. But beyond all these there is an even more acute issue; the paramount need to satisfy the claims, no less ultimate, values; justice, happiness, love, the realisation of capacities to create new things and experiences and ideas, the discovery of the truth. Nothing is gained by identifying freedom proper, in either of its senses, with these values or with the conditions of freedom, or by confounding types of freedom with one another.'[27]

---

26  *Four Essays on Liberty* (1968) at 1.

27  Charles Taylor 'What is wrong with Negative Liberty?' in David Miller (ed) *Liberty* (1991) at 146. In some way the dispute about liberty which has been prompted by the *Ferreira* judgment reflects a clear divide in the philosophical literature between a libertarian position and one that can be sourced in Hegel. In his *Philosophy of Right* (T M Knox (trans)) Hegel objects to the negative concept of liberty favoured by libertarian and liberal thinkers on the grounds that it takes the choice of the individual as the basis from which freedom must begin. Questions of how and why choices are made, are

It is in his insistence that negative liberty is at the heart of the s 11 guarantee of liberty, and in his one-dimensional use of Berlin which ignores the latter's more complex project, that the problem for the South African Constitution lies were Ackermann J's jurisprudence to become hegemonic. In the context employed by Ackermann J, negative liberty is purely an opportunity-concept where freedom is purely a matter of what individuals can do, of the lack of obstacles placed in the way of what is open to the individual. But this is a distorted version of freedom which has all too crudely considered that freedom should merely embrace the exercise of control over one's life without recourse to any other consideration. Freedom is inextricably linked to the ability to determine one's identity and the shape of one's life. Freedom is not merely an opportunity-concept; it is also an exercise-concept. As Charles Taylor puts it: 'If we are free in the exercise of certain capacities, then we are not free or less free, when these capacities are in some way unfulfilled or blocked. But the obstacles can be internal as well as external.'[28]

Taylor's critique of negative freedom is based on its omission of any account of an individual being able to recognize his or her important purposes and to overcome, or at least neutralize, his or her 'motivational fetters'.[29] Read in one context, it is possible to see how this would stimulate Ackermann J's Orwellian nightmare, but in another it raises the question that negative liberty, as employed by Ackermann J, ignores completely the link between freedom and the ability of the individual to actualize self-realization.

This brings me to my second objection, namely the South African Constitution's unequivocal commitment to a society where the self-realization of all members of society can be attained. The point has been grasped by other members of the court. For example, Mahomed DP (as he then was) said in *S v Makwanyane* that '[t]he South African Constitution is different: it … represents … a vigorous identification of and commitment to a democratic, universalistic, caring and aspirationally egalitarian ethos, expressly articulated in the Constitution'.[30] This reading can be clearly

---

then ignored, nor is any consideration given to the manner in which needs, choices and identity are shaped by an individual being part of the community. See Hegel at 104–10.

28  Taylor at 162.

29  1995 (3) SA 391 (CC) at para 262.

30  I am indebted to the important examination of the meaning and scope of transformatist constitutional law of Karl Klare 'Legal Culture and Transformative Constitutionalism' (1998) 14 *SAJHR* 146. This section draws heavily on his insights into the vision of the Constitution.

sourced in the text.[31] There are at least five separate commitments in the text which reinforce this position, namely:

1.  The express provision of social rights and a recognition of the substantive nature of equality. For example, s 1 provides that the Republic is founded on the value of achieving equality. Section 9(2) provides, inter alia, that equality includes the full and equal enjoyment of all rights and freedoms. Section 7(2) commits the government to promoting democratic values, human rights and equality.

2.  Horizontality. The earlier jurisprudence of the court notwithstanding, s 8 extends the scope of the Constitution to private relations. Even under the interim Constitution in terms of which Ackermann J delivered his judgment in *Ferreira's* case, s 35(3) mandated a constitutional audit of all law, even when applicable to private relations.

3.  The Constitution envisages a system of government that is open and accountable. As s 234 states: '[T]he government must actively promote and deepen a culture of democracy.'

4.  The protection of identity. The Constitution strives for a society which treats every person with equal concern and respect. Sections 30 and 31 protect and promote multiculturalism, s 9 protects the vulnerable and weak, and, somewhat more progressively than comparable instruments, expressly gay people.

5.  The importance of being rooted in the history of the country. While the interim Constitution showed a greater sensitivity to the country's history than the 'ersatz' Canadian-styled draft of the final Constitution, particularly in the Preamble and the Postamble, ss 1, 7 and 39(1) are clear indicators of the transformative vision of the final text.

As Klare correctly notes, these factors support an argument in favour of a constitution which is 'social, redistributive, caring, positive, at least partly horizontal, participatory, multicultural and self-conscious about its historical setting and transformative role and mission'.[32] By contrast, Ackermann J's employment of negative liberty is indicative of a commitment to atomistic, individual 'man' and of a world view which over-emphasizes the importance of individuality and autonomous choice as components of the well-being of each individual.

If the objection is that my egalitarian predelicting have clouded my judgement of Ackermann J's approach, an objector still requires the production of an answer which can show a satisfactory fit between Ackermann J's Lochnerian approach

---

31   Klare at 154–5.

32   See, for example, J R Lucas 'Against Equality' (1965) 4 *Philosophy* 296.

and the overwhelming textual support for a commitment to a caring and sharing society in which the autonomy of each individual is only part of the recipe for the establishment of an open and democratic society based on the human dignity, freedom and equality principle.[33] In short, Ackermann J can invoke the support of John Stuart Mill, namely, that 'over himself, over his own body and mind, the individual is sovereign'.[34]

But he would then be forced to confront the same Mill, who wrote in the very same work:

> '*How … can any part of the conduct of a member of society be a matter of indifference to other members? No person is an entirely isolated being; it is impossible for a person to do anything seriously or permanently hurtful to himself, without mischief reaching at least to his near connections, and often far beyond them. …If by his vices or follies a person does no direct harm to others, he is nevertheless … injurious by his example; and ought to control himself for the sake of those whom the sight or knowledge of his conduct might corrupt or mislead.*'[35]

In short, Mill recognized the need for external constraint and, although this auto-critique does not go far enough, it is indicative of the problems with the cruder, atomistic version of liberty. It does not go far enough because it still sees the freedom in a society which permits rich and poor to sleep on the benches of Joubert Park. If freedom consists in doing that which one desires, the lack of capacity is fatal to the ability to fulfil the wish.

Briefly stated, the negative concept of liberty shows little concern for external constraint, it shows little concern for promoting the freedom of the entire community, and in its formalism it ignores the question of capacity to act out one's desires. For these reasons it is not that liberty admits of one answer, namely that which is advocated by Ackermann J; rather, liberty is a more subtle and nuanced concept which admits of reconciliation with the remaining foundational values. Here, the South African Constitution looks to a society in which personal freedom and the right to self-assertion need to be strengthened. But it envisages a new community whose members are no longer pawns of the authority of either the public or the private sphere and where individual destiny is imposed by racism, sexism, class or any other form of prejudice which were the very cancers which

---

33   See Klare at 177.

34   John Stuart Mill *On Liberty* (J M Robson (ed) *Collected Works* vol 18) 224.

35   Mill at 280.

destroyed any possibility of community under apartheid. In adopting the formulation of human dignity, freedom and equality, the Constitution recognizes that we need to reconstruct a sense of community but we also need to be protected from those who wish to impose their version of humanity upon the rest of us. Roberto Unger expresses this succinctly as follows: 'As we free ourselves from entrenched structures of social division and hierarchy, we diminish the quota of dependence and depersonalisation in group life and begin to heal the wounding conflict between the conditions of self-assertion.'[36]

Ackermann J seeks to achieve a dichotomy between a *laissez-faire* conception of liberty and a collective vision of a new society. Self-assertion and individual autonomy must be harmonized with the desire to change our practices and institutions, so that all within the society can have a fair crack at self-assertion, so that for the majority there is no longer 'a disproportion between the intensity of [their] desires and the indignity of the objects on which they must ordinarily fasten'.[37]

In a later work, Berlin himself conceded much of this argument. As he wrote:

*'Total liberty for wolves is death to the lambs, total liberty of the powerful, the gifted, is not compatible with the rights to decent existence of the weak and the less gifted. … Equality may demand the restraint of the liberty of those who wish to dominate; liberty — without some modicum of which there is no choice and therefore no possibility of remaining human as we understand the word — may have to be curtailed in order to make room for social welfare, to feed the hungry, to clothe the naked, to shelter the homeless, to leave room for the liberty of others, to allow justice or fairness to be exercised.'*[38]

For Berlin, however, a clash of values is inevitable, for 'we must say that the world in which what we see as incompatible values are not in conflict is a world altogether beyond our ken: that principles which are harmonised in this other world, are not the principles with which, in our daily lives, we are acquainted; if they are transformed, it is into conceptions not know to us on earth but it is on earth that we live, and it is here that we must believe and act'.[39]

Unfortunately, it is also on earth that constitutional lawyers exist, and it is on the same planet that constitutional judges must adjudicate. To follow Berlin's negative

---

36  Roberto Unger *What should Legal Analysis become?* (1996) at 185.

37  Unger at 185.

38  Berlin *The Crooked Timber of Humanity* (1992) 12–13.

39  Berlin at 13.

concept of liberty is to render the Constitution incompatible with its second leitmotif, equality. But this is exactly what Ackermann J achieved, in order to conclude that the restrictions placed by s 417(2)*(b)* of the Companies Act on an examinee constitute an infringement of his or her freedom guaranteed by s 11(1).

It is somewhat ironic that the intellectual source of the judgment — Berlin — revealed a clear recognition of the tension between freedom (presumably in his terms) and equality when he wrote that it is 'the notion of freedom in its "positive" sense that is at the heart of the demands for national or social self-direction which animate the most powerful and morally just public movements of our time'.[40] For Berlin, positive freedom was the equivalent of the principle of equality which is enshrined in the Constitution. He was concerned that the implementation of 'positive' freedom would enhance the role of the state at the expense of the freedom of the individual. He was particularly concerned that 'the belief that some single formulation can in principle be found whereby all the diverse ends of man can be harmoniously realised is demonstrably false'.[41] For this reason, Berlin rejected the concept of 'positive' freedom as being incompatible with liberty. A government which sought to implement a programme for the attainment of 'positive' liberty would encroach upon the individual's zone of privacy and autonomy. Government would soon know what was good for the individual, and liberty would then be more of a sham than a reality. In contrast, our Constitution enjoins the courts to pursue liberty with equality, even were a negative concept of liberty to be employed. Negative freedom can operate only in a society in which all are equal and free to pursue their own ends, and most certainly not in a society to be reconstructed after apartheid.[42]

In his separate judgment, Sachs J recognizes that '[f]reedom and equality are [at] one and the same time in tension with each other, and mutually supportive'.[43] Unfortunately, the recognition of this tension does not lead to the conceptual

---

40   Berlin *Four Essays on Liberty* at 169.

41   Loc cit.

42   In his very last contribution to this issue Berlin makes a comment that is not only devastating of Ackermann J's interpretation but also reveals the extreme danger of uncritical philosophical borrowing. He writes that negative liberty could be interpreted as economic *laissez-faire*, 'whereby in the name of freedom owners are allowed to destroy the lives of children in mines, or factory owners to destroy the health and character of workers in industry. But that was a perversion of and not what the concept basically means to human beings, …' (*New York Review of Books* 14 May 1998 at 58). *Laissez-faire* could therefore not be crudely equated with liberty.

43   Para 253.

reconciliation that would harmonize the approach developed by Ackermann J with the jurisprudential premise of the Constitution.

But Sachs J has at least begun to indicate the way forward. In *Bernstein & others v Bester & others NNO* O'Regan J said:

> 'The conception of freedom underlying the Constitution must embrace that interdependence without denying the value of individual autonomy. It must recognise the important role that the State, and others, will play in seeking to enhance individual autonomy and dignity and the enjoyment of rights and freedoms.'[44]

There remains, therefore, the challenge of developing a coherent basis for reconciling the tensions and challenges of a Constitution which promises freedom and equality. For O'Regan J, the constitutional guarantee of freedom yields to a greater aim, one which is directed to 'facilitate the achievement of autonomy and equality [which] is explicit within the constitutional framework'.[45] Is this intended to relegate equality to the achievement of freedom, or is the principle of freedom as employed in the Constitution of a lower order, so that together with an equal commitment to equality a democratic society can be created? O'Regan J appears to be concerned with the second question, as her judgment is directed towards a re-examination of a negative concept of freedom employed by Ackermann J.

## CONCLUSION

The conclusion reached by the majority of the court in *Ferreira's* case was that the compulsion to give self-incriminating evidence has to be coupled with an immunity: that such evidence cannot be directly used in a criminal trial and has to be subjected to the further judicial discretion to exclude derivative evidence at a criminal trial. Such finding could not breach the essential content of the rights under s 11(1) or the right under s 25(3). This finding is eminently sensible, as is the declaration of the invalidity of s 417(2)(b) of the Companies Act on the narrow ground, and to the limited extent that incriminating evidence given by an examinee under compulsion of the provisions of s 417(2)(b) will be rendered inadmissible in criminal proceedings against a person previously examined pursuant to its terms.

---

44   1996 (2) SA 751 (CC) at para 150.

45   Para 151.

Ackermann J reached the same conclusion, but on a basis that could set one part of the interim Constitution at war with the other. This conclusion aside, Ackermann J's judgment is probably the first to invoke a broader philosophical reading of the Constitution. This attempt to reconcile the words of the text with the Constitution's premise reveals not only the contestable content of a Constitution but also the extent to which it is an unfinished project whose meaning will change in the light of political development and social experience. In short, the dispute about Ackermann J's approach to s 11 represents the perfect reposte to the plain-language approach advocated by Fagan, as discussed in chapter 2 above. The plain-meaning lobby seeks to achieve constitutional closure by advocating the kind of 'absolute categories or ideals' of which Berlin, ironically, was fearful.[46]

On another level, it would appear that Ackermann J is concerned that a society over-committed to equality may well produce an Orwellian nightmare in which individual freedom is constricted by the zeal of equality advocates to fashion a society based on 'happiness' as defined by them. Significantly, Orwell wrote that the

> 'real objective of Socialism is not happiness [but] human brotherhood. ... Nearly all creators of Utopia have resembled the man who has toothache, and therefore thinks happiness consists in not having toothache. He wanted to produce a perfect society by an endless continuation of something that had only been valuable because it was temporary.'[47]

In short, whereas Ackermann J poses the choice as between autonomy for the individual and the imposition of a particular vision of society by the 'social engineers' — all in the name of equality — Orwell, whose work *1984* provides the fictitious illustration of what occurred in post-war Russia, has a more nuanced set of distinctions in which equality is viewed as being about 'human brotherhood', about a society in which all members are equal in that each is treated with equal concern and respect and all members are sufficiently empowered to enjoy their freedom. For Orwell the holistic vision went completely wrong because it was a total holistic vision. Balancing is required; as Berlin put it 'claims can be balanced compromises

---

46  See Charles Taylor *The Ethics of Authenticity* (1992). See also Stuart Woolman and Dennis Davis 'The Last Laugh; *Du Plessis v De Klerk*, Classical Liberalism, Creole Liberalism and the Application of Fundamental Rights under the Interim and Final Constitutions' (1996) 12 *SAJHR* 361. I am truly indebted to Stuart Woolman for his collaboration in the publication of this article. As is apparent, I have drawn heavily on this piece in which I was significantly influenced by his ideas.

47  George Orwell *1984* (1948) at 332.

can be reached: in concrete situations not every claim is of equal force: so much liberty and so much equality'.[48]

Stated differently, the jurisprudence expressed in *Ferreira* is about the preservation of a set of principles which are immune from democratic debate or contest. A set of principles entrenches a zone of autonomy abstracted from historical or material context and which must be defended against any democratic decision to change them. Neutral principles trump any attempt at democracy. As Bernard Williams and Amartya Sen write, this is 'an outlook favouring social arrangements under which a utilitarian elite controls a society in which the majority may not itself share the beliefs of the elite'.

My difference with Ackermann J illustrates what is meant by a contest of constitutional meaning. For me, Ackermann J's philosophical approach is retrogressive because it stands in sharp contrast to what I consider to be the fundamental underpinnings of the Constitution: the interpretation of liberty and equality within the particular African context of *ubuntu*.[49] Ackermann J has put forward a somewhat different vision, one grounded in a commitment to principles which promote the individual as an anatomized individual rather than as a member of a community. The problem can be stated differently. There is a tension between individual autonomy and collective power. Our Constitution enjoins us to conceive of our society as one in which the collective becomes a source of autonomy rather than a threat to its functions.

The Constitution which ushered in the promise of democracy in 1994 spoke of *ubuntu*, the traditional spirit of humanism expressed in the African notion that people are people through other people. Within this concept the idea is contained that individual selves are not merely socially constructed, but that all their actions are in some way addressed towards other people and communities with whom they are involved or within which they are situated. Since the meaning of action is assigned within socially constructed frameworks of meaning, other individuals to whom the actions are addressed, whether directly or indirectly, can have some-

---

48 'The Pursuit of the Ideal' in *The Crooked Timber of Humanity* (1992) at 17.

49 At the risk of boring readers with my complaint against the prevailing fetish of plain language (as opposed to clear drafting to which unequivocal support can be given), the omission of rich African concepts, such as *ubuntu*, from the final text can presumably be explained by the fact that the overseas expert, while a talented drafter in his own right, clearly employed a Canadian drafter's manual, which did not contain African terminology.

thing meaningful to say about the rightness or wrongness of such action. As Jennifer Nedelsky has noted:

> 'We must develop and sustain the capacity for finding our new law, and the task is to understand what social forms, relationships and personal practices foster that capacity. I use the word "find" to suggest that we do not make or even exactly choose our own law. The idea of "finding" one's own law is true to the belief that even what is truly one's own life is shaped by the society in which one lives and the relationships that are part of one's life.' [50]

The challenge of reconciliation between these two foundational values is recognized by O'Regan J in *Bernstein's* case, namely that a radical constitutional project needs to acknowledge that autonomy can be fostered within a more communitarian vision, in which liberty is not merely a negative buffer to state incursion but rather a positive injunction to a new society. The final Constitution poses similar interpretive challenges for the court. Section 39(1) enjoins a court, when interpreting the Bill of Rights, to promote the values that underlie an open and democratic society based on human dignity, equality and freedom. The Preamble proclaims as an objective of the Constitution that it '[h]eal the divisions of the past and establish a society based on democratic values, social justice and fundamental human rights'. Section 1 states that South Africa is a 'sovereign democratic state founded [inter alia] on [h]uman dignity, the achievement of equality and advancement of human rights and freedoms'.

The emphasis placed upon human dignity and social justice indicates that certain values need to be reconciled to ensure that the interpretive process promotes the integrity of the entire Constitution. As has been argued throughout this work, the values of the Constitution are not immutable, nor is it a simple matter of discovering values from the plain words of the text. They are values that seek to underpin a democracy in which equal participation of all the members of society becomes possible and in which the elected governors of the society are accountable to the people who elected them. By contrast, the convictions that fuel the jurisprudence of *Ferreira v Levin* wish to construct a fence of neutral principles to keep democratic output at bay. The contest regarding the reading of 'freedom' should ultimately be seen within this context.

---

50   Jennifer Nedelsky 'Reconceiving Autonomy: Sources, Thoughts and Possibilities' in A Hutchinson and L Green (eds) *Law and the Community: The End of Individualism?* (1994) at 220–1.

South Africa awaits judgment by the Constitutional Court, not only in which the possibility is raised of giving the values of the Constitution this indigenous perspective but also in which guidance will be given on which model of constitutionalism — neutral value or democratic — is to be followed.

Although decided in terms of the 1993 Constitution, the 1996 Constitution will pose similar challenges. Looking up the meaning of words in *The Oxford English Dictionary* is unlikely to deliver on this promise, a critical engagement with the foundational values of our Constitution. An equal danger, however, is posed in the philosophy which underpins Ackermann J's approach in *Ferreira's* case and the later contribution in *Du Plessis'* case. By arguing for the immunization of private activity from any scrutiny, and the concomitant argument that there can be no meaningful notion of freedom if the state, or anyone else, tries to second-guess choices about the good life, the Constitution's transformatist potential is mangled into a view that masks substantial inequality in social power and renders the concept of autonomy for the majority of South Africans somewhat meaningless.[51] It also has major implications for the interpretation of s 8 and the scope of the Constitution. But that must remain the subject of a separate chapter.

---

51  See, in particular, Jennifer Nedelsky *Private Property and the Limits of the American Constitution* (1990).

# EQUALITY

## EQUALITY: THE SEARCH FOR AN ANIMATING VISION

It is a basic tenet of the overwhelming number of contemporary moral and political theories that human beings are intrinsically of equal worth. As Thomas Jefferson wrote in the American Declaration of Independence, 'we hold these truths to be self-evident that all men are equal and are endowed by their creator with certain inalienable rights and among these the rights of life, liberty and the pursuit of happiness.' The centrality and longevity of the value notwithstanding, its core meaning remains elusive. If, as one commentator has observed, 'every plausible political theory has the same ultimate value, which is equality,'[1] it only goes to show the contest nature of the value. The paramount duty of our Constitutional Court to take sides in that contest for equality is therefore central to our constitutional enterprise.

When the Republic of South African Constitution Act[2] (the interim Constitution) proclaimed the fundamental aim of our Constitutional enterprise to be the achievement of an open and democratic society based on freedom and equality, it introduced the requirement that the policies and programmes of government had to be justified in the public domain in terms of the values of openness, transparency, freedom and equality. In a number of different sections, the Constitution of the Republic of South Africa Act[3] (the final Constitution) reinforces the existence of these values from which a justification for policy must be sought. Section 1 provides that the Republic of South Africa is to be one, sovereign, democratic state founded on the following values:

(a) Human dignity, the achievement of equality and the advancement of human rights and freedoms.

(b) Non-racialism and non-sexism.

(c) Supremacy of the Constitution and the rule of law.

(d) Universal adult suffrage, a national common voters' roll, regular elections and a multi-party system of democratic government, to ensure accountability, responsiveness and openness.

---

1   Will Kymlicka *Contemporary Political Philosophy* (1990) at 4.

2   Act 200 of 1993.

3   Act 108 of 1996.

Section 7(1) provides that the Bill of Rights is to be the cornerstone of democracy in South Africa. It enshrines the rights of all people in our country and affirms the democratic values of human dignity, equality and freedom. Subsection (2) provides that the state must respect, protect, promote and fulfil the rights in the Bill of Rights. The limitation clause (previously s 33 of the interim Constitution, now s 36 of the final Constitution) provides that the rights in the Bill of Rights may be limited only in terms of a law of general application to the extent that the limitation is reasonable and justifiable in an open and democratic society based on human dignity, equality and freedom. Section 39(1) of the final Constitution (previously s 35(3) of the interim Constitution) enjoins a court to interpret the Bill of Rights so as to promote the values that underlie an open and democratic society based on human dignity, equality and freedom.

The elusive nature of equality exposes the poverty of the ordinary language approach to constitutionalism. In a case of interpreting an equality guarantee, the rule and the reasons therefor cannot really be separated.[4] A reasonable person may not agree with a particular justification for a judgment grounded on the principles of dignity, equality and freedom. Such a reasonable participant in a dispute may adopt a different conceptual approach to these principles or may disagree about the weight to be given to each value in the determination of the overall justification. But if our constitutional enterprise seeks to introduce a culture of justification, the corollary is the establishment of a culture of reason. In other words, the test is not so much whether all citizens will agree with a particular justification for a policy of government or to the weight to be given by a court to a particular right entrenched in the Constitution. A court may well ground its judgment in what it considers to be reason but fail to convince disputants that it has an acceptable justification between the outcome of a policy and a coherent interpretation of the entrenched values contained in the Constitution.

The establishment of a culture of reason introduces a tangible measure of content into our constitutional enterprise. We are not merely concerned to protect the right of each citizen to participate in the political arena.[5] We are concerned with the inclusivity of debate about the meaning of those foundational constitutional commitments that lie at the heart of our new society. By requiring that one conception of our Constitution can trump another only by reasoned

---

4    Joseph Raz *The Morality of Freedom* (1986) at 58f suggests that it is the authority of the rule, not the underlying reasons therefor, that should guide the interpretation process.

5    J H Ely *Democracy and Distrust. A Theory of Judicial Review* (1980).

argument, our Constitution 'challenges "the peoples'" self-enclosing tendency to assume their own moral completion as presently [sic] enshrined and thus to deny to themselves the plurality of perspectives on which their capacity for transformative self-renewal depends'.[6] In short, the Constitution seeks to establish a culture of reasoned argument in terms of which one interpretative framework for the foundational values does not deny the possibility of other frameworks but rather sets up the potential for reasoned contest.

It is for this particular reason that the jurisprudential coherence of our constitutional enterprise is dependent upon a conceptually understandable exposition by the Constitutional Court of the fundamental values of dignity, equality and freedom. To date, the court has either been cautious or enigmatic, to the extent that the constitutional debate about the fundamental values of equality and freedom has been fought in a constitutional vacuum. In its early judgments, the court did provide some guidance when it focused attention on the key value of dignity. As O'Regan J said in *S v Makwanyane*:[7]

> *'The importance of dignity as a founding value of the New Constitution cannot be over emphasised. Recognising a right to dignity is an acknowledgement of the intrinsic worth of human beings.... This right therefore is the foundation of many rights that are specifically entrenched in Chapter 3.'*

Similarly, in *Fraser v Children's Court, Pretoria North*[8] Mahomed DP said of the value of equality: 'there can be no doubt that the guarantee of equality lies at the very heart of the Constitution. It permeates and defines the very ethos upon which the Constitution is premised.'

The 1996 Constitution strengthens the need for clarity in respect of the interpretation of these values. By the inclusion of the principle of dignity the text affords the court the opportunity of clarifying the link between the principles of freedom and equality. The landmark philosophical text in which the meaning of dignity is given clear content is Kant's *Foundation of the Metaphysic of Morals*[9] and particularly the second formulation of the categorical imperative:

> *'Man necessarily thinks of his own existence in this way; thus far it is a subjective principle of human actions. Also every other rational being thinks of his existence by*

---

6    Frank Michaelman 'Law's Republic' (1988) 97 *Yale Law Journal* 1493 at 1532.
7    1995 (3) SA 391 (CC) at para 324.
8    1997 (2) SA 261 (CC) at para 20.
9    R P Wolf (ed) (1969) at 53–4.

*means of the same rational ground which holds also for myself; thus it is at the same time an objective principle from which as a supreme practical ground, it must be possible to derive all other laws of the world.'*

The practical importance, therefore, is the following: 'Act so that you treat humanity whether in your own person or in that of another, always as an end and never as a means only.'

By recognizing a person's sense of dignity, one affirms the central intrinsic worth of each human being. Not surprisingly, the fundamental importance of this principle was recognized long before Kant. For example, before the current era, rabbis confirmed the intrinsic value of each human being. Thus, Ben Sira says 'honour thy neighbour as thy self', whilst Hillel suggested that the entire Torah can be encapsulated in the dictum, 'whatever is hateful unto thee, do it not unto thy fellow', confirming the proposition that as all human beings are created in the divine image, each is entitled to human love and each must be treated with equal concern and respect.[10] Different philosophical traditions therefore lead to a similar conclusion, namely that the principles embedded in the Constitution envisage a community based on ethical individualism, that is, a community which is concerned to implement a commitment to equality of participation in the social, economic and political fabric of society and simultaneously to preserve the claim to moral autonomy of each of its citizens.

For constitutional law the importance of these values is that the prevailing conception will ultimately contribute to the definition of the nature of our community. As Ronald Dworkin has written:

> *'If it is true that self-government is possible only within the community that meets the conditions of moral membership, because only then are we entitled to refer to government by "the people", in a powerful communal rather than a barren statistical sense, we need a conception of democracy that insists that no democracy exists unless those conditions are met.'*[11]

In short, by affirming the principles of dignity, equality and freedom as central to the new culture of justification and reason, the Constitution establishes the terrain on which citizens can contest the moral shape of our community as envisaged by the constitutional enterprise. As important as the Western tradition might

---

10   J H Hertz *The Soncino Edition of the Pentateuch and Haftorahs* (1960) at 563.

11   R Dworkin *Freedom's Law — The Moral Reading of the American Constitution* (1966) at 24.

be in determining the content and scope of equality, it should never be forgotten that the African tradition must be considered, with the constitutional emphasis on *ubuntu* which compels the court in a communitarian direction.

Constitutional law has not been excluded in the fiercely contested nature of equality. By way of illustration, in a controversial article, Peter Westen[12] has argued that equality as a jurisprudential concept was not only unnecessary but also misleading and devoid of content. Westen's central thesis is encapsulated in the following passage from his article:

> *'Thus, to say that people who are morally alike in a certain respect "should be treated alike" means that they should be treated in accord with the moral rule by which they are determined to be alike. Hence "likes should be treated alike" means that people for whom a certain treatment is prescribed by a standard should be given the treatment prescribed by the standard. Or, more simply, people who by a rule should be treated alike should by the rule be treated alike. So there it is: equality is entirely "[c]ircular".'[13]*

Stated briefly, if the principle requires a certain treatment of each of the two people, they should be treated alike by virtue of that prior principle and not by virtue of the value of equality. Westen considers that the injunction of equal treatment is a necessary consequence of applying a rule to all cases to which the terms of that rule dictate that it be applied. In other words, the rule and its application are logically posterior to determinations of equality. On its own, equality is devoid of content and meaning.

Considering that equality is central to our Constitution, Westen's argument makes somewhat disturbing reading, particularly because our Constitution clearly intended that a definite content be given to the concept of equality. But what if it is inevitably devoid of content, as Westen suggests? Within the context of our constitutional enterprise, the response must be to reject Westen's argument. Our Constitution enjoins that we care about different treatment of people because we have created a social compact which 'establishes among the citizens' such an equality that they all pledge themselves under the same conditions and ought to enjoy the same rights. By the nature of the compact, therefore, every act of sovereignty, that is, every authentic act of the general will, binds or favours equality for all the citizens'.[14]

---

12. 'The Empty Idea of Equality' (1982) 95 *Harvard Law Review* 537.

13. At 547.

14. J Rousseau *The Social Contract* Book II Chapter IV, cited in F W Coker (ed) *Readings in Political Philosophy* (1929) at 492–3.

The concept of equality lies at the centre of the South African constitutional idea. It is not simply there to be employed as a 'talisman incantation to decide the controversies'.[15] The principle of equality should therefore not be employed as a jurisprudential warcry which lacks any content.

The objective of equality is not merely the recognition of a certain dignity of the human being as such, but it is also to provide him with the opportunity — equal to that guaranteed to others — 'for protecting and advancing his interests and developing his (her) powers and personality'.[16]

Prior to the case of *President of the Republic of South Africa & another v Hugo*,[17] the Constitutional Court had only once engaged in any depth with the challenges posed by the concept of equality.[18] In addition, Ackermann J developed a lengthy analysis of the principle of freedom in *Ferreira v Levin NO*.[19] The particular facts of *Hugo* only added to its potential importance:

On 27 June 1994, the President and two Executive Deputy Presidents signed the Presidential Act No 17, in terms of which a special remission of sentences was granted to certain categories of prisoner, including 'mothers in prison on 10 May 1994, with minor children under the age of twelve years'. Hugo was a male prisoner who was the father of a son under the age of 12 years although by the time the judgment in the court *a quo* was delivered he was 13 years old. The mother of the child had died while Hugo was in prison. He sought an order declaring that the Presidential Act was unconstitutional and directing the President to correct it in accordance with the provisions of the interim Constitution. In short, he alleged that the Act violated s 8(1) and (2) of the interim Constitution in that it unfairly discriminated against him on the grounds of sex or gender and indirectly against his son in terms of s 8(2) because the incarcerated parent was not a woman. In the court *a quo* Magid J found that the Act discriminated against Hugo and his son on the grounds of gender and consequently ordered the President to correct the Act in terms of the provision of the interim Constitution within six months of the date of the order.

---

15  Erwin Chemerinsky 'In Defence of Equality: A Reply to Professor Westen' (1983) 81 *Michigan Law Review* 575 at 578.

16  R Pennock 'Democracy and Leadership' in W Chambers & R Salisbury (eds) *Democracy Today* (1962) 126, as cited by Chemerinsky op cit 586.

17  1997 (4) SA 1 (CC).

18  In *Brink v Kitshoff NO* 1996 (4) SA 197 (CC).

19  1996 (1) SA 984 (CC), which is discussed elsewhere in this work.

On appeal, the Constitutional Court was required to consider two questions:

1. The nature of the powers granted to the President in terms of s 82(1)(*k*) of the interim Constitution, namely the power to pardon or reprieve offenders either unconditionally or subject to such conditions as he or she may deem fit, and to remit any fines, penalties or forfeitures; and

2. In the event that the court found that such power was subject to review, whether the exercise thereof breached any of the rights enshrined in the Constitution.

The court's finding revealed a bold commitment to the culture of justification in its approach to the prerogative powers. The interim Constitution provided for the powers of the President in s 82(1) and, as Goldstone J observed, 'these powers have their origin in the prerogative powers found in earlier constitution but under the new constitutional dispensation there were no powers derived from the royal prerogative other than those set out in s 82(1)'.[20]

In examining the scope for review, the court carefully examined the decision in *Council of Civil Service Unions v Minister for the Civil Service*[21] and observed that the majority of the House of Lords was of the opinion that the exercise of power authorized by the prerogative may be revisable, the decision depending on the subject-matter. Whilst the English courts have developed the range of grounds of review beyond the initial 'list' as set out by Lord Roskill in the *CCSU* case,[22] there remain some areas of 'high' policy 'such as the making of treaties, the defence of the realm and the appointment of Ministers' where the courts do not intervene because the matters are not justifiable.[23]

Goldstone J emphasized that the introduction of a constitutional state in which the Constitution shall be the supreme law of the Republic and that any law inconsistent with its provisions shall be of no force and effect obliged the court to test (s 4 of the interim Constitution) any action by any organ of state against the provision of the Constitution. As he said:

'*It would be contrary to that promise if the exercise of presidential power is above the interim Constitution and is not subject to the discipline of the Bill of Rights. However, it may well be that, because of the nature of a section 82(1) power or the manner in*

---

20   Para 8.

21   [1985] AC 374 (HC).

22   *R v Secretary of State for Home Department; Ex P Bentley* (1994) QB 349, which deals with the prerogative of mercy.

23   De Smith, Woolf and Jowell *Judicial Review of Administrative Action* (1995) at 321.

*which it was exercised, the provisions of the interim Constitution, and, in particular,*
*the Bill of Rights, provide no ground for an effective review of presidential exercise of*
*such a power. The result, in a particular case, may be the same as that in England,*
*but the manner in which that result was reached in terms of the interim Constitution*
*is a different one. On the English approach the courts, in certain cases, depending on*
*the subject matter of the prerogative power exercised, would be deprived of jurisdic-*
*tion. Under the interim Constitution, the jurisdiction would be there in all case in which*
*the presidential powers under section 82(1) are exercised.'*[24]

Having drawn such an emphatic distinction between the English approach and
the more holistic approach mandated by the Constitution, Goldstone J concluded
somewhat more ambiguously:

*'I would emphasize that we are not required to consider the question of the reviewa-*
*bility of other powers which may be exercised by the President under s 82(1). In cases*
*where the President pardons or reprieves a single parent it is difficult … to conceive*
*of a case where a constitutional attack could be mounted against such an exercise of*
*the presidential power.'*[25]

Reduced to its essentials, the subject-matter of the power may dictate that the
matter is not justifiable — a conclusion which is then similar to that adopted by
the English courts. In short, facts rather than principle dictate the outcome.

Nevertheless, the finding is an important indication of the willingness of the
court to hold all public power, including that possessed by the President, to be
accountable to the Constitution. As the magic transition disappears and South
Africans begin to confront the long haul towards an imperfect democracy, this
finding could prove vital in curbing the arbitrary excesses of an executive less sensitive to new constitutional enterprise.

Once it had decided that the Presidential Act was subject to constitutional
review, the court was required to decide whether the Act was in conflict with s 8
of the interim Constitution in that by releasing all mothers whose children were
under the age of 12 years it had discriminated against the fathers of children of
a similar age.

Section 8 of the interim Constitution provided, inter alia, that:

*'(1) Every person shall have the rights to equality before the law land to equal*
*protection of the law;*

---

24  Para 28.
25  Para 29.

*(2)   No person shall be unfairly discriminated against, directly or indirectly, and with-*
*out derogating from the generality of this provision, one or more of the following*
*grounds in particular: race, gender, sex, ethnic or social origin, colour, sexual ori-*
*entation, age, disability, religion, conscious, belief, culture or language;*

*(3)   …*

*(4)   Prima facie proof of discrimination on any of the grounds specified in subsection*
*(2) shall be presumed to be sufficient proof of unfair discrimination as contem-*
*plated in that subsection, until the contrary is established.'*

Accordingly, Hugo argued that, by releasing the mothers of small children
but not the fathers, the President had discriminated against him on the ground
of sex. Mothers had been given a greater advantage than fathers of small children
and this decision was sufficient to establish discrimination within the meaning of
s 8(2) of the interim Constitution. As the Presidential Act *prima facie* discriminated on one of the grounds listed in s 8(2), s 8(4) raised a presumption that the
discrimination was unfair until the contrary was proved.

In an affidavit, the President informed the court that the remission of sentences of mothers with small children would serve the interests of such children.
In support of his assertion, he averred that, generally speaking, mothers are primarily responsible for the care of small children and, accordingly, the remission
policy as implemented in the Presidential Act was rationally and reasonably connected to the promotion of the best interests of the children concerned.

On behalf of the majority of the court, Goldstone J accepted that the Presidential
Act discriminated against men and that, accordingly, s 8(4) required the court to
presume that the discrimination was unfair until the contrary was proved. In dealing with the question of fairness, Goldstone J said:

*'The fact that the individuals who were discriminated against by a particular action,*
*such as the one under consideration, were not individuals who belonged to a class who*
*had historically been disadvantaged does not necessarily mean that the discrimination*
*is fair. The prohibition on unfair discrimination in the interim Constitution seeks not*
*only to avoid discrimination against the people who are members of disadvantaged groups.*
*It seeks more than that. At the heart of the prohibition of unfair discrimination lies a*
*recognition that the purpose of our new constitutional and democratic order is the estab-*
*lishment of a society in which all human beings will be accorded equal dignity and*
*respect regardless of their membership of particular groups.'*[26]

---

26   Paras 40–41. In the employment of dignity as an analytical tool with which to interpret equality as
     contained in s 8 of the interim Constitution, Goldstone J was heavily influenced by the approach

Drawing on the wording of s 8(3) of the interim Constitution, which expressly recognizes a need for measures to alleviate the disadvantages of past discrimination, Goldstone J found that the concept of unfair discrimination does not entail identical treatment in all cases but '[e]ach case … will require a careful and thorough understanding of the impact of the discriminatory action upon the particular people concerned to determine whether its overall impactis one which furthers the consstitutional goal of equality or not'.[27]

Until this point of the judgment, I had serious grounds for optimism that the Constitutional Court was about to develop a substantive concept of equality of a kind which would give clear content to a foundational value and therefore strengthen the culture of justification and reason mandated by our constitutional enterprise. Sadly, however, from this point in the judgment, principle appears to make way for pragmatism. The power of pardon was not to be given the same rigorous constitutional scrutiny as other forms of state power. As Goldstone J noted:

> 'The pardoning power in the interim Constitution … (is) … granted to the President to determine when, in his view, the public welfare will be better served by granting a remission of sentence or some other form of pardon.'[28]

The court must be careful not to interfere with the exercise of the pardoning power and, on the basis of the President's affidavit, the court found that there was sufficient justification to conclude that he had considered carefully the implications of the remission he proposed. In particular, he took into account the interest of the public and the administration of justice.[29]

---

taken by L'Heureux–Dube J in *Egan v Canada* 124 DLR (4th) 609 (SC), a case dealing with rights to a spousal allowance in the case of a gay couple. In dealing with the anti-discriminatory provision in s 15 of the Canadian Charter of Rights and Freedoms L'Heureux–Dube J found that dignity lies at the heart of the concept of non-discrimination. Acknowledging that dignity is a 'notoriously elusive concept', she went on to examine the impugned provisions from the position of the victim as a member of a group which has been rendered socially vulnerable by the approach of society to such group. In short, L'Heureux–Dube J does not invoke an individualistic conception of dignity. The use of the word 'dignity' is perhaps unfortunate in that the judgment is more concerned with the problem of the vulnerable group and the manner in which dominant power seeks to marginalize that group. See, for example, Carl F Stychin 'Novel concepts: A comment on *Egan and Nesbit v The Queen*' (1995) 6 *Constitutional Forum* 101. It is regrettable that Goldstone J borrowed the term 'dignity' from this judgment without attempting to examine it within the context of the Canadian debate about the meaning of anti-discrimination. From this particular employment of comparative law, our equality jurisprudence got off to a most questionable start.

27  Para 41.

28  Para 44.

29  Para 46.

While the release of Hugo might have been discriminatory, Goldstone J observed that

'Male prisoners outnumber female prisoners almost fiftyfold. A release of all fathers would have meant that a very large number of men prisoners would have gained their release. As many fathers play only a secondary role in child rearing, the release of male prisoners would not have contributed as significantly to the achievement of the President's purpose as the release of mothers. In addition, the release of a large number of male prisoners in current circumstances where crime has reached alarming levels would almost certainly have lead to considerable public outcry.'[30]

To those who might have been concerned that the conclusion of the court reduces to the proposition that we should trust the President, Goldstone J said:

'It is true that fathers of young children in prison were not afforded early release from prison. But although that does, without doubt, constitute a disadvantage, it does not restrict or limit their rights or obligations as fathers in any permanent manner. It cannot be said, for example, that the effect of the discrimination was to deny or limit their freedom, for their freedom was curtailed as a result of their conviction, not as a result of the Presidential Act.'[31]

This attempt at explanation notwithstanding, Goldstone J's judgment appears to reduce to the following set of arguments:

1. The President discriminated against prisoners who were fathers with children under the age of 12 years.

2. Accordingly, the President had to discharge the onus of proving that the discrimination was not unfair.

3. The pardoning power was an act of mercy directed to a particular group.

4. In considering the consequences of the pardoning power, the President carefully analysed the implications of this action and took into account the interest of the public and the administration of justice.

5. It was impossible for the President to release all fathers who were in prison, because male prisones outnumber female prisoners almost fiftyfold.

6. The rights and obligations of fathers were not restricted or limited in any permanent manner in that it was not the fact of the pardon which denied or limited their freedom but rather their prior conviction.

7. For these reasons it could not be said that the Presidential Act introduced a system of unfair discrimination as prohibited by s 8(1) and (2) of the Constitution.

---

30   Ibid.

31   Para 47.

Much of this reasoning is highly questionable, as Kriegler J eloquently exposed in a powerful dissent. In his judgment, Kriegler J found that the conclusion of the majority reinforced the gender stereotyping which the Constitution sought to outlaw. Accordingly:

> '[T]he notion relied upon by the President, namely that women are to be regarded as the primary care givers of young children, is a root cause of women's inequality in our society. It is both a result and a cause of prejudice; a societal attitude which relegates women to a subservient, occupationally inferior yet unceasingly onerous role. It is a relic and a feature of the patriarchy which the Constitution so vehemently condemns … Reliance on the generalisation that women are the primary care givers is harmful in its tendency to cramp and stunt the effort of both men and women to form their identities freely.'[32]

Significantly, Kriegler J found that the majority had conflated the inquiry as to whether discrimination was unfair in terms of s 8(2) and (4) with the limitation test as set out in s 33. The conflation is evident in the majority's conclusion that a very large number of men would have gained their release had the pardon been extended to male prisoners. As Kriegler J noted:

> 'we have not been told and have not data to found an opinion as to how many men would or could have qualified for release if the Act had treated the sexes equally. There is ever less room for a finding that the numbers would have caused a public disquiet. The President said nothing of the kind on the papers; no argument to such effect was advanced on his behalf at the hearing and counsel were not asked by the Court to address the subject.'[33]

Kriegler J's judgment represents a legitimate warning that, even if the court adopted a deferential approach to the scrutiny of the Presidential powers, it was still required to insist on a measure of rational justification for the exercise of any of these powers rather than rely on a measure of speculation about the implications of the President's decision.

Clearly stung by Kriegler J's approach to the majority judgment, O'Regan J delivered her own concurring judgment in which she observed:

> '[T]he responsibility borne by mothers for the care of children is a major cause of inequality in our society. Being responsible for the rearing of children is a great privilege, but

---

32  Para 80.
33  Para 72.

*also a great strain. Many women rear children single handedly with no help, financial or otherwise, from the fathers of the children.'*[34]

Accordingly, she correctly cautioned against insisting upon equal treatment in conditions of established inequality, for this may result in the entrenchment of the very inequality which the Constitution seeks to eradicate. On this basis, she found that there were two factors relevant to the determination of unfairness, namely:

(a)  an examination of the group which had suffered discrimination in a particular case; and

(b)  the effect of the discrimination on the interests of the group concerned.

Therefore, the more vulnerable the group adversely affected by the discrimination, the more likely the discrimination will be held to be unfair. Similarly, the more invasive the nature of the discrimination upon the interests of the individual affected by the discrimination, the more likely it will be held to be unfair.'[35]

Given the profound social disadvantage experienced by women who bear the burden of child rearing, she found that a policy which afforded women an advantage in such circumstances could not be considered to be unfair discrimination.

In one respect O'Regan J is undoubtedly correct. In his minority judgment, Kriegler J had urged that there must be a connection between the discriminatory action and the advantage to the previously disadvantaged. Therefore he found

*'from the fact that women have suffered discrimination generally, it cannot be argued that they deserve compensatory benefits in* any *context. I suggest that the relevant context in this case is a penal one, for the effect of the Presidential Act is felt by prisoners. It is not been suggested that women have suffered systematic discrimination in a penal context.'*[36]

This conclusion appears to deny the importance of systemic discrimination suffered by a group, in this case women, and may well compound the difficulty of achieving a society based on equality as envisaged by our Constitution. The eradication of systemic discrimination could well be impeded by the application of a rigid rule 'that reliance upon that generalisation even to afford some advantage to mothers would, except in very narrow circumstances be unfair'.[37] That the court

---

34  Para 110.

35  Para 112.

36  Para 84.

37  O'Regan J at para 113.

did not want to develop a concept of formal equality which would disregard established patterns of privilege and distribution is important, as is the finding that discriminatory practices should be assessed in terms of their impact and effect on human dignity.

However, in the application of these concepts the majority of the Constitutional Court has left a trail of confusion. After all, the court was dealing with a single parent. It is difficult to see how one can distinguish between the impact upon a child prevented from enjoying the care of his or her mother and a child denied the care of his or her single parent, in *Hugo's* case a father. It is equally difficult to understand, let alone support, a process of reasoning which concludes that it is not a practice of unfair discrimination to deny to a single parent who happens to be a father benefits which are accorded to a single parent who is a mother. For one who urges us to contextualize equality, O'Regan J's reasoning in the following passage is particularly surprising:

> 'But in assessing the impact of the discrimination, it must be remembered that their imprisonment resulted, not from the President's Act denying them remission, but from their having been convicted of criminal offences. In addition, they still have the right to apply for special remission of sentence in the light of their own circumstances. The effect of the discriminatory act was, therefore, in my view not to cause substantial harm. That harm would have been far more significant in my view if it had deprived fathers in a permanent substantial way of rights or benefits attached to parenthood.'[38]

Suddenly equality has become an abstract notion without any use of a comparator! The argument that the imprisonment of men resulted from a conviction and not a pardon applies equally to women. The test is whether it is justified to give remission to a woman, whose freedom has also been circumscribed by a sentence, and not to a man because of her sex or gender in circumstances in which the applicant (whether male or female) is a single parent. Refusing to engage in a fair comparison is hardly the way to develop a coherent jurisprudence of equality.[39]

---

38  Para 114.

39  In their defence of O'Regan J, Albertyn and Goldblatt ('Facing the Challenges of Transformation' (1998) 14 *SAJHR* 248–65) write: 'short term measures designed to help women may not always be able to serve the longer term purpose of encouraging men to share the burden. This does mean that those short-term measures are never valid since alleviating immediate suffering/disadvantage is also an important objective.' While one may agree about the importance of such an objective, one has to question whether such a short-term measure is about equality. And on the facts of *Hugo*, why did the women's rights exceed those of the fathers?

There are two disturbing features of this case. First, the majority adheres to a static concept of equality which refuses to recognize new forms of identity. The Constitution contains a clear commitment to the eradication of racism and sexism.

To that end all forms of systemic discrimination must give way to a process designed to redress the legacy of such systemic injustice. Out of this process lies a promise of a new South African community, based on equality between the sexes rather than upon patriarchy. For this reason, where a court is confronted with a set of facts in which such a new identity can be reinforced and encouraged by the judgment of the court, it is subversive of the constitutional commitment for a court to revert to a process of generalization which ignores the transformative call of the Constitution.

Accordingly, a defender of the majority in *Hugo* must be driven back to seek the appropriate level of scrutiny employed by the court when reviewing the exercise of a prerogative power. If the court had made it clear that presidential action should be given as wide a berth as possible and that such actions, save in extreme circumstances, should not be overturned by a court, the outcome of *Hugo* might have been understandable. A reasonable reader could have understood the outcome even if he or she disagreed with it, either on the ground that less deference should be shown to presidential action or because *Hugo* represented an extreme case and hence the decision was a legitimate subject for review.

But the court did not seek to justify its decision expressly in such terms and accordingly its exposition of equality and the application of the principle of equality is so troubling that the outcome represents the very antithesis of the culture of reason. For me, the values of dignity, freedom and equality are clear 'propointers' in the direction of a society in which there is equal distributive concern for each member of the society and that from this individual imperative a community can emerge which is welded together by an active commitment to these foundational values.[40] The decision in *Hugo* does little to contribute to a man's dignity and freedom as a father and hence creates a considerable gulf between the principle of equality as proclaimed by the court and its implementation.

The second disturbing feature concerns the underlying premise, namely, that although the prerogative power is revisable, a remedy is impractical. A remedy would

---

40  Stephen Gardbaum 'Why the Liberal State can Promote Moral Ideas after All' (1991) 106 *Harvard Law Review* 1350.

mean reincarcerating the released women or releasing numerous men. But is this, a case of a right without a remedy, a nod in the direction of executive accountability while throwing up one's jurisprudential hands in despair rather than facing the consequences of the initial finding? All in all, *Hugo* is a journey into pragmatism rather than principle.

The clear problem in the application of its own test for equality must have concerned the court, for it quickly seized the opportunity to clarify its position in a most unlikely factual context in the case of *Prinsloo v Van der Linde*.[41]

The development of constitutional law by the courts does always depend on facts which raise profound questions, but the connection between equality and the Forestry Act surely tested the most talented of lateral jurisprudential thinkers. The case turned on s 84 of the Forestry Act,[42] which provides: 'when in any action by virtue of the provisions of this Act or the common law the question of negligence in respect of a veld, forest or mountain fire which occurred on land outside a fire control area arises, negligence is presumed until the contrary is presumed.'

Among the objections to the constitutionality of this provision which were raised was the argument that this form of reverse onus breached the equality guarantee as provided for in s 8 of the interim Constitution.

Perhaps the court considered that, having begun its engagement with the equality clause in *Hugo's* case, it was opportune to complete its exposition. Whatever the reason may have been, Ackermann, O'Regan and Sachs JJ decided that the argument concerning the constitutionality of s 84 of the Forestry Act required to be analysed in the most careful and detailed manner.

Accordingly, the three judges who delivered the opinion for the majority of the court (Didcott J delivered a separate opinion concurring in the result) commenced with an analysis of s 8(2) of the Constitution. As an introduction to their analysis they warned that s 8(2) could not have been intended to cover all differentiation or the 'courts would be compelled to review the reasonableness or the fairness of every classification of rights, duties, privileges, immunities, benefits or disadvantages flowing from any law'.[43]

Differentiation that does not involve unfair discrimination is an inevitability in a modern democratic society, although the state is expected to perform its

---

41   1997 (3) SA 1012 (CC).

42   Act 120 of 1994.

43   Para 23.

regulatory function in a rational manner. For this reason Ackermann, O'Regan and Sachs JJ concluded that the existence of a rational relationship between the practice of differentiation and the express purpose of the government's policy was a necessary precondition for an infringement of s 8(2).[44]

Finding a rational relationship was not sufficient, however, to conclude the inquiry: differentiation, however rational, could still amount to unfair discrimination. The judges found two sources of discrimination, namely differentiation on one of the 14 grounds specified in s 8(2) and on a residual ground, namely 'people treated differently in a way which impairs their fundamental dignity as human beings, who are inherently equal in dignity.'[45]

Few, if anyone, reading the judgment would have been surprised by the finding that there was a rational connection between s 84 and the express purpose of the government in introducing the measure. There was probably even less of a lifting of any readers' jurisprudential eyebrows when the judges concluded that the differentiation between owners of land inside a fire control area and others 'cannot, by any stretch of the imagination, be seen as impairing the dignity of the owner or occupier of land outside the fire control area'.[46]

The surprise was rather in the effort that had been expended to arrive at this seemingly obvious answer. Section 84 of the Forestry Act did not appear to raise the kind of problem to trigger a complex equality inquiry. As Didcott J observed in his judgment, 'but so complex, so subtle and so delicate a task ought not to be undertaken in a case inappropriate for it'.[47]

The basis of the approach adopted by Ackermann, O'Regan and Sachs JJ required an appropriate case to test its suitability as a coherent framework for analysing and applying the equality guarantee as contained in s 8 of the Constitution.

## THE COURT EXPOUNDS

The next equality challenge provided a more appropriate set of facts. Admittedly, the dispute in *Harksen v Lane NO*[48] might not have caused a major moral debate

---

44 See paras 24–6.
45 Para 31.
46 Para 41.
47 Para 52.
48 1998 (1) SA 300 (CC).

among the citizenry, but the resolution of the argument raised by the applicant at least required a careful analysis of the implications of gender equality.

For the purposes of this chapter the case concerned the constitutionality of certain provisions of the Insolvency Act.[49] Section 20(1) of the Act provided that the effect of sequestration of an estate of an insolvent was to divest the insolvent of his or her estate and to vest it in the master until a trustee was appointed. In terms of s 20(2), once a solvent spouse proves that his or her property was acquired under a marriage settlement, acquired by the solvent spouse during the marriage by valid title against the creditors of the insolvent and certain property protected by the provisions of the Insurance Act,[50] the trustee shall release such property. The applicant submitted that these provisions constituted unequal treatment of solvent spouses and discriminates against them, the effect of which is to impose severe burdens on the insolvent spouse of a kind far beyond that applicable to other persons with whom the insolvent had close commercial dealings.

The court took the opportunity of taking stock of its equality jurisprudence,[51] which it divided into separate s 8(1) and s 8(2) analyses. At the s 8(1) stage, the court is concerned to determine whether differentiation has occurred and, if so, whether there is a rational connection between this differentiation and the legitimate government purpose it is designed to achieve.[52]

Assuming, then, that s 8(1) has not been violated, s 8(2) becomes relevant, because even where the state differentiates in a rational manner, it could still have acted in a manner which amounts to unfair discrimination. Once more the analysis is divided into two parts. First, the court must ascertain whether there has been discrimination and, if so, the second question arises, namely: has the discrimination been unfair?

## DISCRIMINATION

The Constitution envisages two forms of discrimination, namely that specified in a list of 14 grounds in s 8(2), and a general category of analogous grounds. As Goldstone J said in relation to the specified grounds:

---

49  Act 24 of 1936.
50  Act 27 of 1943.
51  Para 41.
52  Para 42.

'There will be discrimination on an unspecified ground if it is based on attributes or characteristics which have the potential to impair the fundamental dignity of persons as human beings, or to affect them adversely in a comparably serious manner.'[53]

The major importance of the distinction between the two categories is that in respect of the specified grounds a presumption operated in favour of the existence of unfair discrimination. In dealing with this stage of the test, Goldstone J referred to the earlier decision in *Prinsloo's* case,[54] namely the reluctance of the *Prinsloo* court to attempt a comprehensive description of those attributes and characteristics which have the potential to impair a person's dignity. He then said:

'These grounds have the potential, when manipulated, to demean persons in their inherent humanity and dignity. There is often a complex relationship between these grounds ... the temptation to force them into neatly self contained categories should be resisted. Section 8(2) seeks to prevent the unequal treatment of people based on such criteria which may, amongst other things, result in the construction of patterns of disadvantage such as has occurred only too visibly in our history.'[55]

## UNFAIR DISCRIMINATION

The court cited its earlier decision in the *Hugo* case, namely:

'To determine whether that impact was unfair, it is necessary to look at the group who has been disadvantaged but at the nature of the power in terms of which the discrimination was effected and, also, at the nature of the interests which have been affected by the discrimination.'[56]

The question of whether the discriminatory provision has impacted unfairly on a complainant requires that a number of factors must be considered, including the position of the complainant in society and whether he or she suffered in the past from patterns of disadvantage; the purpose of the provision; the extent to which the discrimination has affected the rights or interests of complainants, and whether it has led to an impairment of such person's human dignity.[57]

---

53  Para 46.
54  *Supra.*
55  Para 49.
56  Para 20.
57  Para 51.

## APPLICATION OF THE TEST BY THE MAJORITY

The court found that s 21 did not breach the general equality guarantee under s 8(1) in that there was a rational connection between the section and the purpose of the provision: the section was introduced to cater for the inadequacy of the common law and statute in providing the master and the trustees with powers to ensure that all the property of the insolvent spouse 'found its way' into the insolvent estate.[58]

Having found the existence of a rational connection between the differentiation created by s 21 and the purpose behind its enactment, the court proceeded to examine whether the differentiation amounted to discrimination in terms of s 8(2). The court found that the discrimination amounted to discrimination on an unspecified ground in that the solvent spouse's property is dealt with in a different manner from that of others who had commercial dealings with the insolvent.

However, the court found that there was no unfairness, because: (1) the insolvent spouse was not a member of a group which had suffered discrimination in the past and (2) although proceedings under s 21(2) might cause inconvenience to the solvent spouse, there was no significant impairment of the solvent spouse's dignity. As Goldstone J concluded, looked at from the perspective of solvent spouses, it is the kind of inconvenience and burden that any citizen may face when resort to litigation becomes necessary.[59]

## THE MINORITY JUDGMENTS

O'Regan's difference with the majority turned on the application of the approach to s 8(2) which the latter had adopted. Because the effect of s 21 is to result automatically in the estate of the insolvent's spouse being vested first in the master and then in the trustee of the insolvent estate, the basis for 'the differential treatment is the marital status of the spouse'.[60]

Marital status is not one of the 14 grounds specified in s 8(2) and therefore the court was required to examine whether the conduct fell under the residual concept of unfair discrimination. In this connection O'Regan J reminded the majority that:

---

58   Para 58.
59   Para 67.
60   Para 88.

*'[W]e have interpreted section 8(2) as a clause which is primarily a buffer against the construction of further patterns of discrimination and disadvantage. Underpinning the desire to avoid such discrimination is the Constitution's commitment to human dignity. Such patterns of discrimination can occur where people are treated without the respect that individual human beings deserve and particularly where treatment is determined not by needs or circumstances of particular individuals, but by these attributes and characteristics, whether biologically or socially determined.'*[61]

O'Regan J found that there had been an entrenched practice of discrimination 'in the context of marital status'.[62] In the context of s 21 the effect of provisions which discriminated against solvent spouses as opposed to any other party with whom the insolvent spouse had a commercial relationship was substantial in that all such persons' property, including property of 'an intrinsically personal nature', would 'suddenly and without notice to (such) spouse' vest in the master and then the trustee.[63] For this reason O'Regan J concluded that impairment of the solvent spouse's interests was sufficiently substantial to constitute unfair discrimination.[64]

Madala and Mokgoro JJ concurred in the judgment of O'Regan J. Sachs J, however, delivered his own minority judgment. In disagreeing with the majority that the dignity of the solvent spouse was not sufficiently impaired to constitute a violation of s 8(2), he said that s 21's 'underlying premise is that one business mind is at work within the marriage, not two. This stems from and reinforces a stereotypical view of the marriage relationship which, in the light of the new constitutional values, is demeaning to both spouses.'[65]

## EVALUATION

*'Because so much conflict over the content of law takes the form of a struggle of the distinction in the treatment of people, equal-protection doctrine occupies a special place in the system of ideas. It is not merely another topic within the law; it is also, by synecdoche,*

---

61  Para 92.

62  Para 95.

63  Para 96.

64  This conclusion necessitated an inquiry into the justification for the invasion of the right under s 8(2), but as this aspect of the judgment deals with the general limitation clause, it falls outside the scope of this chapter.

65  Para 120.

*the problem of law itself just as property is not simply another right but the exemplary instance of rights.'*[66]

The three cases reviewed represent the court's attempt at an 'incremental development of equality jurisprudence' in which the court will 'examine on a case-by-case basis the way in which a challenged law impacts on persons belonging to a class contemplated by section 8(2)'.[67] This description of the court's approach makes understandable the energetic attempt by the majority in *Prinsloo* to clarify thier approach in *Hugo*, notwithstanding that the facts did not so require. In short, these three cases represent a single text in which the court has set out the framework in which it proposes to develop a body of equality jurisprudence. Given the test it has unveiled, it would appear that it is the application rather than the establishment of a meaning of equality that will be dealt with in an incremental manner. Unfortunately the manner in which the court has gone about the business of applying its test in both *Hugo* and *Harksen* has so muddied the jurisprudential waters that the meaning of the foundational principle of equality is all but clear.

In *Hugo*, the court held out the promise of a principle of equality that was grounded in a history of racial and gender stereotyping and which could support the development of a society that would substantively redress this burden of history. In applying its test to the facts, it retreated into such a formalistic position that it almost destroyed the potential of its test. It could be argued that the court was faced with a practical problem of a remedy in that, were it to have found that the President had disregarded the guarantee contained in s 8(2), it would have been required to order the release of many male prisoners or to return to prison many women who had been released pursuant to the presidential order. These were difficult options, but the problem should have been addressed at the stage when the court examined its capacity to review the prerogative power and not at the determination of the equality test. In short, the court sought to curtail the remedy which flowed from its initial decision to review the prerogative power by an incoherent application of its equality test — hardly the way to set about the business of developing a coherent equality jurisprudence.

In *Harksen*, the problem was unrelated to the remedy. Where the two decisions are similar is in their inability to grasp the need to transcend previous stereotypes.

---

66  Roberto Mungabeira Unger 'What Should Legal Analysis Become?' (1996) 59 *Modern Law Review* 1 at 84.

67  Sachs J in *Harksen's* case *(supra)* para 124.

Sachs J captures the problem when, in his analysis of s 21, he suggests that

> '[b]eing trapped in a stereotyped and outdated view of marriage inhibits the capaci-
> ty for self-realisation of the spouses, affects the quality of their relationship with each
> other as free and equal persons within the union, and encourages society to look at
> them not as "couple" made up of two persons with independent personalities and shared
> lives but as "couple" in which each loses his or her individual existence.'[68]

The majority in *Harksen* failed to grasp this point. Goldstone J applied a formalistic
test in that the only question which required an answer concerned the extent of
the inconvenience suffered by the solvent spouse rather than the effect of the
stereotyping to which Sachs — referred. The majority applied a formal consequentialist test, namely which consequences flowing directly from the Act were
suffered by the applicant.

In her minority judgment O'Regan J claims to apply an impact test that is a
similar consequentialist approach to that adopted by the majority. It is this claim
that renders her judgment somewhat incoherent. Having concluded that it was
not the case that s 21 did not 'implicate a pattern of discrimination rooted in one
of the patterns established in our past ...',[69] O'Regan J then proceeds to assert
that the consequences of the application of s 21 do unfairly discriminate against
the solvent spouse.[70] The difference between the two judgments turns on whether
the Act imposes inconveniences inherent in litigation or unfair discrimination, a
factual assessment which hardly clarifies that this is a dispute about principle rather
than formal consequence.

It is left to Sachs J to articulate that this dispute is more than about the impact
of the Act but about identity and their citizenship. It concerns the reinforcement
of patriarchy and a stereotypical view of a marriage relationship. This idea, pro-
moted by the Act, lies at the heart of its conflict with the equality guarantee contained in s 8. The Constitution promises that citizenship and the concomitant
ability of all to participate in the shaping of society. This cannot be achieved when
imposed concepts of identity deny equality of citizenship.

Equality jurisprudence must concern the examination of concepts to analyse
whether they promote an outmoded set of values or those mandated by the Constitution.
In *Hugo*, the majority mechanistically applied their equality test so as to exclude

---

68  Para 124.

69  Para 95.

70  Para 100.

men who wish to assume responsibility for child rearing. In *Harksen*, the majority again showed no willingness to fashion a jurisprudence in which legal concepts and their application do not reinforce the existence of values totally out of kilter with the promise of the Constitution as contained in the vision of an open and democratic society based on dignity, freedom and equality.

One can appreciate the desire of the court to approach the vexed question of equality with care (although the extravagance of the majority in *Prinsloo* might justify a contrary conclusion to such an approach); therefore the attraction of the incremental approach. However, when the court sets out a comprehensive test as to the application of s 8(1) and (2),[71] then there is a legitimate expectation that the test, the underlying constitutional values as ascertained by the court and the application of the test will reveal a clear measure of coherence.

## ANOTHER STAB

The court took the opportunity of canvassing these issues in the case of *The City Council of Pretoria v Walker*.[72] In 1994 the townships of Mamelodi and Atteridgeville were amalgamated with Pretoria. The council decided to continue levying a flat rate for services in the old township areas until meters had been installed, whereas residents of the old Pretoria area were charged on a differential basis related to plot size. Walker decided to pay at the same flat rate charged to township residents, notwithstanding that he resided in the old Pretoria area. The council sued him for outstanding rates. He contended that he was being discriminated against in that he was being charged at a higher rate than the township residents — even those in the old townships who had meters installed — and, further, that the council attempted to recover rates only from the old Pretoria residents.

Langa DP, on behalf of the majority, commenced with an examination of a rational connection between differentiation and a legitimate government purpose and, given that he so found, there was no breach of s 8(1). The inquiry therefore turned to s 8(2) as to whether there was differentiation that amounted to discrimination and, further, whether this was unfair. Langa DP found that, as race had been a factor, there had been discrimination and that the council had therefore to rebut the presumption of unfairness.

71   *Harksen's* case para 53.
72   1998 (2) SA 363 (CC).

In developing an inquiry into unfairness, it is important that a court considers the interplay between the discriminatory measure and the person or group affected by it. In this investigation, the court must recognize discrimination, even in respect of whites, but the difference in forms of discrimination and entrenchment of privilege was crucial to the inquiry. While both the majority and the minority judgment of Sachs J found that the imposition of a flat rate was not unfair discrimination, the latter found that s 8(2) was triggered only by differentiation which imposes identifiable disabilities or threatens to reinforce problems of disadvantage or to reduce the dignity or equal concern or worth of the affected persons. Langa DP disagreed. The wording compelled a two-stage inquiry, the first part being to determine whether there had been differentiation, direct or indirect, on the grounds of race.[73]

Sachs J's approach has the benefit that it seeks to avoid a conflation between discrimination and differentiation, although the coupling of the words 'unfair' and 'discrimination' does support the majority approach. The response is to find that discrimination has a prejudicial connotation and that the presumption of unfairness throws the onus upon the discriminator to show absence of unfairness, assessed in terms of the value of equality itself. Viewed in this light, Walker suffered discrimination if his race was used as a factor in the decision but, viewed from the intrinsic morality of equality, there was no unfairness in that the principle rests upon anti-subordination rather than being supportive of privilege.

Where there is clear merit in Sachs J's approach is where he points more clearly in the direction of substantive equality. As he reasons in respect of the presumption of unfairness, it 'makes no sense at all when invoked to shield continuing advantage gained as a result of past discrimination from the side winds of remedial social programmes designed to reduce the effect of such structured advantage'.[74] Sachs J recognizes the dynamic quality of equality in that it is a value that acts as a pointer towards a particular form of society, one in which advantage can only be gained fairly and without a breach of the foundational values of the Constitution.[75]

Put briefly, the jurisprudence of equality requires an animating vision which guides and informs the interpretative process. As argued in chapter 1 above, this vision will doubtless be contested, but once outlined the vision can be contested

---

73  Para 35.

74  Para 109.

75  Ibid.

or justified. Its value for our constitutional context can be gleaned from a passage from the work of Michael Walzer:

> '[T]he experience of subordination — of personal subordination, above all — lies behind the vision of equality. Opponents of the vision often claim that the animating passions of egalitarian politics are envy and resentment, and it's true enough that such passions fester in every subordinate group ... but envy and resentment are uncomfortable passions; no one enjoys them ... the aim of political egalitarianism is a society free of domination. This is the lively hope named by the word equality; no more bowing and scraping, fawning ... no more masters, no more slaves. It is not a hope for the elimination of differences; we don't all have to be the same or have the same amount of all things. Men and women are one's equals when no one possessor controls the means of domination.'[76]

In *Walker*, for example, Langa DP is the more consistent, perhaps, when he acknowledges, that whites being held to a tariff and blacks not is discriminatory, because 'to ignore the racial impact of the differentiation is to place form above substance'. But Sachs J's approach appeals rather more because it attempts to engage with equality in a value-orientated manner rather than following a rigid textual approach. This becomes a particular problem when the court tries to pigeon-hole a differential tax policy into an offence against dignity — a difficulty inflicted on itself because of its formalistic treatment of the general protection of equality in s 8(1) of the interim Constitution or s 9(1) of the final Constitution, namely that it is merely a guarantee of equal treatment before the courts.[77] The potential to explore difference as a result of the law and extend the analysis to a positive means of achieving an egalitarian vision is lost in such an analysis, as is the possibility of examining equality as a guiding value rather than an adjunct of the more individualistic foundational value of dignity.

---

76  See Michael Walzer *Spheres of Justice — A Defence of Pluralism and Equality* (1983) at xiii.

77  That is not to say that there are not difficulties in the judgment of Sachs J. Thus I find his conclusion that the council's policy of collecting back taxes was not unfair discrimination a surprising sanction of arbitrariness. Part of the difficulty with this judgment is that its own style is so different from the norm that I find that each scheme requires intricate deconstruction. Thus, in the first sentence, Sachs J compliments the majority judgment of Langa DP. Whereas the usual approach is to praise the learning and research of the judgment, Sach J says 'Langa DP analysed the difficult issues in this case ... with composure and sensitivity'. Perhaps the difference in style reflects my own lack of transformation!

## CONCLUSION

My argument has been that, sadly, this has not occurred and as a consequence the promise that the underlying value of equality can provoke a transformation of social values and the legal concepts that sustain such a venture remains as distant as it did when the court commenced hearing these cases.

In its analysis of whether the Pretoria City Council's practice of imposing rates amounted to unfair discrimination, the court placed great emphasis on its earlier use of dignity. While it is easy to understand that discriminatory revenue practice affects an individual, I would have thought that it is his or her pocket which is hurt to a greater extent than is the person's dignity. The loss of dignity must be traced, therefore, to the unfairness of the practice, which leads to circularity rather than explanation. It would appear that a better approach is to be found in the conclusion that such discrimination has a clearly detrimental affect on the targeted group's ability to perform as citizens in the same manner as their fellows. Unfairness than can be employed to test whether such a practice does have a detrimental affect or, in the *Walker* case,[78] actually supports the possibility of equal citizenship. The uncritical use of dignity to understand equality gives an individualistic slant to equality of a kind that is incongruent with the need to balance individual and community, concepts which lie at the heart of the South African constitutional idea.[79]

## EQUALITY: THE NEED FOR A FRESH APPROACH

The Constitutional Court has got us off to an unpromising start in our search for a coherent equality jurisprudence. In *Hugo*, the court introduced the principle of dignity to interpret equality without ever explaining whether it was the absence of a prior constitutional right to equality or the breach of the self-standing dignity right that had been infringed. By the time of *Prinsloo*, O'Regan, Sachs and Ackermann JJ had managed to introduce the idea that dignity was the central idea animating the concept of unfair discrimination. If discrimination constitutes differentiation which is unfair, the three judges tell us that what makes for unfairness is an infringement of dignity (or as Goldstone J says in *Harksen's* case, an

---

78  *Supra.*
79  See, in general, Karl Klare (1998) 14 *SAJHR* 146.

impairment to one's dignity or an infringement of a comparably serious nature — in which formulation dignity has become the comparator!). Why unfairness is not linked to the breach of the equality guarantee itself is never made clear. How would the judges deal with the case of the welfare department only handing cases of those born on the first ten days of the month.[80] One would have to stretch the concept of dignity extremely wide to accommodate this form of unfairness. By contrast if the court had recourse to the idea that equality is less about sameness and more about justification of difference it would have been able to provide content to the basic equality guarantee in s 9(1) rather than employing the section as a gatekeeper for the discrimination provision of s 9(3) and distinguish between practices that offend dignity, those that offend equality and those that offend both.

In some unintended way, the court has provided support for the Westen thesis in that in any set of circumstances the enquiry into a breach of the equality guarantee necessitates an investigation into whether another independent moral right (dignity or a comparable right) has been breached.[81] Nowhere does one find any attempt to examine the basis of the equality right itself. Now, the defender of the court's adventure may reply that the court wishes to distinguish between a positive duty placed on the state as a corollary of the bearer's right to equality and the proposition that, to date, the court has been concerned only with discrimination, that is, the shadow side of equality. But if this is so, this defence does not explain why the court has found the need to put all its discrimination eggs in the dignity basket. Surely a better approach would have been to argue in favour of a jurisprudential direction in which exclusion cannot take place other than on rational or appropriate grounds and that further grounds are only appropriate only when they are of a kind that all in society have an equal chance of satisfying.

The court has tried to set out the kind of formula for the determination of equality which in itself reveals the influence of the previously hegemonic Roman-Dutch framework of setting out the formulation of a principle and then engaging in a mechanistic application of it. The contested nature of equality necessitates an acknowledgement of the contest and the need to engage with both sides. The point is made with great clarity by Bernard Williams as follows:

---

80  I am indebted to my colleague, Anton Fagan, for this idea.

81  I base this conclusion on my reading of the court's equality judgments in which Westen's articles play no role.

*'a highly rational and efficient application of the ideas of equal opportunity, unmitigated by the other considerations, could lead to a quite inhuman society. ... On the other hand, an ideal of equality, of respect that makes no contact with such things as the economic needs of society for certain skills and human desire for some sorts of prestige would be condemned to a futile Utopianism and to having no rational effect on the distribution of goods, position and power that would inevitably proceed. ... it is not really known how far ... these conflicting claims might be reconciled ... it is all the more obvious that we should not throw one set of claims out of the window; but should rather seek, in each situation, the best way of eating and having as much cake as possible.'*[82]

By conflating equality with dignity or its variants the court has failed to engage with the component parts of equality, let alone achieve any working balance. Accordingly, we still await a judgment that deals with the substantive imperative of the equality guarantee or its scope and limitations, both internal and external.

---

82  Bernard Williams 'The Idea of Equality' in P Laslett (ed) *Philosophy, Politics and Society* (1969) at 130–1.

# THE CONSTITUTION
# AND PRIVATE LAW

## THE CONSTITUTION AND PRIVATE LAW:
## THE CUTTING EDGE OF LEGAL TRANSFORMATION?

*'Lawyers ... have pictured law as reason encoded in the doings and dreams of power just as economists have seen actual market economies and their law as approxima-tions to a pure system of rationality and reciprocity. They have sung for their supper by singing in their chains. Hope and insight may nevertheless succeed where indig-nation and history worship failed, and draw the lawyers and economists into the work of giving eyes and wings to the institutional imagination.'[1]*

During the 1960s the dominant forms of positivism in South Africa and their authoritarian potential were cruelly exposed by a distinguished and courageous group of three: Tony Mathews, Barend van Niekerk and John Dugard. They placed the link between law and politics on the South African legal agenda and from this platform the next generation, the most important of whom was Etienne Mureinik, introduced the work of Dworkin into legal debates.

South African lawyers swallowed legal positivism whole. More recently, a younger generation of academics, correctly critical of John Austin, have espoused the newer forms of positivism which emanated from Oxford in the writings of Hart and Raz and which gave rise to a legal *Weltanschauung* that refused to acknowledge that jurisprudence should examine the arbitrariness and violence in law's adju-dicative and enforcement process.

Notwithstanding a body of immensely creative work which lay its founda-tions bare, positivism retained its footing, even after the introduction of the new constitutional era. As an illustration of positivism, recourse can be had to the work of two of the finest of the younger generation of legal academics, Alfred Cockrell and Anton Fagan. In a recent review of the South African Bill of Rights, Cockrell holds up the following argument of Fagan as 'the best way to ... save the prac-tice of constitutional review from the charge of democratic illegitimacy', namely

---

1   Roberto Unger 'What should Legal Analysis become?' (1996) 59 *Modern Law Review* 1 at 23. This chapter emerges from earlier work undertaken with Halton Cheadle, who, in my view, is South Africa's foremost exponent of transformist law.

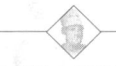

'constitutional rules make a difference to how the court should decide constitutional cases'. In other words, the decision of the court will be different as a result of this extraordinary insight from a decision which would have been reached had it been free to pursue 'an all things considered' moral judgment![2] Now, this statement is surprisingly trite, such that one can only assume that it means more than the literal words suggest, particularly because it is dressed up as representing such a ground-breaking constitutional insight. What it appears to suggest is that the legal decision can and must be carefully demarcated from a political decision: politics and morality shall never mix with law! For all its eloquence, the argument is the same as that which has dominated South African jurisprudence from its earliest days; the spirit of the Constitution appears to have passed by as a jurisprudential irrelevance. Legal business shall continue as usual.

The tenacity of a dormant legal tradition is not unexpected. In a recent work, Roberto Unger[3] suggests that the range of legal imagination can be reduced to two conceptions of law. The first is rooted in 19th-century legal science. It consists of a system of property and contract law which promotes private autonomy and a system of public law which enforces a carefully constructed ring in which compliance with the Queensberry Rules will entail no legal interference. But a series of inevitable social impediments, which economists would term 'externalities', required changes to legal doctrine. Therefore a range of ad hoc additions was made to the conceptual edifice which was predicated on anything but coherence and determinacy. This form of development is denied and legal scholars spend great energy in an attempt to contrast the certainty, clarity and rationality of private law with the 'circumstantial and controversial efforts of the regulatory and redistributive state as if the rules of property and exchange were any less arbitrary than the provision of tax and transfer'.

Unger refers to the second approach, which is prevalent in contemporary legal thought, as 'rationalising legal analysis'.[4] Whereas free enterprise assumptions shape the first concept of law, a weak and incoherent set of social democratic compromises form the basis upon which rationalizing a legal analysis emerges. Within this model, law is seen as a flawed but crucial embodiment of fundamental principles

2   A Cockrell 'The South African Bill of Rights and the Duck/Rabbit' (1997) 60 *Modern Law Review* 513 at 534.

3   Op cit.

4   Unger at 15.

of justice and right — the underlying principles which dictate that each person should be treated with equal concern and respect run, albeit tentatively, throughout the entire body of law. For Unger, much of modern legal scholarship follows this model. As an example, he focuses on a typical form of a law journal article which represents any part of the body of legal rules and doctrine as an expression of a connected and coherent set of principles and policies. The article then criticizes the established body of rules as inadequate for the achievement of these principles and concludes with a proposal for law reform with which to achieve a better equilibrium between the existing body of law and the ideal conception, with the objective of making the best sense of this body of law.

For Unger, neither of these models makes any tangible legal contribution to the transformation of society. Critical legal scholarship demands dialectically linked moments of mapping and criticism. Mapping is an attempt to describe in detail the structure of the entire body of law, whether it be principle or exception. This process takes place in the absence of the spin doctors who employ rationalizing legal analysis. Thereafter, he suggests that critique should take over to penetrate the disharmony between the social and political ideals and commitments of society and those legal institutions that supposedly give meaning to these ideals but effectively constrain their realization. By way of these two processes we can look at the way 'in which the ideal conceptions expressed in policies and principles or the group interests represented by programmes and strategies get truncated in their fulfilment and improvised in their meaning by their revised institutional forms'.[5]

I want to develop an argument that accepts, as a result of mapping, the inevitability of the politics–law link and by way of criticism allows us to understand the nature of the dichotomy between promise and reality. From this perspective it is suggested that s 8 of the 1996 Constitution represents a constitutional mandate to engage in mapping and critique in order to bring our existing body of law into harmony with the new *Grundnorm* that is the 1996 Constitution. The Constitution mandates an exploration of our existing legal institutions, an analysis of the disharmony between their reality and the new values and commitments of the Constitution and the consequent attempt to bridge that gulf.

---

5   Unger at 22.

# THE DISPUTE REGARDING THE APPLICATION OF THE 1993 CONSTITUTION

The application of Chapter 3 of the 1993 Constitution to both customary law and common law arose out of a compromise between those parties who wished to have all constitutional rights enforced not only against the state but also against private citizens. In terms of this traditional approach the Constitution was seen primarily as a fundamental law that restricted government and subjected its action to judicial scrutiny. Accordingly, constitutional challenges were to be confined to legislative and administrative action only. Those who argued in favour of this approach based their justification on the premise that the primary function of a constitution is to curb unfettered public power and that the abuse of private power can and should be addressed through legislation.

The intention of the compromise was to ensure that the Bill of Rights would not apply directly to private relationships but that it would apply to all law in force, namely common law and customary law. In addition, s 33(2) expressly subjected the common law and customary law to the rights contained in the chapter and rendered any common-law limitation on such rights unconstitutional, unless such limitation conformed to the requirements of s 33(1).

Advocates of the vertical approach relied almost exclusively upon s 7(1). Section 7(1) provides that Chapter 3 'shall bind all legislative and executive organs of state at all levels of government'. In turn, organs of state are defined in s 233(1) as including any statutory body or functionary. In contrast, s 4(2) provides that '[t]his Constitution shall bind all legislative, executive and judicial organs of state at all levels of government'.

The discrepancy between s 7(1) and s 4(2) was therefore seen to lend support for concluding that, because the judiciary is not bound by Chapter 3, no constitutional duty is imposed upon it to apply private law in cases involving third parties.

But s 7(2) provides textual support for the conclusion that Chapter 3 applies to all law, from whatever source. Certain provisions, such as s 23 dealing with rights to information, expressly qualified the scope of the right to information held by the state. Without rehearsing all the arguments on both sides, the applicable provisions were ambiguous and open to both interpretations. Once ambiguity was admitted, the verticalist argument found favour among many lawyers, because it reflected a deep commitment to a rigid division between private and public law embedded in our legal system. André van der Walt has observed that one of the results of the traditional private-law method is that a set of largely unstated private-law values is embedded deeply in the structure of South Africa law, which 'by simply accepting existing social values … [underestimates] the basically conservatist and repressive effort of hidden power relations'.[6] Far from being neutral, these values reflect and promote a specific view of the person, a society and the relation between them. South African lawyers working within this system of rights accept that there is a clear division of the public and the private spheres, of law and politics. Viewed within this perspective, private-law rights form a wall which divides the two spheres in order to protect the individual against interferences by the collective will.

## DU PLESSIS V DE KLERK:[7] THE DISPUTE SETTLED

Kentridge AJ's arguments in support of his finding on application were based essentially on a literal reading of the text. Section 7(1) — that '[t]his Chapter shall bind all legislative and executive organs of the state at all levels of government' — is read as supporting the proposition that 'Chapter 3 is intended to be binding only on the legislative and executive organs of the state'.[8] Kentridge AJ declared that had the drafters wished to bind the judiciary and subject all private common-law disputes to constitutional scrutiny, they could have expressly so provided. Kentridge AJ referred to s 35(3), namely that '[i]n the … the application and development of the common law … a court shall have due regard to the spirit, purpose and objects of this Chapter' to reinforce the restrictive reading of s 7(1) on the ground that had the chapter been designed to apply to all common-law disputes, s 35(3) would have been unnecessary.

In support of this conclusion, Kentridge AJ found that although the limitation clause (s 33(1)) applies to all law of general application, including 'common law', 'applying section 33(1) to private relationships governed by the common law would

6   André van der Walt 'Marginal Notes on Power Legends: Critical Perspectives on Property Theory' (1995) 58 *THRHR* 396 at 417.

7   1996 (3) SA 850 (CC).

8   Ibid.

create insurmountable obstacles'.[9] The focus of the judgment therefore turned to the operation of the common law. As Kentridge AJ said:

> 'The common law addresses problems of conflicting rights and interests through a system of balancing. Many of these rights and interests are now recorded in the Constitution and on any view that means that as a result of the terms of the Constitution the balancing process previously undertaken may have to be reconsidered. A claim for defamation, for instance, raises a tension between the right to freedom of expression and the right to dignity. The common law compromise has been to limit both rights to a certain extent, allowing damages to be recovered for what is regarded as "unlawful expression" by allowing "dignity" to be infringed in circumstances to be privileged. Section 33(1) could hardly be applied to such a situation.'[10]

Kentridge AJ observed that the current common law of defamation is designed to resolve the 'tension' or 'conflict' between such rights as the 'right to freedom of expression and the right to dignity'. The common law provided a compromise by limiting both rights to some extent by 'allowing damages to be recovered for what is regarded as "unlawful expression" but allowing "dignity" to be infringed in circumstances considered to be privileges'.[11]

A further difficulty raised by Kentridge AJ concerned the problem which would follow upon 'a declaration by the court that a rule of the common law was invalid on the basis that it was unconstitutional'. In his view, such a declaration would necessitate the reformulation of the relevant common law.[12] As the court derived its jurisdiction from s 98 exclusively, it could not rewrite the common law, a task left by the Constitution to the ordinary courts.

For these reasons Kentridge AJ concluded that Chapter 3 was to apply thus:

(a) Constitutional rights under Chapter 3 may be invoked against an organ of government but not by one private litigant against another.

(b) In private litigation any litigant may none the less contend that a statute (or executive act) relied on by the other party is invalid as being inconsistent with the limitations placed on the legislature and the executive under Chapter 3.

(c) As Chapter 3 applies to the common law, governmental acts or omissions in reliance on the common law may be attacked by a private litigant as being

---

9   *Supra* at para 55.

10  At para 56.

11  At para 55.

12  At para 52.

inconsistent with Chapter 3 in any dispute with an organ of government.[13]

From the judgment it is not clear what difference exists between the common law which is subject to constitutional review when the state is an affected party and the common law applied to private litigants where, according to the Constitution, it is not applicable. After the Constitutional Court's jurisdictional difficulties when adjudicating upon the common law had been discussed exhaustively, these very same difficulties disappear in the judgment as soon as the common law is invoked in a dispute between the government and a private litigant.

Kentridge AJ never made it clear why s 98 circumscribes the power of the court when it actually states that the Constitutional Court is the court of final instance over all matters relating to the interpretation, protection and enforcement of the Constitution and for this reason — to the extent that the common law violates the spirit, purport and object of Chapter 3 — the Constitutional Court can alter or develop the common law accordingly.

The inconsistencies in the judgment might be explained away as the inevitable outcome of working with a difficult and somewhat contradictory text. But this drives towards a more accurate explanation of the outcome; that, to a considerable extent, it was a product of judicial choice. This conclusion is fortified by Kentridge AJ's view that, traditionally, bills of rights have been inserted in constitutions to strike a balance between government power and individual liberty, to constitute a precaution against state tyranny.[14] A vertical approach is therefore the constitutional norm and, short of the most unambiguous use of language to show that South Africa did not want to follow such norm, the court would keep us within the comfort of traditional constitutional usage.

The most eloquent support for the argument that Kentridge AJ's judgment is a matter of choice is to be found in the dissent by Kriegler J, supported by Didcott J. Kriegler J found that the text sustained a horizontal argument. As he said, 'on a reading of s 7(2) alone, the scope of application of Chapter 3 with regard to law therefore seems clear. It governs all law in force during the currency of the Constitution. There is no qualification, no exception. All means all.'[15] Kriegler J found further support for this conclusion. He referred to s 33(2), which provides that, save as provided

---

13  At para 49.

14  At para 45n74.

15  At para 130.

for in s 33(1) or any other provision of this Constitution, 'no law, whether a rule of the common law, customary law or legislation, shall limit any right entrenched in this chapter'.

Kriegler J noted:

> 'The sweep of s 33(2) harks back to the generality of s 7. If the chapter were indeed to operate only vertically, or only indirectly horizontally, why was it necessary or indeed appropriate to declaim the preservation of rights in such unqualified terms?'[16]

Kriegler J dismissed the jurisdictional difficulties which appear to be so insurmountable to Kentridge AJ by observing that s 98 of the Constitution created the Constitutional Court as the final arbiter on all constitutional matters, including the common law.[17]

## THE 1996 CONSTITUTION AND HORIZONTALITY

Perhaps the most surprising aspect of the majority approach to the Constitution in *Du Plessis'* case[18] was that the judgment was delivered at a time when the Constitutional Assembly had already agreed to a formulation which subjected private power to constitutional scrutiny. As this decision was widely known, the majority of the court had placed themselves at intellectual odds with the new Constitution. The extent to which the intellectual position of the majority can continue to prevail depends on the nature of the formulation contained in s 8.

It was the articulated approach to the role of law and the state as much as the restrictive interpretation of the text in *Du Plessis* on the issue of application that supports the conclusion that a particular legal vision rather than the clarity of the courts lay at the head of the judgment in the *Du Plessis* case.[19]

Section 8(1) binds the state in its different manifestations to the provisions of the Bill of Rights. The specific inclusion of the judiciary will give rise to its own difficulties, but in so far as its inclusion has any relevance to the question of the application of the Constitution to private persons, it removes the basis of an argument that the provisions in Chapter 3 do not apply to private persons. As discussed,

---

16  At para 133.

17  At para 148.

18  *Du Plessis v De Klerk* 1996 (3) SA 850 (CC).

19  See the analysis in ch 2 above. A less understandable position is that assumed by Langa and O'Regan JJ, who concurred in the judgments of both Kentridge AJ and Mahomed DP notwithstanding the vastly different jurisprudential approaches taken in the two judgments.

the arguments against the horizontal application of the interim Constitution which were based on the failure to include 'judiciary' in s 7 of the interim Constitution are not persuasive: the manner in which the law articulates with the courts is different from the manner in which it articulates with the other branches of the state — the legislature and the executive. When it is stated that the legislature is bound by a right, that means that it cannot pass laws which violate that right. When the executive is bound, it means that the executive cannot act in breach of the Constitution. This means in each case that the legislature and the executive do things that the courts have to measure against the Constitution. Can the same claim be made in respect of the courts? Their conduct — the processing of law claims and the passing of judgments — is not extraneous action to be tested against the Constitution: it is constitutive of the law, including the Constitution itself.

Section 8(2) reads:

> 'A provision of the Bill of Rights binds a natural or a juristic person if, and to the extent that, it is applicable, taking into account the nature of the right and the nature of any duty imposed by the right.'

This section puts beyond dispute that the Bill of Rights can bind natural or juristic persons. Accordingly, the majority decision in *Du Plessis* that the interim Constitution does not bind private persons has been quite deliberately cured by the wording of this section in the new Constitution. The Constitution applies to all law, binds the legislature, executive and judiciary, and binds private persons. The only difference with regard to private persons is that the determination of applicability has been made subject to a specific formula contained in s 8(2).

From the analysis developed in chapter 1 regarding the nature of constitutional interpretation, it follows that the new text affords no guarantees as to how far judges should go in binding private persons to the strictures of the Bill of Rights. Those who fear the Constitution's incursion into private law will use the formulation employed in this section to restrict the application of the Bill of Rights to private persons. Those who recognize that power is not the sole prerogative of the state, particularly as the state privatizes many of its functions, will use the discretion to provide a remedy to bring private conduct into line with the Constitution when the legislature fails to do so.

In terms of the analysis developed in this book, the context of the section is important. It is therefore significant that the role of private power in the creation of apartheid South Africa informed certain of the judges in the *Du Plessis* case.

Thus Mahomed DP said:

> '*I would have remained profoundly uncomfortable if the construction favoured by Centrifuge AJ meant, in practice, that the Constitution was impotent to protect those who have so manifestly and brutally been victimised by the private and institutionalised desecration of the values now so eloquently articulated in the Constitution. Black persons were previously denied the right to own land in 87% of the country. An interpretation of the Constitution which continued to protect the right of private persons substantially to perpetuate such unfairness by entering into contracts or making dispositions subject to the condition that such land is not sold to or occupied by blacks would have been for me a very distressing conclusion. These and scores of other such examples leave me no doubt that those responsible for the enactment of the Constitution never intended to permit the privatisation of apartheid or to allow the unfair gains of apartheid or the privileges it bestowed on the few, or the offensive attitudes it generated amongst many, to be fossilised and protected by Courts rendered impotent by the language of the Constitution.*'[20]

Even more directly, Madala J said:

> '*Ours is a multi-racial, multi-cultural, multi-lingual society in which the ravages of apartheid, disadvantage and inequality are just immeasurable. The extent of the oppressive measures in South Africa was not confined to government/individual relations, but equally to individual/individual relations. In its effort to create a new order, our Constitution must have been intended to address these oppressive and undemocratic practices at all levels. In my view our Constitution starts at the lowest level and attempts to reach the furthest in its endeavours to restructure the dynamics in a previously racist society.*'[21]

As argued in chapter 1, the South African Constitution holds the potential for a transformatist reading, one that is concerned with the abuse of power, wheresoever sourced, and with the promotion of a maximum measure of public deliberation. Section 8(2) states that the provisions of the Bill of Rights 'bind' natural and juristic persons if the provisions are 'applicable'. At first blush this appears to admit only of a circular consequence: 'Applicable' exists when it is applicable. However, the word 'applicable' has three meanings in this context — all of which could be consistent with the use of the term in s 8(2):

(a)  the provisions apply that this have reference to;

(b)  they are capable of being applied, and

(c)  they are fit or suitable for application.[22]

---

20  At para 75.

21  At para 163.

22  See the definition in *The Shorter Oxford Dictionary*.

The word 'bind' means something quite different — 'to subject to a specific legal obligation'. Far from being circular, the question of whether a private person is bound depends on the answer to whether the provisions apply to private persons. That answer lies first in interpreting the right in each case. The better reading is that the word 'applicable' is used in the sense of 'capable and suitable in s 8(2)'. The formulation leads inevitably to an enquiry into the capability and suitability within the context of the Constitution and hence to the interpretative issues canvassed in chapter 1 above.

The first use of the term — 'the provision *applies* to natural or juristic persons' — is narrow and directs the court to look at the text and determine whether or not the provisions explicitly or implicitly apply to natural or juristic persons. There are instances of explicit application — s 9(4) prohibits discrimination by any person; s 15(2) imposes obligations on state-aided institutions in respect of religious observances; and s 29(3) places obligations on private schools. But s 8(2) requires that, in determining whether or not the provisions of a right apply, the court must take into account the nature of the right and the nature of the duty imposed by the right. That clearly points to an interpretative process that goes beyond the strict construction of the text alone and to whether the right is capable of being applied or whether the right is suitable for horizontal application. Therefore the nature of the rights and the nature of the duties will determine that the rights of arrested, detained and accused persons are neither capable of being applied to natural or juristic persons nor suitable for horizontal application. The difference in the tests is reflected in their application to rights such as the right to a clean environment, but whether they are suitable is a different question. In other words, the suitability criterion is less mechanical and confers greater discretion on the courts. It is as wide a criterion as it is capable, but is potentially narrower. Of course, whether a right is capable of application is an inevitable part of the enquiry into its suitability for horizontal application. It is here that the terrain of struggle between verticalists and horizontalists will be located.

If the courts are likely to determine the applicability of rights after an assessment of their suitability, the question arises as to how a court decides whether it is suitable that a right bind private persons. The text enjoins a court to take account of the nature of the right and the nature of the duty imposed by the right. The nature of the right may reveal that it is a right capable of being applied to private persons — the right to dignity (*injuria*, defamation); the right to freedom and security of person (delict); the right to privacy,[23] the right to an environment that is not harmful to health or well-being (nuisance), the right to property, and children's rights. The common-law recognition of any of the rights does not always cover the whole ambit of the constitutional right, but the fact that part of the right is capable of application suggests that the right is suitable for application to private persons. The fact that legislation is commonly used to give effect to a right as between private persons may also assist in this enquiry. Anti-discrimination legislation is common in many democratic societies. Typically, that legislation prohibits discrimination by private persons. Accordingly, the right to equality can be, and often is, applied horizontally. Labour relations rights and environmental rights are often given effect to between private persons by legislation. In other words, the fact that certain of the rights find horizontal expression in the common law and in statute gives an indication of the suitability of a right to horizontal application.

Having determined that the right is capable of application to private persons, the broader enquiry as to the suitability of its application still remains. The nature of the duty imposed by the right will be an important consideration in determining suitability. It would seem that in some instances the duty imposed by a right would be particularly onerous to a private person. For example, the nature of the duty contemplated in s 26(2) — namely to take reasonable measures to give everyone access to housing — may, quite apart from the implications of the text, militate against imposing the duty upon private parties. The right to life may impose a duty of care that on the face of it goes considerably further than our current duty to rescue a person in a life-threatening situation. The potentially onerous nature of the duty may constitute grounds for not imposing the duty, though the proper place for balancing the rights of the drowning man and the duty on the passer-by can be located in s 8(3) and the balance struck in the common-law rules governing liability in rescue cases probably constitutes reasonable and justifiable limitations on the right to life and the correlative duty to save a life.[24]

It is evident that an analysis in terms of s 8(2) must involve an examination of the test that provides for the right in question. Certain rights are clearly not

---

23  See, for example, *Financial Mail (Pty) Ltd v Sage Holdings Ltd* 1993 (2) SA 451 (A).

24  Section 27(3), which states that no-one may be refused emergency medical treatment, may create new common-law obligations.

capable of or suitable for application to private persons. They are the rights of arrested, detained and accused persons in s 35. Then there are those rights that specifically contemplate horizontal application. Let us consider some examples.

Section 9(4) states: 'No person may unfairly discriminate directly or indirectly against anyone ....' There are other provisions that contemplate the infringement of rights by private persons. Section 12(1)*(c)*, for example, states that everyone has a right to freedom and security of person, including the right to 'be free from all forms of violence from either public or private sources'. Section 15(2) requires of state-aided institutions, though private, to conduct religious observances in a particular way. Section 23 speaks to trade unions, employers and employer organizations. Section 28 speaks to parents, guardians and employers. Section 29(3) places explicit obligations on private schools. Section 32(1)*(b)* recognizes a right to access to information held by private persons.

The scope of Chapter 2 of the Constitution still remains undetermined to the extent that interpretative work is required. Notwithstanding that many of the provisions make explicit reference to private persons, there are persuasive arguments against horizontality. For example, in s 9(4) the right not to be discriminated against applies to private persons. But the second sentence specifically states that '[national] legislation must be enacted to prevent or prohibit unfair discrimination'. That can be interpreted as a clear constitutional preference for legislation as the appropriate means of implementing the right horizontally. For this reason, those seeking a limited constitutional scope may argue that the provisions of s 9(4) are not intended to apply or that they are, therefore, not suitable for application to private persons. Similarly, s 12(1)*(c)* refers to private sources of violence. That can easily be interpreted in the light of s 7 as placing an obligation on the state to protect and promote and fulfil the right and not to place a constitutional obligation on employers or owners of football stadiums to take steps to prevent violence on the shopfloor or on the football field.

A similar enquiry is required in respect of the socio-economic rights in ss 26 and 27. An analysis sourced in s 8(2) suggests that these rights are not rights that are infringed by private persons. They flow from a social democratic vision of the role of the state — that the state should provide basic facilities and services to ensure equality of its citizenry in order to participate properly in the democratic process that the Constitution structures and protects. Moreover, the text itself specifically imposes a duty on the state to take measures to achieve the progressive realization of these rights. Given the potentially onerous nature of such a duty on private persons, the likely outcome of this analysis must be that these rights are not suitable for horizontal application.

But if there is interpretative work to be undertaken in determining the scope and meaning of s 8, and hence the scope of Chapter 2, such work will depend upon the chosen interpretative theory. In this enquiry I have followed the approach advocated in Chapter 2.

The nature of some of the constitutional guarantees provides the clearest of pointers in favour of suitability. Where there is uncertainty, the enquiry into suitability will be determined by an examination of the right viewed within the context of an analysis of the right within the overall conception of the Constitution. The court must then seek justification in the overall values of the Constitution — openness, democracy, dignity, equality and freedom.

Clapham provides some indication of the importance of these values in the analysis of the limits of human rights in the private sphere. He suggests that,

> *'when we confront a situation involving a human rights claim, an appeal to the twin concepts of dignity and democracy will enable us to see the limits of the right in question. For example [in] … the case of the protester in the private shopping precincts (this being the only forum in the town) democracy demands that there is full participation and representation of different ideas in the community. … But if we turn to the theoretical case of a coven of witches demanding to speak at a Christian prayer meeting, there is no question of democracy being threatened where the witches are free to disseminate their views via alternative means.'* [25]

Clapham therefore concludes that a constitutional right should apply to the private sphere as follows:

> *'[W]here the right involved is justified by the goal of democracy there has to be a public element in order to justify protection of the right. But where the right can be justified by an appeal to dignity we do not need such a public element, consequently the right must always be protected.'* [26]

The fundamental values of the Constitution should act as guidelines to which rights are suitable to promote application because they enhance the kind of society envisaged in the fundamental values enshrined in the Constitution.

---

25  Andrew Clapham *Human Rights in the Private Sphere* (1993) at 145–6.

26  Clapham at 146.

# SECTION 8(3): A QUESTION OF JUDICIAL DISCRETION?

Section 8(3) reads:

> '(3)  When applying a provision of the Bill of Rights to a natural or juristic person in terms of subsection (2), a court—
>
> (a)  in order to give effect to a right in the Bill, must apply, or if necessary develop, the common law to the extent that legislation does not give effect to that right; and
>
> (b)  may develop rules of the common law to limit the right, provided that the limitation is in accordance with s 36(1).'

Once the s 8(2) analysis is complete and a court has satisfied itself that the provision of the Bill of Rights applies to a natural or juristic person, it must engage in a four-stage analysis in terms of s 8(3), namely:

1.  It must satisfy itself that there is no legislation that gives effect to the right as between private persons.
2.  It must then determine whether there is not already a common-law rule that gives effect to the right as between private persons; if there is, it must apply that common-law rule.
3.  If there is no legislation or common-law rule giving effect to the right, the court must develop rules of the common law to give effect to that right.
4.  In applying or developing a common-law rule, the court may limit the right provided that the limitation is in accordance with s 36(1).

The application of this four-stage analysis can be illustrated by the following example. Following the precedent of the MCC (Marylebone Cricket Club), a South African cricket club (SACC) which tenaciously holds on to its colonial heritage refuses to admit a woman as a member. The court must decide whether the prohibition on unfair discrimination in s 9(4) is suitable for application to private persons. There is no legislation giving effect to the right not to be unfairly discriminated against by such institutions. If, however, the case were an application for a job at the club, such as that of a coach, the enquiry would have revealed that there is legislation that gives effect to the right.[27]

The *second* stage of the enquiry will also reveal that there is no common-law rule giving effect to the right. The *third* stage then requires the court to develop a rule to give effect to the right. The rule is, at this stage of the analysis, relatively easy to formulate. It is a delict on the part of an association to discriminate

---

27  Item 9(1) of Schedule 7 of the Labour Relations Act, 1995.

unfairly against an applicant who seeks to join the association. The *fourth* stage constitutes an elaboration of the rule. There are other constitutional rights involved in the development of a rule of this kind — the right to privacy and the right to freedom of association.[28] The first phase of the s 8(3) analysis involves determining the existence of legislation. But this inevitably involves the determination of the extent of the right. For example, the Labour Relations Act, 1995 purports to give effect to the right to fair labour practices in s 23(1) of the Constitution. But the definition of an unfair labour practice in item 2(1) of Schedule 7 of the Labour Relations Act is not as extensive as the definition of the 1956 Act, which it replaced, and the jurisprudence it spawned. For example, under the old definition, the courts developed collective bargaining unfair labour practices such as the refusal to bargain in good faith. The new definition limits unfair labour practices to individual employment practices and although there are specific provisions in the Labour Relations Act that prohibit certain collective unfair labour practices, the Act does not confer a justifiable remedy for a refusal to bargain. Accordingly, there appears to be room to argue that the Labour Relations Act, 1995 does not give effect to the whole right to a fair labour practice as it might have been understood as a result of the

---

28  It may be that our courts will follow the US Supreme Court and distinguish between different kinds of association, granting a remedy in respect of associations that are not private or intimate but which decline to do so in respect of associations that are. See *Roberts v United States Jaycees* 468 US 609 (1984), in which the court recognized a spectrum of associations from the 'selection of one's spouse' to the 'choice of one's employees'.

The criterion for determining whether an association ought to be protected from legislative (or in our case common-law) intrusion is the private and intimate nature of the association. To evaluate in any particular case whether an association was of a private or an intimate nature, the court proposed *indicia* such as size, purpose, policies, selectivity and congeniality. The court observed that 'determining the limits of state authority over an individual's freedom to enter into a particular association ... unavoidably entails a careful assessment of where that relationship, objective characteristics, ... a spectrum from the most intimate to the most alienated of personal attachment' (at 620). In *Roberts* a Minnesota statute prohibited sex discrimination. The law had been applied to the Jaycees, a national civic organization which restricted its voting membership to men. The Jaycees challenged the constitutionality of the legislation on grounds that it infringed the right to freedom of association. The Supreme Court held that the local chapters of the Jaycees were 'neither small nor selective'. Much of the activity central to the formation and maintenance of the association involves the participation of strangers to that relationship. Accordingly, ... the Jaycees chapter lack the distinctive characteristics that might afford constitutional protection to the decision of its members to exclude women' (at 621).

See also *Rotary International v Rotary Club of Duarte* 481 US 537 (1987) (Rotary not an intimate association); *Hishon v King & Spalding* 467 US 69 (1984) (law firm not an intimate association); and *Runyon v McCrary* 427 US 160 (1976) (private school that advertised in the yellow pages and by mass mailing not a private or selective association).

jurisprudence arising from the statutory definition in the 1956 Act.

In order to determine whether legislation gives effect to a right in the Bill, the court is requested to engage in a further enquiry. Assume that Parliament passes a Civil Rights Act. A section excludes from its scope sports clubs. An international cricketer, in this case a woman, wishes to join the SCC, the newly established equivalent of the MCC. She is refused permission.

If the courts do not accept that a correct interpretation of s 9 justifies such discrimination and that such curbs fall within the scope of the provision, the next issue is whether the Act has limited the right. That requires an analysis of the Act. If the court is satisfied that the Act can limit the right, then the legislation crowds out any claim based on the excluded part of the right. If it does not, then the court has to develop a common-law rule to give effect to the right. The law of delict would again be an appropriate vehicle for the development of the rule.

The second phase of the enquiry is to determine whether any common-law rule gives effect to the right. As discussed, many of the rights in Chapter 2 are already given effect to by the common law.[29]

If there is no legislation or common-law rule giving effect to the constitutional right, then the courts have to develop a common-law rule. The word 'develop' reflects the nature of the legal revolution. The common law is presumed to be immanent and judges find it rather than develop it. But is there immanence after a legal revolution? Kelsen[30] notes that 'the judicial decision is the continuation of the common law and not the beginning of the law creating process'. However, this continuation does not remain unquestioned in the light of a legal revolution. As Kelsen notes, the basic norm of the legal system must be effective in the sense of being applied consistently by and large by the citizenry in order for the legal system based on such basic norm to operate. Thus 'as soon as the old constitution loses its effectiveness, and the new one has become effective, the acts that appear with the subjective meaning of creating or applying legal norms are no longer interpreted by the presupposition of the old basic norm, but by presupposing the new one'.[31]

---

29  A Civil Rights Act would probably render many of the constitutional challenges to equality somewhat redundant; alas, it has not seen the light of day after more than four years.

30  *The Pure Theory of Law* (1967) at 255.

31  Kelsen at 210.

The 1993 Constitution introduced a new *Grundnorm* and with it a legal revolution. Accordingly, the common law must develop in terms of this new *Grundnorm*. To this extent it is not as immanent as it might have been prior to the Constitution! Accordingly, the existing body of common law is not necessarily found whole but requires to be reshaped and recast in the light of the new norm.

Take the law of contract. The rules of contract provide a basis from which to develop appropriate rules. If a landlord terminates an indefinite lease because she discovers that her tenant is a scientologist, the common-law rules as they stand entitle her to terminate the agreement on due notice.[32] Provided that due notice is given, she may terminate for any reason. The development of that rule may mean that a party to a contract may terminate the contract on notice for any reason other than for a reason which amounts to a violation of a constitutional right. It would amount to no more than an extension of the existing rule that an act in contravention of legislation can be null and void. The application of that rule in respect of the termination of a contract is now no longer controversial.[33]

The injunction in s 8(3) to develop the common law is hardly a revolutionary initiative: our courts are continually engaged in the development of the common law. As Corbett CJ has observed:

> '[T]he policy decisions of our courts which shape and at times refashion the common law must also reflect the wishes, often unspoken, and the perceptions, often but dimly discerned, of the people. A community has certain common values and norms … It is these values and norms that the judge must apply in making his decision. And in doing so, he must become "the living voice of the people" … he must integrate society to itself.'[34]

The judgment of Rumpff CJ in *Minister van Polisie v Ewels*[35] is particularly illustrative in this context. A private citizen had been assaulted by a police sergeant who was not on duty but who was in a police station under the control of the police. When the victim sued the Minister of Police, he was met with an exception. In upholding the claim, the Appellate Division found that the common law would recognize a delictual claim for a negligent omission, notwithstanding earlier precedent:

---

32  Termination of a contract on other grounds is not relevant and accordingly has not been included in the summary of the rule.

33  See *National Union of Textile Workers v Stag Packings (Pty) Ltd* (1982) 3 *ILJ* 284 (T).

34  M M Corbett 'Aspects of the Rule of Policy in the Evaluation of our Common Law' (1987) 104 *SALJ* 52 at 67.

35  1975 (3) SA 590 (A).

'[D]it skyn of die stadium van ontwikkeling bereik is waarin 'n late a onregmagtige gedrag beskou word ook waneer die omstandighede van die geval van so 'n aard is dat die late nie alleen morele verontwaardiging ontlok nie maar ook dat die regsoortuiging van die gemeenskap verlang dat die late as onregmagtig beskou behoort te word en dat die gelede skade vergoed behoort te word deur die persoon wat nagelaat het om daadwerklik op te tree.'[36]

*Ewels* illustrates the manner in which the judiciary can and has developed the common law by adapting basic principles to changing circumstances. The courts have worked with the concept of public policy, *boni mores* and the legal convictions of the community and they have applied these concepts to give new content to common-law concepts when 'confronted with a legal problem in the common law for which there is no precedent or authority and where the judge has thus to step into the unknown'.[37]

Section 8(3) now mandates a similar approach in terms of which the courts are to employ the constitutional commitments of the Constitution in the development of the law.[38]

But the challenge to the courts does not end there. The process of limitation required by s 8(3) will demand a fresh and unique approach to the limitation clause.

In practice the limitation inquiry will amount to the proper balancing of rights and values. For this reason, the goal of constitutional invasion of the zone of autonomy conjured up by the judgments of Kentridge AJ and Ackermann J in *Du Plessis'* case is easily exorcised. The right against unfair discrimination has to be balanced against the right to freedom of association, the right to privacy and the value of personal autonomy. That balance has been relatively easily found in other jurisdictions.

Where the central principles of the Constitution mandate the existence of a right *strictu sensu* which imposes a correlative duty, the outcome of the application process could alter the nature of the legal relationship and bring the application of the law into the hitherto more unfettered zone of a liberty against which other individuals had no right.

---

36  *Supra* at 597A–B.

37  Corbett at 44.

38  For other examples of judicial development of the common law, see *Bayer South Africa (Pty) Ltd v Frost* 1991 (4) SA 559 (A) at 568–9 (delictual liability for negligent misstatement in the course of contractual negotiations); *Administrator of Transvaal & others v Traub & others* 1989 (4) SA 731 (A) (recognition of doctrine of legitimate expectations as part of our administrative law).

In the process of the limitation stage, the court will be required to examine the justification for such right or liberty which is a product of the earlier stages of the s 8 inquiry.

## THE CHALLENGE AHEAD

The framework advocated in this chapter will unquestionably be contested.

There is already an indication that these sections will be interpreted restrictively. In their commentary, for example, De Waal, Currie & Erasmus distinguish between the direct application of s 8 and the indirect application contained in s 39(2) as follows:

> 'The purpose of direct application is to determine whether there is on a proper interpretation of the law and the Bill of Rights any inconsistency between the two. The purpose of indirect application is to determine whether it is possible to avoid any inconsistency between the law and the Bill of Rights by a proper interpretation of the two.'[39]

In respect of the effect upon the common law, it is suggested that there is no difference between the two approaches.[40] Not only does this conclusion differ from that of Kriegler J in *Du Plessis'* case,[41] namely that the indirect application contained in s 39(2) (previously s 35(3)) applied where there is no direct challenge based on one or more of the rights and freedoms 'protected in Chapter 2', but it ignores the potential for a cause of action to be grounded in an express provision of the Bill of Rights. The difference depends more on approach than on text. In short, those who compaigned against the indirect approach in favour of the mediated approach to the interim Constitution were generally saying that the traditional incremental development of the common law can easily accommodate the mandate to the courts under s 35(3) (now s 39(2) of the final Constitution) to apply the spirit, purport and objectives of the Constitution to the development of the common law. Indeed, the Constitution has not altered the inexorable development of the common law by generations of judges: one would be ill-advised to interpret the Constitution in a manner that might allow judges to engage in critique and development as advocated in this chapter.

---

39   J de Waal, I Currie and G Erasmus *The Bill of Rights Handbook 1998* (1998) at 38.

40   De Waal et al at 45.

41   At para 142.

# A TRANSFORMIST PRECEDENT

Notwithstanding the more limited scope of the indirect approach, it was, of course, possible for judges to strike out in that direction from the moment of the passing into law of the 1993 Constitution. The paucity of positive response to this precedent, however, supports the submission that a more direct form of mandate is required in the Constitution if the rights of the latter are to infuse the common law with fresh content. There are exceptions to this pessimistic conclusion; in particular, the judgment in *Holomisa v Argus Newspapers Ltd*,[42] which represents the finest precedent we have of the kind of jurisprudence that should be inspired by the new Constitution. The facts were set out by the court as follows:

> '[T]he Johannesburg Star *newspaper published a prominent report about [General Holomisa] ... headed "Holomisa is linked to infiltration of APLA Hit Squad". At the time [Holomisa] was the military ruler of Transkei ... In August 1994 he issued summons against the defendant which publishes the* Star *claiming damages for defamation ... He pleaded that the allegations in the report in the* Star *meant and were understood to mean that he had engaged in acts aimed at racially inspired killings of white people and in a conspiracy to murder a South African official in Transkei ... The particulars of the claim asserted that the report was "false and defamatory" ... and that the defendants published it "wrongfully and unlawfully and with intention to defame the plaintiff and damage his reputation".'*[43]

The defendant excepted to the claim and raised the question whether public officials could claim compensatory damages for defamation on the same basis as ordinary litigants. The exception invoked the free speech and expression guarantee of the Constitution, s 15(1) which provides that every person should have the right to freedom of speech and expression, which shall include freedom of the press and other media and freedom of artistic creativity and scientific research.

In support of its exception, the defendant contended that Chapter 3 of the interim Constitution applied directly to litigation between private parties. Cameron J referred to s 7(1), namely that the chapter shall bind all legislative and executive organs, and contrasted it with s 4(2), namely that the Constitution shall bind all legislative, executive and judicial organs of state. He also referred to s 33(4), which

---

42  1996 (2) SA 588 (W).

43  At 593E–H.

provides that this chapter shall not preclude measures designed to prohibit unfair discrimination by bodies and persons other than those bound in terms of s 7(1).

Cameron J concluded that 'these provisions seem to make it incontestably plain that the Constitution envisages that certain bodies and persons would not, without further legislative provision, or further development of the common-law, be bound by the fundamental rights chapter'.[44]

In short, Cameron J concluded that Chapter 3 did not have direct horizontal application. The chapter did not provide a direct cause of action to the plaintiff nor could it be used directly for ascertaining the limits of the plaintiff's capacity to claim compensation for defamatory statements made about him.

In his judgment Cameron J refrained from an evaluation or an analysis of the scope of Chapter 3. He relied rather upon s 35(3), which he saw 'nor merely [as] an interpretative directive, but a force that informs all legal institutions and decisions with the new power of constitutional values'.[45] Accordingly, s 15(1), which guarantees the right to freedom of speech and expression, and s 10, the constitutional guarantee of dignity, infuse the law with defined values. The question therefore arises as to how these values affect the plaintiff's claim as well as the development of the common law of defamation.

By using the framework provided by 35(3), the starting point became the existing rules of common law. Cameron J therefore commenced his judgment with an examination of the development of the law of defamation from the case of *Whittaker v Roos and Bateman*.[46] In *Whittaker's* case the concept of the *animus injuriandi* was given an objective test, namely that the defamer must have intended to produce the effect of his act or, in the words of Innes J, 'that the aggressor had in view the necessary consequence of his conduct'.[47] In *Maisel v Van Naeren*[48] advocates of the purist Roman-Dutch School began their attack on the existing law of defamation.

---

44  At 596H.

45  At 598D.

46  1912 AD 4.

47  *Supra* at 124.

48  1960 (4) SA 836 (C). This development is a clear illustration of the over-arching influence of a political project upon the law. As Martin Channock has written, 'Roman-Dutch law was created in opposition to English law (and African law) as part of the writing of a national self-narrative': 'Race and Nation in South African Common Law' in P Fitzpatrick (ed) *Protecting Human Rights by Bills of Rights* (1994) at 265.

In *Maisel*, De Villiers AJ said:

> '*In as much as dolus, or* animus injuriandi *as it is called in relation to injuriae, is an essential for liability under the* actio injuriarum, *it is likewise an essential for liability for defamation. This basic situation is not affected by the fact that a claim may be added under the* actio legis Aquiliae, *for patrimonial loss (Voet 47.10.18); for the patrimonial loss thus sought to be recovered is that which flows from the* injuria, *and there can be no* injuria *without* animus injuriandi ... *it is essential that the alleged wrongdoer should be conscious of the wrongful character of his act ... of some other object.*'[49]

In *Naidoo v Vengtas*[50] the Appellate Division began to follow the approach in *Maisel* and assert the necessity for a subjective test to determine the existence of *animus injuriandi*, that is the intent to defame by a state of mind that willed the consequence of the statement.

This change in approach made an action for defamation against the media extremely difficult because a subjective belief that a report was made in good faith became a justifiable defence. In short, our courts dispensed with the requirement of *animus injuriandi* in cases concerning the mass media's publication of defamatory statements because of the view that the former requirement was ill-suited to the effects of modern communication. In *Suid-Afrikaanse Uitsaai Korporasie v O'Malley*[51] the Appellate Division responded to this problem, stating that strict liability was the appropriate basis for a defamation action involving the media.

In cases subsequent to *O'Malley*, the Appellate Division steadily moved away from emphasizing the importance of *animus injuriandi* as a means for determining liability for *injuria*. Cameron J suggests that the proper assessment should not involve the *animus injuriandi*; the assessment of liability 'should take place in relation to the criteria of wrongfulness, and not fault. This conforms with the trend away from the wrongdoer's subjective state of mind, and to an objective assessment of the justification for his or her conduct.'[52]

Cameron J was not yet free to use the concept of wrongfulness in order to develop the law of defamation as urged by the excipient. Facing him was a large

---

49  *Supra* at 842.

50  1965 (1) SA 1 (A).

51  1977 (3) SA 394 (A).

52  *Holomisa (supra)* at 601G.

and formidable obstacle in the form of the judgment of the Appellate Division in *Neethling v Du Preez*.[53] In *Neethling* Hoexter JA had said:

> '[S]ince it is entirely of his own accord that the defendant elects to vilify the plaintiff, justice demands that he should do so at his peril; and that in an action for defamation he should have to establish what he should have troubled to verify before he maligned the plaintiff.'[54]

Accordingly, the court found that the defendant was required to prove the truth of a defamatory statement on a complete balance of probability in order to raise a successful defence.

Cameron J acknowledged that, were it not for the new Constitution, he would have been bound by this judgment, but 'the terrain of the law in South Africa has profoundly changed. All South African courts must now, as a first duty, take into account the provisions of the Constitution particularly its fundamental rights provisions.'[55] Section 35(3) therefore required careful attention, for it impelled a court fundamentally to reconsider rules of any common law where these might conflict with a right guaranteed in terms of Chapter 3.

In particular, the constitutional aspiration of an open and democratic society depended upon 'vigorous mechanisms of public scrutiny and public debate, not only to nurture the new structures, but to guard against excesses in their exercise'.[56]

But if s 35(3) allowed the court to re-examine the law of defamation, the Constitution itself contained two seemingly conflicting rights, namely, freedom of speech, on the one hand, and, on the other, the right to dignity, which entails the right to a reputation and the consequent protection of such reputation against an unjustified attack. Cameron J conceded that:

> '[T]he determination of a right's constitutional importance in each situation unavoidably involves the evaluation of competing values. The value whose protection most closely illuminates the constitutional scheme to which we have committed ourselves should receive appropriate protection in that process.'[57]

Cameron J emphasized that in the development of a South African democracy committed to the principles of openness and accountability the guarantee of freedom

---

53 1994 (1) SA 708 (A).

54 At 770.

55 *Holomisa (supra)* at 603D–E.

56 At 605I.

57 At 607I–608A.

of speech in general, and the role of the media in particular, in assisting in the nurturing of such a democracy would prove to be critical factors.

However, the safeguarding of freedom of speech does not grant the media a licence to publish what they wish. As Ronald Dworkin has noted:

> 'But if free speech is justified on principle, then it would be outrageous to suppose that journalists should have a special protection not available to others, because that would claim that they are, as individuals, more important or worthier of more concern than others.'[58]

But if the constitutional guarantee of freedom of speech makes the role of the media easier in the promotion of dialogue and debate, the further question arises as to its impact upon the right to dignity and reputation. Cameron J was alive to this difficulty by observing that the common law asserted in *Neethling* gives a primacy to the value of reputation over that of freedom of speech and that 'seems to me to be difficult to reconcile with the importance the Constitution's structures and values attach to freedom'.[59] Given the importance placed upon freedom of speech in the Constitution and the protection given to political speech by virtue of the necessity requirement which forms part of the limitation test (s 33(1)), the court found that the Constitution attached greater weight to freedom of speech and expression. To allow the plaintiff merely to prove the publication of defamatory matter and then to oblige the defendant to justify such publication would run counter to fundamental principles enshrined in the Constitution. The Constitution therefore required of the common law a greater measure of protection to be given to those who published statements than was afforded to them under the law as set out in the *Neethling* judgment.

In attempting to give content to his submission, counsel for the excipient sought to rely on the decision of the United States Supreme Court in *New York Times Company v Sullivan*.[60] In its judgment, the Supreme Court found:

> '[A] rule compelling the critic of official conduct to guarantee the truth of all his facts and assertions—and to do so on pain of libel judgments virtually unlimited in amount—leads to a comparable self censorship. Allowance of the defence of truth, with the burden of proving it on the defendant, does not mean that only false speech will be deterred. Under such a rule, would-be critics of official conduct may be deterred from voicing their

---

58  Cited by Cameron J at 610F.

59  At 611D.

60  376 US 254 (1964).

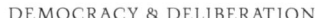

*criticism, even though it is believed to be true and even though it is in fact true, because of doubt whether it can be proved in court or fear of the expense of having to do so.'*[61]

Accordingly, the Supreme Court found that the proof demanded to succeed in a defamation action required the plaintiff to show that the defendant had made the defamatory statement with actual malice, that is, with knowledge that it was false or with reckless disregard of whether it was false or not.

A notable feature of the *Holomisa* judgment is its refusal to follow American authority slavishly. Cameron J pointed out that *Sullivan's* case had to be seen within the context of a deliberate strategy of intimidation by civil libel suits against the press. By the time the Supreme Court decided *Sullivan*, public officials had brought nearly US$300 million in libel actions against the press. Further, *Sullivan's* judgment was based on the First Amendment of the American Constitution, which 'seems to me to differ greatly from even our post-Constitution understanding of a free speech'.[62]

Accordingly, the approach to the law of defamation would be to compel a publisher to establish the existence of reasonable conduct in publishing a report such as the taking of steps to check the accuracy of the impugned material or by establishing that the publisher was otherwise justified in publishing without taking steps defined as adequate.

The concept of reasonableness rather than the *animus injuriandi* as the test for negligent conduct therefore becomes an important balancing tool. Through the standard of reasonableness, a powerful mechanism is developed

> *'for resolving the difficulties inherent in protecting reputation while at the same time giving recognition to the role the Constitution accords free speech and expression. It will not be reasonable to publish most untrue statements of fact. Only due enquiry and the application of reasonable care will mark such conduct out for protection.'*[63]

As the *Holomisa* case dealt with the publication of a report of a political nature, the Constitution tilted the balance in favour of the newspaper, given the more burdensome onus to be discharged when such speech is justifiably limited in terms of s 33 of the Constitution. For this reason Cameron J concluded his judgment by finding that 'a defamatory statement which relates to "free and fair political activity

---

61   *Supra* at 279.

62   *Holomisa (supra)* at 614.

63   *Holomisa (supra)* at 617.

is constitutionally protected, even if false unless the plaintiff shows that, in all the circumstances of its publications, it was unreasonably made"'.

Cameron J was able to harmonize the law of defamation with the Constitution without recourse to direct application, but the 1996 Constitution makes it difficult for the judiciary to ignore these implications.[64]

## CONCLUSION

Even for the most committed verticalist, s 8 presents a new challenge. It forces lawyers to break from their conceptual chains and to re-examine the South African legal system and its established rules and principles afresh. South African lawyers will now be required to analyse the common law, examine its scope and promise and test whether it meets the particular constitutional commitment enshrined in Chapter 2. Not even the relative safety and certainty of indirect *Drittwirkung* sourced in German precedent is available, for s 8 raises the possibility of a new cause of action where silence or absence previously prevailed. Unger's mapping and critique no longer languishes as an ideological frustration against elegant analysis and no praxis. Section 8 enjoins our court to fuse the gaps between laws, idealistic commitments and its more depressing reality as expressed in the ageing content of existing common-law concepts. Previously the legal system held out the principles of private law as timeless, transcending boundary and history. It was not for lawyers to concern themselves with institutional arrangements and political disputes; lawyers were there to implement our rich heritage, not to prefigure the structure of society.

Now, in contrast, each legal dispute holds the potential for an engagement with a new process which is designed to harmonize existing law with the deepest commitments of the Constitution.

The challenge extends to the very heart of our present system. The potential for horizontal application calls into question the private–public divide which previously lay at the centre of the legal system. But it does so not by creating a direct, separate constitutional cause of action; it does so rather by ensuring that a newly

---

64  The Supreme Court of Appeal has more recently offered its own approach to freedom of expression. In the light of my criticism of the judgment in *National Media Ltd v Bogoshi* 1998 (4) SA 1196 (SCA), the discussion is more appropriately located in the following chapter.

created constitutional action must be mediated through our common law. In this fashion the legal apartheid between an egalitarian constitution and a *laissez-faire* common law is destroyed — itself a major justification for concluding that the 1996 Constitution promises to transform the entire body of the South African legal system from the 19th-century premises which still characterize much of our jurisprudence towards a coherent legal system based on the principles of human dignity, equality and freedom.

But legal tradition is nothing if not tenacious. There is comfort in shibboleths, certainly in tried and tested 'scholarship' and clarity of 'truth' in old ideology. It is to this clash between legal tradition and the transformist demands of the 1996 Constitution as set out in this chapter to which we now must turn.

# ESCAPING THE CHALLENGE OF THE CONSTITUTION:
## PRIVATE LAWYERS AND BUSINESS AS USUAL

*'If we do not tackle the basic problem of the transformation of humanity, or at least if we do not see that part of its activities that is our specialist concern in the context of this transformation, which is still in progress, then we as historians are engaged in trivialities or intellectual or other parlour games.'*[1]

*'A young person being trained in legal doctrine in a peripheral part of the twentieth century could still experience these charms almost undiminished, in the form of the long fossilised project of nineteenth century legal science, perennially rehearsed in those faraway places. He could study Roman Law through the unhistorical lens of the traditional Romanists, reading Savigny on possession as if the German bureaucrat and the Roman jurisconsults were nearly contemporary co-discoverers of the same legal order. He could be thrilled by the sense of participation in a form of consciousness that seemed both archaic and indispensable, preceding the social sciences, giving birth to them, and yet continuing to perform a mission they were powerless to accomplish. Identifying with the ancient priesthood of the jurists, he could see in their work a halting escape from the accidents, absurdities and atrocities of history. We can laugh at him now, but we cannot so easily sever our anxieties from his sympathies.'*[2]

As was apparent from chapter 1, s 8 of the Constitution compels the development of an integrated legal system in which no one set of legal concepts can be left to develop in ignorance of the Constitution and its fundamental commitments. My argument about application can be summarized thus: a rigid split between the public domain and the private domain and the formal notion of autonomy which infuses a *laissez-faire* approach are false. Real autonomy has its sources in both socially constructed and politically maintained forms of life which are inextricably bound up with each other. But the common law significantly shapes all private and public relationships. The final Constitution insists on the requirement that all inquiries as to the constitutionality of a particular law or relationship be tested against this shared public philosophy and not artificially suppressed as a result a

---

1   Eric Hobsbawm *On History* (1997) at 64.
2   Roberto Unger *What should Legal Analysis Become?* (1996) at 183.

misguided belief that the guarantees in the Bill of Rights apply only to those actions and relationships which can be traced back to the state.

In *Du Plessis v De Klerk*[3] Ackermann J adopted an entirely different perspective in order to justify a restrictive enterprise. He wrote that

> '[W]hat also needs to be considered carefully is the impact, on the legislative process, of a directly horizontal application of Chapter 3 to private legal relationships. In each case when a final pronouncement of this nature is made through this Court, Parliament will be bound by this Court's judgment. The Court has after all pronounced on the meaning and application of the Constitution in a particular context. Should Parliament wish to alter the law, resulting from such a direct application of the Chapter 3 rights by this Court, it will have to amend the Constitution. I consider this to be a most undesirable consequence needlessly inhibiting the normal piecemeal statutory modi-fication of the common law. It is one which directly flows, however from the holding which in essence constitutionalises the entire body of private law.'

When a court pronounces on the implications of a section in the Bill of Rights, it must follow that the common law should be moulded accordingly, if at all possible. It could never, in my view, have been the intention of the framers to constitute Chapter 3 as a special code, to which the private common law is directly subject. In short, the incremental development of the common law in the light of the constitution is mandated.[4] But this is hardly a revolutionary step. That s 8(2) provides that the provision of the Bill is binding if and, to the extent that it is applicable indicates a process of a case-by-case development which is hardly different from the manner in which the law has been developed previously, *save* that this time there is principle to guide such development.

To accomplish this task we need to explore the values embedded in the existing body of law. The Constitution asks us to test this body of law by engaging with two fundamental imperatives: cooperation, being the construction of a society in which reciprocity and *ubuntu* prevail, and the demand for personal freedom and self-assertion. As Unger expresses it:

> 'we need other people and need to be protected from them. We must be able to par-ticipate wholeheartedly in particular societies and cultures, in particular societies and cultures, in particular forms of experience and consciousness, yet we cannot surrender

---

3    1996 (3) SA 850 (CC) at para 111.

4    See also Sachs J at para 179; a particularly ironic conclusion, given his earlier writings such as *Advancing Human Rights in South Africa* (1992).

*our powers of desire or insight to any of these versions of humanity or to any collection of them.'*[5]

Accordingly, this necessitates a process of deconstruction of our existing law. We need to examine the extent to which the law as it existed when the Constitution became the fundamental law, is predicted as these foundational values whereas all public law was massively influenced and shaped by apartheid, private lawyers have often insisted in the universality of the principles of this body of law. But even if the concepts are universal, the further questions occur as to the content of this law and its compatability with the dual imperatives. Until recently, there was not only no such activity but no demand for it. Perhaps for this reason, South African legal history could best be analysed in terms of the sharp contrast between the manner in which social historians have sought to engage with their subject in the manner suggested by Hobsbawm and the descriptive exercise of a legal past which exists on a timeless horizontal plane. In short, while students of social history study the richly crafted works of Van Onselen, Bundy, Delius and Peires, over the years law students have been fed a far leaner intellectual diet of description of events and summaries of the work of the 'ancient legal priests'.

As discussed throughout this work, 1994 heralded a new dawn for South African law. Whatever side taken in the debate about the exact scope of the interim Constitution, there is surely no escaping the far-reaching implications for private law now that the final Constitution has been adopted. In any event, even under the interim Constitution, s 35(3) provided that, in the interpretation of any law and the application and development of the common law and customary law, a court shall have due regard to the purport and objects of this chapter (that is, the Bill of Rights). In short, the section introduces new principles which mandate all judges to fill old forms with new content. The section created not so much a new source of law into the realm of private adjudication but a set of first-ranking principles by which all existing rules of common law had to be assessed and justified. Clearly the process of assessment called upon legal historians to locate the origins and role of existing doctrine in order that the constitutional mandate could be implemented.

For this reason alone the most recent historical enterprise, *Southern Cross*, an examination of civil and common law in South Africa, promised much.[6] Its

---

5   Unger at 185.
6   Reinhard Zimmermann *Southern Cross: Civil Law and Common Law in South Africa* (1996) at 5.

failure is illustrative of the gap between constitutional challenge (as outlined above) and the more mundane reality of South African legal scholarship. But that is to run way ahead of the discussion in this chapter. The promise of this major work, published after the constitutional enterprise had been launched, was considerable. After all, the editors were Zimmermann, author of a magisterial text on the law of obligations, and Visser, who had earlier edited a collection on legal history to which he had penned a superb introduction (to which I shall return later). These two distinguished academics assembled a wonderful cast to contribute to their production. It is difficult to conceive of a better line-up in the fields chosen for analysis of South African private law. Now at last the unhistorical lens through which generations of South African lawyers had viewed particularly private law would be replaced by a microscope which would throw up all existing doctrine in the sharpest historical relief.

Unfortunately, however, the most respected directors and the most distinguished of casts do not always make the best productions. Sometimes the plot is simply too weak, occasionally the actors do not do the material sufficient justice, perhaps the difficulty lies with miscasting of certain actors or the overall direction is not sufficiently tight. In some ways *Southern Cross* suffers from all these deficiencies.

In my view, however, the core problem stems from the direction. And it is in the direction that the deep ideological roots of South African law can be found. In their introduction Zimmermann and Visser suggest that this book is the 'first attempt to write a doctrinal history of South African law'. Although the meaning of doctrinal history is not expressly defined, the authors give the term some meaning in the following sentence: '[a]s far as general discussions of the history of South African law are concerned, they focus mainly on what one may call the "external history" rather than the history of the specific legal institutions.'[7] Earlier we are informed that we need to transcend a national legal enterprise because of the existence of common legal tradition in Europe, an analysis of which will allow us to understand similarities, differences and divergences of national legal development.

It appears, therefore, that a doctrinal history is an 'internal account', a narrative of doctrinal development, the law working itself pure as it obeys an inexorable

---

7   Much of the discussions relating to *Southern Cross* are based on a review of the work. I appreciate that many readers will not have ploughed its many pages, nor, as I make clear, do I necessarily recommend such a course of action. I do consider, however, that this work represents a most excellent example of the present state of academic ploy and hence I have adapted the review for this illustrative purpose. I trust that the book does not have to be read to understand the thrust of the dispute.

process of change from feudalism to capitalism, status to contract and pragmatism to conceptual coherence. Only the most myopic breed of advocates of this approach would wish to forget the effect of apartheid on the South African legal system and thus early in their introduction Zimmermann and Visser it make clear that 'there can be no doubt that private law was a structural part of the system of domination in South Africa'.[8]

So far so good! However, a few sentences later the following appears:

> '[We] realised that the internal development of the law of obligations and property would reveal very little of the societal forces surrounding it, because South African lawyers, like their counterparts all over the world tend to create law primarily with reference to the intellectual concerns raised in statutory documents, authoritative court decisions, and learned treatises.'[9]

For this reason, we are told, the first two chapters dealing with Roman-Dutch law in its historical context and the history of African land dispossession were commissioned to provide the external context into which the doctrinal development can be located.

We thus arrive at the problem of direction. To suggest, as if it were common intellectual cause, that lawyers create law in some ahistorical, depoliticized void and that intellectual development can be analysed without careful consideration being taken of socio-economic forces is truly breathtaking in its simplicity, revealing the tenacity of the crude positivist hold on South African legal scholarship. The intention is clear — all but two of the invited contributors can forget about engaging with 'the material conditions, symbolic systems and tacit assumptions in which (legal concepts) were embedded'.[10] In *Southern Cross*, Eduard Fagan, writing about Roman-Dutch law in its South African historical context, and Tom Bennett, analysing the history of African land dispossession, are left to carry the contextualized can while the doctrinalists can proceed to do the 'real thing'.

Simply stated, the debate is about the kind of history worth reading. For my part, I fail to see how two chapters, however well written, can be offered as an excuse for writing about the development of crucial areas of law without any engagement with influences beyond the texts. In short, history and formalism meet in a neat embrace. Why, one may ask, is this approach so attractive at the very

---

8   At 5.

9   At 5–6.

10   Robert Gordon 'Forward: Arrival of Critical Historicism' (1997) 49 *Stanford Law Review* 1023 at 1025.

time that our legal system has been subjected to a constitutional mandate to change and when our society is undergoing the most painful process of self-examination? A persuasive answer is to be found in a work which represents the kind of history I would consider rises to the challenge posed by Hobsbawm, namely Morton Horwitz's *The Transformation of American Law, 1780–1860*, particularly where he writes '[f]or the paramount social condition that is necessary for legal formalism to flourish in a society is for the powerful groups in that society to have a great interest in disguising and suppressing the inevitably political and redistributive functions of law'.[11] Expressed differently, I wish to resist an intellectual project that seeks to construct a Chinese wall between a so-called internal and external account of history.

If we do not tackle the basic problem of the transformation of human external history, we will continue to have a much impoverished conception of our legal history. Doubtless Hartians will argue in favour of the importance of the internal model and criticism of this approach should not be construed as the advocacy of a purely external account. It has been the very argument of this book that external and internal factors so intertwine that an explanation that fails to take account of these connections is unable to provide a holistic account of legal development. Indeed, by including two 'external' chapters the editors of *Southern Cross* have made such a tacit concession.

Outside of the two initial chapters, these concerns hardly earn a footnote. We are told that the new Constitution will increase the impetus towards recognizing 'societal considerations' as contained in the Bill of Rights and that such a trend is reflected in the contributions of a number of the authors.[12] The point is that such reflection is more marked in its absence than in the chapters that follow. This is not surprising in a work that argues for the legitimacy of a project in which doctrine can be wrenched so violently from its social moorings.

The almost awestruck manner in which the transnationalism of law is proclaimed as a fact is perhaps less surprising for its pretence at original comment as for its inability to examine how the broader nationalistic project of the 18th and 19th centuries affected all social development, including law. The fact that different systems derived from the Continent and England were used to develop

---

11  At 206.

12  *Southern Cross* at 6.

a body of law in this century is of contemporary relevance. In particular, this enquiry holds implications for the recent rise of the global economy in the last decade of the 20th century and the attendant drive toward regionalism, particularly in law. The movement of law outside the confines of the national state is important for the future of constitutionalism and its promise of human rights. If one is committed to the notion of 'legal science'[13] as are the editors of *Southern Cross*, it is hardly surprising that these implications of a transnational legal system are simply ignored.[14]

But the directors are not to blame for all the performances, because some lawyers still wish to live in the earlier era. Thus J P van Niekerk's tedious description of how the purity of the Roman-Dutch law of insurance was replaced by English law is the very apotheosis of Rip van Winkel jurisprudence. Van Niekerk's passionate enthusiasm for a Roman-Dutch legal revival in the area of insurance, notwithstanding that the commercial reality in this area is that the insurance industry has been dominated by English practice, arguably throughout the period reviewed by Van Niekerk. In many ways the insurance industry, particularly marine insurance, represents the earliest example of economic globalization, with English precedent dominating both the core and the periphery, including South Africa. Of this Van Niekerk has nothing to say save for a brief description of the influence of the practice of English insurance companies.[15]

Van Niekerk greets the key judgment of Joubert JA in *Mutual and Federal Insurance Co Ltd v Oudtshoorn Municipality*[16] with considerable enthusiasm. He writes: 'Roman-Dutch law constitutes the basis from which, by historical and

---

13  The introduction to *Southern Cross* talks of 'legal science' as if there is no controversy surrounding the term. We are then informed that the concept of disciplinery divide should be rejected — legal science will have to be supported by a legal scholarship that transcends both national boundaries and disciplinary divides (such as those between legal history, comparative law and modern legal doctrine) (at 1). Small wonder, therefore, that the predominant view of legal scholarship is so ill suited to the approach of mapping and critique which lies at the heart of the constitutional idea enshrined in the Constitution.

14  See the contrasting analysis by Habermas in Balakkrishnan (ed) *Mapping the Nation* (1996) at 287, who suggests that the tension between the universalism of an egalitarian legal community and the particularism of the nation can be solved when the constitutional principles of human rights and democracy give priority to a cosmopolitan understanding of the nation as one of citizens over and against an ethnocentric interpretation of the nation as a prepolitical entity. It is within this context that the idea of legal integration has considerable purchase.

15  See *Southern Cross* at 439n15.

16  1985 (1) SA 419 (A).

comparative methods, a viable system of South African insurance law may be developed.'[17] Accordingly, Joubert JA is seen as having struck a great blow in favour of this headlong dash into the archives to discover some further arcane text — this while the balance of the world responds to the demands of an increasingly uniform set of commercial principles. But even if I do Van Niekerk's essay an injustice, his chapter is hardly a history, and it certainly contains no analysis of how and why the law developed in the fashion it did. If Zimmermann and Visser's claim about the influence of intellectual concerns of lawyers upon legal development is to be taken seriously (and as a causal factor which explains legal development as opposed to the causal influence it should be taken seriously), Van Niekerk offers us precious little. The least one could have expected was some analysis of the role of Joubert JA in the Appellate Division, particularly in the court's development of private law during the 1980s. *Oudtshoorn Municipality* was not the only case during this period when Roman-Dutch authority was controversially invoked. In this connection, the analytical treatment of the judgment of Joubert JA in *Bank of Lisbon and South Africa Ltd v De Ornelaby*[18] by Zimmermann[19] stands in sharp contrast to the rather awestruck manner in which Van Niekerk considers *Oudtshoorn Municipality*.

An equally disappointing contribution, even if assessed solely in terms of the editors' definition of history, is that on the judiciary by Stephen Garvin. This is an area where South African legal scholarship has served us well, particularly well as a result of the pioneering work of John Dugard and the more recent work of Hugh Corder[20] and David Dyzenhaus.[21] In the context of private law mention must also be made of one of the truly outstanding contributions to a South African law journal, namely Edwin Cameron's piece on L C Steyn entitled 'Legal Chauvinism, Executive-mindedness and Justice. L C Steyn in Perspective'.[22]

For this reason alone, Garvin's contribution adds little to our understanding of the role of the judiciary in the development of the law. The best that can be said of this list of biographical detail of South African judges is that such an

---

17 At 476.
18 1988 (3) SA 580 (A).
19 At 235ff.
20 *Judges at Work* (Juta, 1984).
21 *Hard Cases in Wicked Legal Systems* (1991).
22 (1982) 99 *SALJ* 38.

enterprise serves little purpose in a book devoted to historical enquiry. So far the collection has revealed two faces of the old legal approach, namely an obsession with old authorities, confirming the adage that those who rely on this approach are but chroniclers without analytical skill but possessed of a facility for grasping many languages, and the deliberate refusal of private lawyers to consider the ideological role played by the judiciary.

An area which lends itself to rich historical analysis of the way in which the development of legal concept and its meaning was deeply embedded in material conditions, economic and legal discourse and ideology is the field of Aquilian liability. This is hardly an original submission; indeed, Danie Visser wrote something almost identical in his introductory essay to which I have already made reference, namely '[t]he vicissitudes of liability for pure economic loss are very likely to be related to, first, the complex variety of ideologies that have influenced our law and, secondly, to the dialectical relationship between these ideologies and material society.'[23] Visser then goes on to lay out a set of challenges for historians canvassing the development of the law of delict, including the ideological 'underpinnings of the reluctance to allow liability for negligent misstatements and pure economic loss'[24] the influence of the Purist movement and the effect of complex policy factors on judgments.

Annél van Aswegen promises the reader that her purpose 'is to identify trends in, and where possible reasons for, the peculiarly South African slant to the early development of liability under the *actio legis Aquiliae* in this country'.[25] She certainly describes how the law changed and how Roman-Dutch principles showed considerable resilience in the face of the more general influence of English law; but, alas, there is not so much as an attempt to provide any indication as to the reasons — be they doctrinal, ideological or material — for this development.

In his contribution Dale Hutchison does little more than extend the narrative into the late 20th century. All too often the reader is offered no more than the theory of the 'great man of history'. For example, Hutchison informs us that the courts resisted the pressure to abandon Aquilian principles in favour of English law and this was 'thanks in no small part to the wisdom, learning and vigilance

---

23  'The legal historian as Subversive; "Killing the Catoline Geese"' in D Visser (ed) *Essays on the History of Law* (1989).

24  At 5.

25  At 562.

of Sir James Rose-Innes'.[26] That a dominant intellectual such as Rose-Innes exerted a profound influence on the law is not at all surprising, but what other factors were at play during this period? To what extent did the rapid economic changes driven through the dominance of mining and leading to a process of industrialization have an influence on the conceptual and doctrinal development in a legal area which by the very nature of the liability imposed would have manifest its effect on economic behaviour. What, for example, explains the difference between the 'liberal' attitude to the recovery of economic loss as reflected in the French and Austrian codes and the restrictive approach adopted by 19th-century German and English law? To what extent did a *laissez-faire* ideology have an impact on legal development? The nature of the subject-matter cries out for an engagement with these questions, particularly when the descriptive part of the exercise is as elegantly crafted as the contribution of Hutchison.

The history of delict has received a sufficiently sensitive treatment elsewhere to have acted as a guide to the contributors to *Southern Cross*. Morton Horwitz has analysed the development of the American law of tort by examining the general and specific legal intellectual climate as well as putting forward the intriguing suggestion about the role of the trade union movement in promoting legal protection against loss caused by industrial accident. Such protection, he asserts, in turn influenced the development of protective labour legislation that was utterly antithetical to the prevailing *laissez-faire* environment. The question arises: what has been the role of the South African trade union movement in the shaping of elements of the law of delict which would have a bearing upon worker protection. Not only is the issue of unions and protective legislation and its potential for influencing either or both substantive law and legal discourse considered neither by Hutchison nor by Van Aswegan but the broader question does not even gain a mention in Fagan's chapter, which was designed to provide the external context. This is somewhat surprising because Fagan raises the fascinating question of the relationship between purism and politics and emphasizes that 'due attention should be given to the historical and political matrix from which the purists claim to Roman-Dutch law's right of pre-eminence arose'.[27]

---

26  At 600.

27  At 63.

These questions necessitate some answer in relation to the developments in our law of delict which followed upon *Minister van Polisie v Ewels*.[28] As Hutchison notes, at roughly the same time as the judgment in *Ewels* was delivered, certain English judges 'began to express the need for a consideration of policy factors in determining the existence of a duty of care in the tort of negligence'.[29] Is the relationship between politics and doctrine at all relevant to the development of the understanding of these significant changes in our law? Even if the aim of the enquiry is more suitable to a chamber piece than to a symphony designed to look only at legal discourse and the changes therein, it is surely essential to focus upon some understanding of 'the resurrection of the old requirement of *iniuria* in its new guise of wrongfulness'[30] Given the scope of our new Constitution, this enquiry has assumed important practical implications for freedom of expression as a fundamental value in a deliberative democracy and the balance to be struck with the right to privacy.

There can be few areas of law where the relationship between politics and doctrine is so overt as in labour law, a point which clearly emerges from Fagan's reference to the industrialization of the country and Jordaan's brief discussion of the labour market in the Cape of Good Hope.[31] However, the implications of this history are scarcely analysed or integrated into the overall account. The exploitation of workers, overwhelmingly black and mainly disorganized, was obviously sustained by the law; but whereas labour legislation often receives academic attention, the role of the common law in the reproduction of these conditions is rarely canvassed. Its significance can, however, be glimpsed from some of the material unearthed by Jordaan. Thus in relation to forfeiture of wages in cases of desertion or justified dismissal the more protectionist position of the Roman-Dutch law was jettisoned for the English law, where forfeiture was the norm rather than the exception.

Specific performance is a critical remedy in the area of labour law in that if an employee can obtain such relief from the courts, even the possibility thereof acts as a deterrent against the overwhelming power possessed by the employer. This point is perhaps best illustrated in the consequences of the decision of Van Dijkhorst J in *National Union of Textile Workers v Stag Packings (Pty) Ltd*,[32] in which

---

28 1975 (3) SA 590 (A).

29 At 639.

30 At 632.

31 At 389ff.

32 1982 (4) SA 151 (T).

the learned judge held that wrongful dismissal should give rise to the same remedy as pertains to the general law of contract regarding wrongful rescission. After *Stag Packings*, employers who wished to dismiss workers where there was a particularly adversarial relationship with the employer but who had acted within their rights had to consider carefully the economic implications of reinstatement. It is therefore hardly surprising that until *Stag Packings* in 1982 our courts accepted the English position which so greatly advantaged the unfettered power of the employer.

In concluding his analysis Jordaan suggests that the reception of English law of employment took place either where the position in Roman-Dutch law was uncertain or where it was silent on the point in issue. Can this pass as a comprehensive explanation? The evidence even assembled by Jordaan suggests some interesting further possibilities. When the law relating to forfeiture of wages and specific performance is examined, the application of English law fitted far more comfortably with the prevailing *laissez-faire* judicial world view which would have been unable or unwilling to consider imbalances of power between employers and employees, a point richly illustrated in the judgment of the Appellate Division in *Boyd v Stuttaford and Co.*[33] The development of this body of law affords clear possibilities for exploring the relationship between prevailing economic conditions, political struggle, particularly union activity and legal discourse, in order to develop a more comprehensive explanatory framework for legal growth and change. Some of this work has been attempted in other jurisdictions, as noted by Jordaan.[34] As so much of Jordaan's own work is located in a broader vision of legal scholarship, I can only assume that the initial direction to authors explains the failure in *Southern Cross* to explore the explanatory possibilities outlined above.

It could well be argued in reply to my criticisms of *Southern Cross* that I have missed the plot or that I should assess the work on the basis of its stated objectives rather than by imposing my own. After all, if you go to the movies and see a film by Ingmar Bergmann, you should not dismiss it by invoking the standards to be applied to a film by Groucho Marx! An assessment of a work of this nature is doubtless shaped by the conception of history which the reviewer brings to the reading of the work, however faithfully she attempts to follow the express intentions of the authors. For my part I seriously question a history of law which

---

33  1910 AD 101.

34  Adrian Merritt 'The Historical Role of Law in the Regulation of Employment: Abstentionist or Interventionist' (1982) 1 *Australian Journal of Law and Society* 56.

refuses to acknowledge that law is deeply embedded in the social and economic structures of society. Furthermore, 'the fact remains that history has moved away
from description and narrative to analysis and explanation; from concentrating
on the unique and individual to establishing regularities and to generalization.[35]
My fundamental objection to *Southern Cross* is its refusal to explore the law within
the context of the society in which it operated and hence after a read of more
than 800 pages I am scarcely the wiser as to how and why South African private
law developed in the manner described in the book. Viewed within the perspective
of this work, this historical approach which can seek to justify a narrow doctrinal
approach represents the very antithesis of what a transformist constitution demands,
namely an enquiry into the deeper political, historical and philosophical foundations of the law as a precursor to understanding that which has underpinned
the power of law and hence that which can undermine values of the new enterprise.
But my objective is hardly novel.

Of course, there is a more than respectable historical tradition which argues
to the contrary of my preferred conception. The historian R G Collingwood wrote:

> '[T]he historian need not and cannot (without ceasing to be an historian) emulate
> the scientist in searching for the causes or laws of events. For science, the event is dis-
> covered by perceiving it, and the further search for its cause is conducted by assigning
> it to its class and determining the relation between that class and others. For history,
> the object to be discovered is not the mere event, but the thought expressed in it. To
> discover that thought is already to understand it.'[36]

Closer to the ambit our specific enquiry, Alan Watson has argued for the critical
influence of legal traditions as transmitted by lawyers in the shaping of the law.[37]
But Watson warns against uni-causal explanations, particularly when he concludes
that the conditions for legal change may be reduced to nine factors, namely source
of law, pressure force (an organized person who or group which believes that a
benefit results from a practicable change in the law), opposition force (an organized
person who or group which resists such change), transplant bias (the receptivity
of a system to a particular outside law), law-shaping lawyers, discretion, the generality factor (the greater the generality factor in a proposed change, the greater
the difficulty of finding agreement in the appropriate rule and hence the greater

---

35  Hobsbawm at 63.
36  *The Idea of History* (1946) at 214–15.
37  *The Making of the Civil Law* (1981).

the difficulty of effecting change), inertia in favour of the status quo, and felt needs by the pressure force which outweigh the inertia factor. These factors all interact with each other and out of this process of interaction emerges some sense of understanding. As Watson says:

> '[T]he legal history of a particular country is bound up with the societal pressures for legal change and the forces that opposed change. But an exclusive focus on the history of one legal system fails to give due weight to what that system has in common with other civilian systems and what separates these from common-law systems. Only by widening the focus can one see how important is the role played by the legal tradition itself in legal change.'[38]

Watson correctly emphasizes the importance of legal elites and legal discourse in the shaping of the law but at the same time his study of the making of the civil law remind us of the need to search widely for our explanations into legal development.[39]

But let us be even more generous and accept the possibility of a pure doctrinal history which looks only internally at the questions posed in the introduction to the book, namely what were the mechanisms that brought about the particular amalgam of common and civil law, and to what extent has this interaction shaped that various branches of the law? The work fails even if assessed purely in terms of this objective.

Each of the chapters analysed in this work may well describe the interaction between civil and common but the reader is hardly the wiser as to the mechanisms that gave rise to the precise nature of the amalgamation unless the entire reason can be attributed to 'the vigilance of jurists steeped in the Roman-Dutch tradition such as Kotze and Innes'.[40] Take the chapter on employment. On more than one occasion Jordaan cites a fascinating study on the development of a similar body of law in Australia by Adrian Merritt. Merritt shows how the Australian master and servant legislation played a key role in the development, particularly in the way in which the courts were influenced by this legislation as they gave content to the rights and duties which flowed from the contractual relationship between

---

38  At 189.

39  See also Harold Berman *Law and Revolution* (1983), a work which provides a cogent account of the rise of Roman law, thereby making out a compelling case for the inextricability of the link between external and internal history.

40  At 194.

employer and employee. As a result the 'contours of the "employment" contract had been shaped by six decades of regulation of "employees" in terms of concepts designed in feudal and post-feudal days for servants'.[41]

South Africa had similar legislation. As Albie Sachs has written, master and servant legislation in 1841, 1856 and 1873 was made applicable to all 'masters and servants' regardless of race, although inevitably the latter were black and the former white. The effect of this legislation was that 'the State with its extensive resources could now be called upon to exercise systematically, publicly and on a large scale the sort of control over labour which the farmers had formally exercised haphazardly, in private and on an individual basis'.[42]

While Jordaan does make mention of master and servant legislation and while many of the early cases referred to in his chapter discuss this legislation, there is no attempt to examine the extent to which the conception of the employment relationship advanced by this legislation (repealed only in 1974) might have influenced the reliance on either English law or Roman-Dutch law and, perhaps more significantly, the degree to which the concepts employed by the courts were so shaped.

Some of the contributions come much closer to an exploration of the 'mechanisms that brought about the particular forms of competition coexistence, or fusion which exist in that area of law'.[43] In particular the contributions by Zimmermann on good faith and equity, Lubbe on voidable contracts, Cockrell on breach of contract and Lewis on interpretation of contracts are scholarly analyses rather than pure description and in each case there is a sense of implication of the past for the future. That these chapters do not satisfactorily answer the questions posed in the introduction can probably be explained by the methodologically flawed framework adopted by the editors. To take but one example. In concluding a fine analysis of the development of the law relating to breach of contract, Cockrell refers to the question of the influence of the commercial appropriateness of this area of law to the development of doctrine. He then remarks that there is insufficient evidence to allow for such 'instrumental appraisal'. What a pity that the chapter itself was not extended in scope to canvass this important question!

Similarly, Carole Lewis refers to the diachotomy in the law of contract, in that

---

41  Merritt at 83.

42  *Justice in South Africa* (1973) at 40. One hopes it is not too much to expect that Sachs' work, now no longer banned, will be made part of any legal history course in South Africa.

43  At 4.

'in deciding whether a contract has come into existence our law has moved from *verba* to *voluntas*; from objective formalism to ascertaining real consensus. However, in determining the meaning of a contract we have moved from *voluntas* to *verba*'[44]

In analysing these developments, Lewis suggests that the 'time has now come for an overhaul of the South African approach to the interpretation of contracts,'[45] the object being to reconcile our law of contract with the demands of social justice and fairness. To this I can only say 'Amen' save for posing the question whether an overhaul is needed in circumstances where the principles and concepts of the common law, based on their historical origins and scope, cannot be adapted to do the same job — hence the point (amongst others) of a critical history.

This mammoth book was published at a key moment in our legal history, the introduction of a new constitution which, as acknowledged by the editors,[46] has profound implications for the existing body of law. For this reason alone the dispute about choice of historical methodology has considerable relevance. Admittedly, only the interim Constitution[47] had been passed at the time of publication, but the draft final Constitution had been made public and the editors were aware of its contents.[48] For this reason it is fair to assume that the dramatic significance of both constitutions, but particularly the final Constitution, was in the public domain. While the Constitutional Court had ruled in favour of a verticalist interpretation of the application provision of the interim Constitution,[49] the final Constitution has mandated an audit by the courts of the common law in order to ensure that the rules thereof are in accordance with the spirit, purport and objects of the Bill of Rights. As Zimmermann and Visser observe, '[S]outh African private law will therefore in future be shaped in the image of the Constitution.'[50]

The final Constitution has strengthened this imperative. Section 8 has, Ackerman J's attempt at playing King Canute notwithstanding, swept away the

---

44  At 195.

45  At 216.

46  At 6.

47  Act 200 of 1993.

48  See at 6n27.

49  *Du Plessis v De Klerk (supra)*. Section 35(3) of the interim Constitution (s 39(2) of the final Constitution). See the concerns expressed about this issue by Mahomed DP (as he then was) in *Du Plessis'* case.

50  At 6.

majority finding in *Du Plessis* and has made all our law subject to the Constitution. When a court is seized of a dispute involving private parties, the section sets out a series of steps that form the basis of the inquiry, namely: (1) Is the particular right as guaranteed by the provision in question suitable or appropriate for application to a private dispute? (2) In the determination of the first question, the court must consider the nature of the right and the duty which flows correlatively from such right; (3) Once the court is satisfied that the right does so apply to the dispute before it, it may be able to conclude that the existing common-law applies or, if not, the court must develop the common-law to the extent that there is neither a legislative nor a common-law provision which gives effect to the applicable constitutional guarantee. In the course of this development the court can limit this transmuted constitutional right provided that the limitation can be justified in terms of the limitation provision (s 36(1)).

This is a potentially revolutionary provision. Agreed that the development of constitutional law will be mediated through the common law and further that the requirement of suitability (s 8(2)) will admit into any enquiry questions about autonomy from legal interference;[51] and that the limitation test can serve to dilute the effect of this provision. However s 8 has effectively put our common law on terms so that, in a variety of circumstances, its scope, content and ambition will have to be made congruent with the Constitution. In addition, s 39(2) enjoins a court, even where there is no applicable constitutional provision to be employed in a dispute, to ensure that the common law meets the demands of a society based on dignity, freedom and equality.

At the very least our law will seek to ensure that the exercise of social, political and economic power can be justified on rational grounds and that every rule of the common law is in harmony with the fundamental values of our new constitutional state, namely a society which is grounded in openness and democracy and is committed to the promotion of the values of dignity, freedom and equality. This poses fascinating challenges for our law. It demands of lawyers that they consider the nature of each rule of the common law and whether the particular provision is in harmony with the Constitution. How these rules have developed and what values they promote raise important questions, particularly for those engaged in historical enquiry. Visser had pointed presciently to this very challenge in his earlier article.

---

51  *Du Plessis'* case at para 79.

*'[I]f legal history is written and taught merely to add further justification for current-ly accepted notions it becomes a mundane, sterile activity; but if it is used to reveal alternative structures and ideas that are possible, it can assist in breaking down the restrictive, artificial barriers which every legal system tends to develop.'*[52]

Visser's earlier vision of the role of legal history is somewhat radical when assessed in the light of the constitutional provisions analysed above. In particular, s 8 of the final Constitution does not require 'alternative structures' as much as it does the development of existing common-law concepts to bring the latter into harmony with the Constitution. In this, the new venture finds support from the real doyen of the purist movement in South Africa, J C de Wet, who in 1948 wrote in rela-tion to the debate about legal development:

*'Ons het heel weinig regsinstellings wat werklik modern genoem kan word. Dis waar die reg voortdurend aan die ontwikkel is, maar die ontwikkeling is nie soseer die skepping van nuwe beginsels nie, as die toepassing van bekende beginsels op nuwe verhoud-ings. Ons skrywers het nie geaarsel om subtiliteite te verwerp, en met beroep op natuurlike billikheid die Romeinse reg te vervorm waar dit nie meer deug nie.'*[53]

From an entirely different political tradition, the Austrian theorist Karl Renner, in his almost forgotten text, separated the form of legal institutions from the social functions which they perform. For Renner the social function of the law may dif-fer significantly while the concepts and institutions of the law remain relatively constant. Thus the content of law could and did change, often fundamentally as the economic structure of society changed. This change could be effected by a change in the application of an existing legal concept or by the combination of various legal institutions in different ways. In this context Renner writes:

*'Thus a simple economic category is equivalent to a combination of various legal cat-egories, there is no point-to-point correspondence. A number of distinct legal institu-tions serves a single economic process. They play a part which I will call their eco-nomic function.'*[54]

Both of these tendencies can be illustrated by South African examples. The concept of *boni mores* as employed by the Appellate Division in the *Ewels* case or the con-cept of *bona fides*, described by Zimmermann as 'the most potentially powerful

---

52  Visser at 19.

53  J C de Wet 'Gemene Reg of Wetgewing' (1948) 11 *THRHR* 1 at 5.

54  *The Institutions of Private Law and their Social Functions* (1949) at 57.

agent for bringing equitable considerations to bear upon the law',[55] have a history of response to changing times. Our law is replete with examples of a combination of legal institutions as a response to the changes of economy. To what extent does this help to explain the interaction between civil and common law? To take but one example: although almost totally ignored in *Southern Cross*, there are growing indications of an overlap between public and private law in response to a concern with the exercise of power. Hence the public-law doctrine of legitimate expectations has found its way into the hitherto pristine world of private law.[56]

Of course there is an important comparative literature which should have stimulated certain of the contributions to *Southern Cross* to consider this overlap particularly in the field of contract. In his monumental work *The Rise and Fall of Freedom of Contract*, Phillip Atiyah observes that the importance of the law of contract has declined in three distinct ways, namely the role of contract has declined, free choice as a source of legal rights has waned in importance so that there has been a decline in promise-based liabilities and a concomitant increase in benefit- and reliance-based liabilities, and, thirdly, the manner in which exchange has been effected by means other than contract. As Atiyah concedes, it is the increased importance of the welfare state (written in 1978) which has been at the heart of the decline of the role of contract. Whatever the merits of this argument in the context of the globalization of the 1990s, the point remains that there *is* important work which should assist South African lawyers to examine changing concepts and institutions and the reasons therefore.

An understanding of the historical development of our law, the manner and reasons for the change of content of concept and institution must become part of the intellectual toolkit of lawyers as the legal profession attempts to meet the challenges posed by ss 8 and 39(2) of the Constitution. These sections in essence make two different demands, namely: (1) When faced with an alleged cause of action which is not grounded not on any existing common-law rule or a provision of any statute, a court will, if it is satisfied of the suitability of a constitutional right to the private dispute *in casu*, have to explore the nature and scope of the relevant common-law rules to test their applicability and if there is a need to develop the common law then as set out above, adapt existing common-law material to

---

55  *Southern Cross* at 239.

56  See, for example, the significant work of Martin Brassey in the area of labour law: in particular, see M S M Brassey 'The Common Law Right to a Hearing before a Dismissal' (1993 ) 9 *SAJHR* 177.

that end; (2) Where there is no applicable constitutional provision, a court faced with a dispute between two private parties shall develop the relevant common law so that it is congruent with the fundamental constitutional values of human dignity, freedom and equality.

The previous categories of private and public are breaking down, even in countries where there is a written constitution.[57] In short, the design of *Southern Cross* at this time of legal development reflects a previous mindset. It is also illustrative of the importance of narrative and it argues in law. *Southern Cross* reflects what Robert Cover would have termed 'the dominant narrative', and it argues that South Africans were fortunate to be bequeathed such a narrative.

In accomplishing these tasks a court will need to examine the very essence of the existing common law. If the concepts that make up the body of South African law have altered in response to the great social and economic developments since they were originally sourced, the nature and explanation for such change can well assist in the process of mediating the new constitutional commitments with the existing body of law. One area where that possibility arises, partly owing to the influence of contemporary legal scholarship is in the area of property law where both André van der Walt[58] and Carole Lewis[59] have questioned the absolutist concept of ownership within our law. In this work the possibility is raised of a development away from the absolutist conception, developments which, he argued, could be justified in terms of Dutch and German law. Lewis and Van der Walt have therefore afforded South African lawyers the opportunity of questioning the absolutist position of ownership, thereby allowing a historical examination to point the way forward in the direction of employing the concepts of limited interests in our law to meet justified competing claims. In this way existing concepts of property can be employed in the new constitutional context, an approach which is in sharp contrast to the almost entirely descriptive chapter on ownership by John Milton which appears in *Southern Cross*, representing traditional ideas of property law.

South Africa faces something of a legal revolution if the provisions contained

---

57  See, for example, the recent decision of the House of Lords in *O'Rourke v Cambden LBC* [1997] 3 WLR 86 (HL) in dealing with the question of when a private right of action arises from a breach of a public-law duty.

58  (1992) 8 *SAJHR* 431.

59  1985 *Acta Juridica* 241.

in ss 8 and 39(2) are to be taken seriously. But it is a limited revolution in the sense that the intention of the Constitution, as gleaned from a holistic reading of it, is to have the justification and supervision of the exercise of power, even where sourced in private hands, accomplished through the provisions of our common-law. In many cases that will mean a dramatic rejection of precedent, although probably no more so than some of the changes documented in *Southern Cross*. In particular the fundamental values as contained in s 39(2) will impose substantial demands. After all, the values of freedom, equality and dignity are not always easily reconciled. Isaiah Berlin, influential in the Constitutional Court's thinking on freedom,[60] argued in his essay 'Two Concepts of Liberty' that although freedom was in essence a negative value, that is freedom from restraint, there were good grounds for restricting freedom as he defined the concept. Hence it could be justified that citizens should be taxed so that others should be fed and housed; but such a justification could not be found in the muddled concept of positive freedom but rather in another competing value such as equality. It may well be that the competing values are more easily reconciled in a society based on communitarian values, such as to be found in African philosophy and views of society. Indeed, the concept of *ubuntu* was central to the vision which inspired the interim Constitution and the trans-formation of African values into our private law is a matter requiring careful analysis.

This investigation into the core values of the Constitution becomes central to the development of the common law. For this reason an historical investiga-tion into the key assumptions of the common law, and in particular how far embed-ded the common law is in an individualistic set of assumptions about society, is fundamental to an enquiry about the appropriateness of the existing body of common law to a society to be built in the image of the Constitution as understood in terms of the content given to these values.

Viewed in this light, *Southern Cross* must be judged a failure. It provides little in the way of an understanding of the 'heterodoxy of the forces determining the structure of legal thought as well as the variety of effects that the law produces in social reality'.[61] Much of the explanation, if any, rests on the background of the pre-siding judge.[62] Unfortunately the key chapter on the judiciary contains no more than

---

60  *Ferreira v Levin NO; Vryenhoek v Powell NO* 1996 (1) SA 984 (CC).

61  Visser in *Essays on the History of Law* at 21.

62  See, for example at 194, 239ff, 694ff; in particular, see the 'goody' vs 'baddy' theory in relation to Jansen JA and Joubert JJA at 256 and 314.

a cryptic set of biographical details so that the true value of this mode of enquiry cannot be tested. Further, the impact of the new Constitution appears in the minds of few of the authors and then only enigmatically. The majority of the contributions provide little assistance in a constitutional audit of private law.

In short, *Southern Cross* is less a history and far more a celebration of the accommodation of civil and common law into one system. Arguably for this reason it appears to present our legal system as representative of an onward progression, a history which shows a narrative of the timelessness of our legal principles and of continuity, albeit with a few corruptions and lapses along the journey. Accordingly, the presentation of the material offers little guidance for the challenges that lie ahead.

The opportunity to examine the proposition regarding the universal nature of legal concepts where content, not concept change has been wasted. Even a casual reading of this book shows that all too many South African lawyers do not laugh with Unger at those who identify with the ancient legal priests. As disturbing for the users of the critical lens as this book may be, perhaps more disturbing has been the way in which the most talented of the younger brigade of lawyers hold on to the previous intellectual paradigm. Mention has already been made of Fagan's enthusiasm for ordinary language. In the context of this chapter mention can be made of an unpublished paper by Alfred Cockrell on the impact of the Bill of Rights on private law. The ink on the interim Constitution was hardly dry and Cockrell had employed his extraordinary legal talent to argue in favour of the narrowest application of the Constitution to private law. As could be expected, the article was carefully researched and eloquently written, but it represented a clear choice for a parsimonious Constitution and a clarion call in favour of the 'majesty' of the 'timeless' common law. The words admitted of different interpretations, as the various judgments in *Du Plessis v De Klerk*[63] revealed. A choice had been made in the formulation of what proved an important source for the verticalist debate and it is that choice which informs *Southern Cross*.

But the imperative for a constitutional mandate will remain a vital need for careful enquiry. As an advocated solution, the Renner approach — that concepts remain constant and content changes — is by no means widely accepted. For example,

---

63   *Supra.* For the record, I find Cockrell's work on private law to be of considerable benefit in the development of the problem, hence my disappointment at his approach to the interim Constitution.

in his recent work, Jurgen Habermas has written of the shifting basis of law. He argues that the concepts of Roman law serve to define negative liberties of legal subjects to secure the property and commercial intercourse of private people., whereas the republican concept of politics necessitates law which assists in the promotion of community. In the context of a constitution which promotes a case for the development of community, the veracity of this division becomes a major question in any reflection on the state of South African law.[64] So the blockbuster might be dismissed as another Hollywood disaster, and forgotten. Alas, *Southern Cross* is not so easily forgettable. It represents a particular vision of legal development and legal education in South Africa. Ironically, some of the distinguished contributors to the book would most certainly not share this vision, one which wants 'business as usual', which would construe the provisions of ss 8 and 39(2) of the Constitution as narrowly as possible in order to preserve the majesty of a vision of the common law which is conveniently presented as timeless so that, all too often, even the Renner approach of constant form/varying content cannot be tested. The fact that public law is not shown in this production is arguable testimony to a vision of law and society in which the public and private are rigidly separated and power is a problem only when government is involved.

There is a battle to be fought around the nature of legal development in this country. It is an intellectual and political engagement, the outcome of which will go some way to shaping law in this country. If the agenda of the editors of *Southern Cross* and their supporters wins in the legal academies, the danger could well be that the political pressure to develop a society which is committed to an attempt, at the very least, of reconciling the fundamental constitutional values with the common law will result not in the dramatic development of our common law but rather in its rejection. If so, the protagonists of the approach which runs through the design of *Southern Cross* will have helped to destroy far better than they could imagine. In this context *Southern Cross* is an extremely important work, for it represents what at this moment is a dominant strain in academic life and hence an argument with which the transformative vision of ss 8 and 39(2) will be confronted.

*Southern Cross* is about law under the pre-constitutional era. It constitutes an elegant description of a seamless web. Fagan, who was charged with giving 'context' to the doctrine, correctly notes that 'the typical description of the growth of a European system of law in Southern Africa as a somewhat smooth and seamless

---

64   See, for example, Habermas 'Human Rights and Sovereignty' 1994 *Ratio Juris* 1.

process has tended to obscure the extent to which that growth paralleled the establishment of a more general European hegemony'.[65]

In short, we should thank whoever we consider to have supernatural power over our world for the great gift of this universal system that has come from a jurisprudential Sinai (perhaps the Dutch East India Company might be in with a meaningful claim!). Content and concept are rolled into one to constitute an irresistible object against deconstruction. But the very challenge posed by the Constitution points in the other direction.[66] If our legal system is to contribute to the establishment of an open and democratic society based on human dignity, freedom and equality, we need to test the very roots of every concept that has functioned in our system. Follow the scholarship promised in *Southern Cross* and it will lead to a continuation of legal business as usual.

In another context, admittedly, but of relevance to the project intimated by s 8 of the Constitution is the following argument of Nicola Lacey, namely:

> '[T]here is a powerful argument for broadening the horizons of critical legal theory to encompass the tracks and sidings. This would allow a wider conception of legally relevant practices in the search for glimpses of empathy for and recognition of the Other and hence for insight about how to weaken the arbitrary, excluding and hierarchical in the operations of legal power. It would also give us a more acute appreciation of the continuing exclusions inherent in institutional changes with rosy theoretical credentials.'[67]

We need to examine our private law to find those exclusions, whether in individualistic notions of contract or property, the arbitrary conceptions of compensation in delict, the lack of rationality and openness in the exercise of private power of the insurer or the necessity for justifiable balance between democratic deliberation and dignity. These are the challenges posed by a society which aspires to be open, caring and egalitarian. *Southern Cross* purports to be work which seeks both to contribute to the understanding of the Western legal tradition generally and to produce a doctrinal history of South African private law in particular. In so doing it has reinforced the prevailing form of private-law scholarship which

---

65 At 33.

66 Not to say that this challenge has been picked up by all constitutional commentators. See, for example, the way in which De Waal and Currie in De Waal et al *The Bill of Rights Handbook 1998* (1998) argue that the new Constitution will make little difference to the law relating to restraint of trade or to the dominance of freedom of contract, even where such power is directed toward a racist end so that equality as a principle must give way. (at 37 and 52).

67 *Unspeakable Subjects* (1998) at 163.

has constructed Chinese walls between 'doctrine' and 'societal forces'[68] and, implicitly, at the very least has left academic private lawyers ill equipped to meet the challenges posed by the new Constitution.[69]

More recently there has been some scholarship which captures much of the idea set out by Unger. In a profound contribution to a conference dealing with the limits of the law of obligations, the very same Alfred Cockrell has engaged with the problem of second guessing the parties to a contract.[70] He notes that though there is no established doctrine to justify a general doctrine of second guessing an exercise of contractual power, there are certain 'propointers', including the doctrine of *arbitrium boni viri*, that is, the reasonable decision[71] and the doctrine of reasonableness.[61]

On a more general level the courts have given jurisprudential direction to these discrete concepts by the use of the doctrine of good faith. In this way Jansen JA in *Tuckers Land and Development Corporation (Pty) Ltd v Hovis* found a doctrine of anticipatory breach existed in our law. As he stated, 'there appears in any event to be no real difficulty in ascribing such an obligation to flow, by operation of law, from the *bona fides* underlying contractual relations in our law'.[73] In similar fashion Smalberger JA employed the concept of public policy to find that 'agreements that are clearly inimical to the interests of the community, whether they are contrary to law or morality or run counter to social or economic expedience will accordingly on the grounds of public policy not be enforced'.[74]

---

68  *Southern Cross* at 5–6.

69  Perhaps the best contemporary example of the effect of this form of scholarship on legal development is the neglect which the judgment of Cameron J in *Holomisa v Argus Newspapers Ltd* 1996 (2) SA 588 (W) has suffered. In his judgment, Cameron J used s 35(3) of the interim Constitution to construct a new form of defence against an action for defamation which, in certain circumstances, would permit a newspaper to publish a falsehood in respect of political activity unless the plaintiff can show, in the circumstances, that the statement was unreasonably made. In this same judgment Cameron J provides a superb example of how to re-examine existing delictual concepts and to shape them in the legal image of the Constitution. Once legal writing refuses to build the analytical mechanism to engage in such exploration, it is small wonder that the jurisprudence ossifies into a celebration of the timeless.

70  The conference has now been published in 1997 *Acta Juridica*. Cockrell's contribution is published as 'Second-guessing the Exercise of Contractual Power on Rationality Grounds' 1997 *Acta Juridica* 26.

71  See, for example, the decision in *Benlou Properties (Pty) Ltd v Vector Graphics* 1993 (1) SA 179 (A).

72  See, for example, *Boland Bank Bpk v Steele* 1994 (1) SA 259 (T).

73  1980 (1) SA 645 (A) at 651.

74  *Sasfin (Pty) Ltd v Beukes* 1989 (1) SA 1 ( A) at 8.

From this Cockrell has shown that there is a significant strand in our law which is prepared to justify curbs on unbridled exercises of power. As he points out, the Constitution now provides a sounder legal foundation to expand and deepen this approach, for

> '*a constitutional right to equality which applies … in the horizontal realm must be respected by a contractor in the exercise of a contractual power such that a failure to respect that right would render the exercise of power liable to judicial second-guessing on constitutional rationality grounds*'[75]

The constitutional mandate to infuse all our law with the values of freedom, equality and dignity will inevitably have a profound effect on private law, the 'bitter-einders' who still dominate academic life notwithstanding. Freedom cannot be abstracted from equality to produce a justification for unbridled autonomy which in the contractual context is an invitation to exercise superior power to destroy any form of reciprocity which lies at the heart of the contractual relationship. Simultaneously the value of equality cannot be expanded to destroy voluntary behaviour. Accordingly, when confronted with an apparently irrational contract the courts need to behave carefully. But where one party, albeit of a formally private nature, possesses the kind of social power similar to a public body, and seeks to foist an interpretation on a contract that would have the effect of destroying the legitimate contractual expectations of one of the parties, the position should change. Then the interventionist strand within our constitutional value schema must take hold. This position had indeed been put forward as the basis of the principle of good faith derived *ex lege* by Van Huysteen and Van der Merwe prior to the Constitution as follows: '[a] contractant is … entitled to have his expectation protected, not because he himself regarded it as part of *bona fide* conduct, but because his expectation conforms with what the law regards as such between contracting parties'.[76]

It will be argued that the attempt to employ the doctrine of good faith in the field of contract is a nonsense if it presupposes a contradiction in terms, namely an altruistic model of contract. But good faith is far less about altruism and substantially about reconciling self-interest or, as Adams and Brownsword put it: 'the pursuit of self interest is permissible only so long as it is compatible with the

---

75  Cockrell at 48.

76  'Good Faith in Contract: Proper Behaviour amidst Changing Circumstances' (1990) 1 *Stellenbosch Law Review* 244 at 248.

legitimate interests of others (most proximately, the legitimate interests of one's fellow contracting party, but also the legitimate interests of third parties)'.[77]

One of the concerns that some private lawyers express with the constitutional influence on private law is the latter's potential to destroy a system that has borrowed the best from the Continent and Britain, a point made often in *Southern Cross*. Indeed, an eminent colleague, upon reading my critique of *Southern Cross*, complained that were my 'obsession' with the Constitution's influence on private law to hold sway, South Africa would develop a legal system wholly inappropriate to the challenges of globalization and its constraints upon the scope for nation states to develop their own legal responses to socio-economic challenges in their society!

The value-laden nature of such comments aside, the manner in which ss 8 and 39(2) of the Constitution were drafted is testimony to the need to develop fresh content for old legal concepts rather than attempting the revolutionary response of rejecting even the concepts which are central to much of Anglo-European private law. In a creative response to this issue, Hugh Collins argues in favour of the discovery of analogous branches of the law in which a particular issue has been addressed already. As Collins says, the idea 'does involve the adoption of loose analogies, such as the comparison between the position of third party beneficiaries of contracts and claims for pure economic loss in tort. It also involves the instrumental use of principles and concepts derived from one subsystem in another in order to further an intended policy objective'.[78] As an example, Collins refers to the law relating to negligent misrepresentation and the way in which developments in this field, following upon *Hedley Byrne and Co Ltd v Heller and Partners Ltd*,[79] can be used to justify and develop the legal imposition of a duty of care to counteract imbalances of information within the contractual context. So legal change does not need to be radical in that it can come about by means of the use of concepts that exist currently in the law and where they have been used in a similar context. In this way doctrines from public law such as legitimate expectations employed in cases dealing with private bodies such as jockey clubs and stock exchanges, the delictual concept of wrongfulness used to balance autonomy with intervention or in the case of defamation, balancing the personal right to privacy against the collective

---

77  J Adams and R Brownsword *Key Issues in Contract* (1995) at 215.

78  'Learning between the Doctrinal Subsystems of Contract and Tort' 1997 *Acta Juridica* 55 at 65.

79  [1964] AC 465 (HL).

interest in freedom of expression can all be employed in the context of protecting contractual interests.

In contrast, much of the balance of the contributions to the conference simply fail to explore these challenges. A reversion to the old appears to be too powerful a force! Thus Annél van Aswegen ends an analysis of the contractual–delictual divide by informing us that 'an increasing overlap between the two is apparent and freely accepted, which indicates that the traditional paradigms are becoming increasingly blurred'.[80] But the divide still exists primarily, it would appear from her argument, because the distinction conforms in broad terms to the main tenets of the classical view. '… The law of contract regulates voluntarily assumed relations between parties to a contract … while the law of delict consists of generally applicable rules of conduct regulating fortuitous relations between strangers'.[81] Van Aswegen, is of course, correct in all these conclusions, yet there is no attempt to explore what effect the Constitution of 1996 will have on the *laissez–faire* assumptions which underpin this divide or to examine how values affect conceptual legal development.

But if Van Aswegen stops at the threshold, Hutchison and Van Heerden do not even recognize the path to such a threshold. They are concerned that a blurring of the delictual–contractual divide will require:

*'the distortion of well-established principles of either delict or contract, depending on how one labels the action. In our opinion any such step should have to be preceded by a thorough consideration of all its implications for the legal system as a whole'.*[82]

The purists ride again save that their purism is not aimed at the preservation of Roman-Dutch law in its pristine 18th-century innocence but rather at a fixed content to our present body of private law. Ideological influences are ignored because, after all, the law is pure and hence the Constitution should be left to the murky quarters inhabited by public lawyers, rather than create a nuisance for private lawyers.

At least these contributions have the advantage of coherence. The prize for the most vehement but confused exposition of the dinosaurian position must go to P J Visser, who, while observing that the *boni mores concept* will retain its status

---

80   'The Concurrence of Contractual and Delictual Liability for Damages: Factors Determining Solutions' 1997 *Acta Juridica* 75 at 96.

81   Van Aswegen at 92.

82   Dale Hutchison and Belinda van Heerden 'The Tort/Contract Divide seen from the South African Perspective' 1997 *Acta Juridica* 97 at 119–20.

'as an agent in shaping and improving the law of delict to deal with new challenges '[argues] that it will in its future development be influenced by the bill of rights'.[83] So far so good. But a few sentences later Visser writes:

> 'the more delictual principles are transformed through the agency of constitutional law, the greater the danger that the law of delict may lose its distinct character as a part of private law. Such a drastic change could hardly have been the intention behind the adoption of a Bill of Rights. The current law of delict is the result of developments spanning thousands of years in order to achieve a just legal balance between various interests by providing remedies when specific requirements are met.'[84]

Two fundamental objections to this approach should suffice. First, if the content of core concepts such as *boni mores* and *bona fides* in our private law are incongruous with the fundamental values of our Constitution, then they must be 'transformed' precisely because laws, however long they have been in existence, which do not promote a society based on dignity, freedom and equality have no place in post-apartheid South Africa.[85] *En passant*, the idea that the content of legal concepts has remained static for thousands of years represents an anti-history of a kind not even found in *Southern Cross*.

Secondly, and related to the first objection, is the problem of the veracity of the proposition that the law of delict as Visser would preserve it contains remedies that have achieved a correct balance between competing interests. As an illustration of the problems inherent in this claim, Visser could have referred to an article in the same issue of the journal in which his contribution was published. There J W G van der Walt showed compellingly how the German law of defamation

---

83   P J Visser 'The Relevance of the Bill of Rights in the Field of Delict' 1998 *TSAR* 530 at 535.

84   Visser at 536.

85   A thoughtful contribution to the debate is to be found in L Hawthorne 'The Principle of Equality in the Law of Contract' (1995) 58 *THRHR* 157, where the author, unlike the majority of contributors to either *Southern Cross* or the *Acta Juridica* colloquium, is prepared to examine how the present law of contract is based on a market vision of egotistic individuals, each of whom wishes to maximize his or her self-interest and how the constitutional imperative in respect of equality insists that the distributive consequences of the bargain be taken into account. By taking this imperative seriously the doctrines of duress, undue influence, good faith and *boni mores* can all be invoked to shape a law of contract that is more in harmony with the values of the Constitution than in the law heralded by all too many private lawyers. It is astonishing that the trumpeters of comparative law in this country have rarely (to my knowledge never) engaged with arguably the most compelling analysis of the value-laden nature of the 'neutral' dominant model of contract of Robert Hale. See, in particular, 'Bargaining, Duress and Economic Liberty' 1943 *Columbia Law Review* 603; *Freedom through Law: Public Control of Private Governing Power'* (1952). See also N Duxbury 'Robert Hale and the Economy of Legal Force' (1990) 53 *Modern Law Review* 421 and Duncan Kennedy *Sexy Dressing etc* (1993) Ch 3.

represented a republican example of reinforcing a deliberative democracy whereas the jurisprudence of the Appellate Division before the introduction of the Constitution was 'a privatist law of defamation that would strengthen the hand of a totalitarian government'.[86] Accordingly, the notion that the law of delict was in a pristine state prior to the Constitution which should, for that reason, give this area of law as wide a berth as possible, is not justified. Once one concedes the need for a constitutional audit of such law, Visser's desire for legal apartheid between private law and the Constitution becomes unsustainable.

So the challenges posed by Cockrell and Collins as to how to deconstruct our legal assumptions and then to develop conceptual mechanisms to render our private law congruent with the promise of the Constitution are effectively spurned by the main body of academic scholarship — after all, business must continue as usual!

The resistance to the demands of transformation has most recently come from a new liberal quarter in the form of two Borkian inspired Americans who have returned to their corporate roots after plying their new liberal wares as clerks in the Constitutional Court. In a recent contribution, Sprigman and Osborne[88] have mounted a spirited defence of the verticalist position as set out in *Du Plessis v De Klerk (supra)*. Taking account of the difficulty of reducing complete incoherence to some form of meaning, it would appear as if the two authors contend that s 8 of the final Constitution can be read to sustain a similar indirect position to that adopted by the majority in the *Du Plessis* case. The entire argument appears to represent a determined effort (to put it in its best possible light) to ignore the difference between interpretative development as indicated by s 39 and direct constitutional cause of action. The approach advocated in this work, which draws upon the earlier work of Cheadle and I, is for the mediated approach in which the justification for the cause of action is to be found in the Bill of Rights, but the form of the cause of action is sourced in the common law. Were Sprigman and Osborne to be correct, there would be a conflation between the meaning of s 8 and s 39 to such an extent that the former would be *pro non scripto*.

The reason given for this extraordinary exercise in textual amnesia can be found in the article. Like their intellectual paterfamilias, Bork, these two United States

---

86   J W G van der Walt 'Truth and Public Interest in German Defamation Litigation against the Media' 1998 *TSAR* 483 at 493. In fairness Van der Walt does argue that there were developments prior to *Pakendorf v De Flammingh* 1982 (3) SA 146 (A) in which the courts adopted the approach eloquently summarized in the article.

88   (1999) 15 *SAJHR* 25.

lawyers wish to resist the model of constitutionalism. Direct rule (whatever that may mean — probably in the style of Henry Hyde!) constitutes the favoured approach.[89] Distrust of the unelected judiciary is the real problem for our Wall Street friends. Horizontality would require too difficult a balancing exercise between competing rights as if this problem would never occur in the case of vertical disputes. Accordingly, the two retired clerks write that 'by requiring that the values of the constitution be mediated through the actions of the representative branch of government, the inclement counter-majoritarian effects of judicial review may be mitigated, and the promise of an 'open and democratic society … may be progressively realised'.[90] How, precisely, is this mediation to take place? Who is to ensure that the values of the Constitution will effect private power? Rhetoric aside, we are never informed. The essential problem with this new-liberal agenda is that it wishes away the effects of private power — an astonishing sleight of hand in a world where the clients of Osborne's Wall Street firm are often more powerful than nation states. (I have classified Sprigman and Osborne's intervention as new-liberal, being short-hand for an ideological position sourced in a desire to immunize private power from the imperative of justification.) This view, either deliberately or otherwise, refuses to draw a distinction between autonomy into which sphere the law and state should not interfere and the arbitrary exercise of power, whether sourced publically or privately. The straw person argument about the Orwellian state derives directly from the refusal to make this distinction. In brief, the range of privacy rights focuses upon protecting a domain of autonomy for each individual in society. It is this range of rights that acts as a protective shield for the unique identity and personal choices of each person without prescribing to them. The creation of enabling conditions for individual autonomy requires that power from whatever source does not destroy such conditions. That the constitutional exercise requires a recognition of this difference and hence compels a process of balancing is what complicates the exercise. Sprigman and Osborne offer an easy solution — wish the relationship away!

Relationships of an economic and social nature are fundamentally affected by the law — particularly in a society ravaged by apartheid. The very point of s 8 of the Constitution is to ensure that private law is rendered congruent with the Constitution and its values. Were we to maintain only the vagueness of the radiating

89  At 42–4.

90  At 50.

effect of s 39, a legal apartheid between private and public law would operate as in the past and private power could continue to be exercised in the same capricious, arbitrary fashion. Sprigman and Osborne can complain, as does the IMF, about the 'pernicious myth' that their argument is sympathetic to *laissez-faire*, but the criticism remains justified for as long as they wish private power to be exercised in an unfettered fashion. Indeed, their very enterprise is directed to water down the egalitarian commitments of the Constitution by a studious misreading of s 8 and ignorance of the socio-economic and cultural rights and the substantive commitment to equality contained in Chapter 2. Only in this way can they assert that 'it is misleading to claim that the 1996 Constitution is essentially egalitarian or essentially libertarian. It is both, and neither.'[91] Apparently not even these authors have the chutzpah to claim that the Constitution is libertarian: the argument that the Constitution is but an exquisite act of neutrality is the best comfort they can offer their corporate and ideological chums.

There is, however, an even more ominous aspect to the Sprigman/Osborne intervention. The last sentence of their article reads as follows:

> *'there is a pungent irony in the fact that those who claim to be personally committed to a progressive social and economic agenda, a the very moment when the legislature is for the first time firmly in the hands of the majority of South Africans, would so energetically advocate a massive enlargement of judicial power'.*[92]

Leaving aside the understandable ignorance of the Yuppie wing of Wall Street, when it comes to South African history and the centrality of constitutionalism to the struggle (certainly from the time of the African claims and the Freedom Charter), this opportunistic attempt at tarring opposition with the racist brush is deeply disturbing. It represents a form of closure — the constitutional model is not to be the subject of contest in that any attempt to debate whether South African democracy has gone further than a majoritarian model is met with the cry of 'racism!'. During the apartheid era, closure in legal circles was effected by arguing that any alternative to the dominant legal model was not part of legal science but a communist attempt to pollute law with politics. Now, racism is employed to achieve the same result. Perhaps one should not be surprised that this has occurred, for the last thing the new (and old) bourgeoise would want for South Africa is

---

91   At 43.

92   At 51.

a social-democratic constitution which transforms the very legal framework that currently underpins their favoured framework!

On the conceptual level, the analysis can also be attacked for its conventional model of judging. If the process of judging is seen as reflective of white middle-class males, then the judiciary will remain imprisoned in a limited, regressive perspective. But, if the judiciary reflects the full diversity of society, the possibility is opened for an enlargement of perspective in which power is subjected to broader analysis and the culture of justification can be sourced in the best aspirations of society seen in its diversity rather than as a white (or black) middle-class male unity.[93]

# THE SUPREME COURT OF APPEAL AND THE IMPACT OF THE CONSTITUTION

The Supreme Court of Appeal has indicated that, although business cannot continue as of old, the Constitution will continue to exist in the shadows of the common law. In *National Media Ltd v Bogoshi*[94] the court faced a constitutionally inspired argument directed at overturning its repressive jurisprudence of defamation actions against the media.[95] In rejecting the earlier approach to press freedom in the *Pakendorf* case,[96] Hefer JA said on behalf of a unanimous court:

> 'If we recognise, as we must, the democratic imperative that the common good is best served by the free flow of information and the task of the media in the process, it must be clear that strict liability cannot be defended and should have been rejected in Pakendorf. Much has been written about the 'chilling effect of defamation actions but nothing can be more chilling than the prospect of being mulcted in damages for even the slightest error.'[97]

---

93  See, in general, Hannah Arendt *Lectures on Kant's Political Philospohy* (1982); Jennifer Nedelsky 'Embodied diversity and the Challenges to Law' (1997) 42 *McGill Law Review* 93.

94  1998 (4) SA 1196 (SCA).

95  The jurisprudence of the Appellate Division (as the court was then called) during the leadership of Chief Justices Rumpff, Rabie and Corbett may well come back to haunt our developing democracy. See, in particular, the parsimonious approach to press freedom in the judgment of Corbett CJ in *Argus Printing and Publishing Co Ltd v Esselen's Estate* 1994 (2) SA 1 (A) at 25.

96  *Supra.*

97  At 1210.

The court held that the publication of defamatory material will not be considered to be unlawful if it is found on the facts that it was reasonable to publish the particular report in that way and at that time.[98]

Having so found, the court, almost as an afterthought, reverted to the Constitution. Relying on the Canadian decision of *Hill v Church of Scientology of Toronto*[99] the court interpreted s 35(3) of the interim Constitution to represent a constitutional confirmation that the common law should be developed incrementally to comply with the fundamental values of society, as currently encapsulated in the Constitution. On this basis Hefer JA held that the proper approach to the Constitution was to develop the common law in the time-honoured manner of incrementalism and then decide whether such law was compatible with the Constitution; as the decision in *Bogoshi* had achieved a proper balance, as compelled by the Constitution between freedom of expression and the right to dignity on the basis of the common law, there was no need for further consideration of any constitutional questions.

On the line of reasoning adopted by Hefer JA the Constitution will generally be irrelevant. The advocated approach amounts to this: common law will be developed incrementally in terms of the changes necessary to render the law compatible with current societal values. Once the result has been achieved, the court should examine the compatibility of the result with the Constitution. But as the current societal values are contained in this Constitution (or in the evolving interpretation of it which in itself is permeated by the values of the society at the time of such interpretation), the procedure advocated by Hefer JA at best represents a jurisprudential sleight of hand. The advocated approach can be examined in terms of the following two alternatives: if the starting point is to examine the existing principle of the common law in the light of 'current societal values', then it is clear that the common law has to be audited in terms of the spirit, purport and objects of the Constitution. If the approach of the court is that the principles of the common

---

98  At 1212. The judgment itself is extremely confusing. It appears that the appellants relied upon exception sourced in wrongfulness, but the court concentrated on the fault requirement. Hefer JA justified this approach thus: 'The third defence raises the question of fault, albeit in the framework of lawfulness.' Whatever this oblique passage may mean, it is regrettable that the court did not use the concept of wrongfulness as did Cameron J in *Holomisa* to marry the constitutional commitment to freedom of speech with its common law of defamation, that is, by the employment of the concept of *boni mores*. See *Holomisa (supra)* at 617E.

99  (1995) 126 DLR (4th) 129 (SCC).

law are immanent and that the court discovers them, then the *Pakendorf* court must have possessed a poor team of discoverers whose discovery was cherished by the Appellate Division — and, indeed, some of the same personnel for more than a decade!

The claim that the common law is discovered in its pristine immanence is the jurisprudential equivalent of the claim that Father Christmas lives in Lapland! Once this legal fiction gives way to the obvious starting point for analysing judicial development, namely the variety of influences which concentrate upon the judge hearing the case and fashioning the law, it follows that the common law is shaped by judges and not by immanence. Values therefore play a significant role in this process. In the present context it follows that the Constitution and the values contained in it are crucial to these developments. To pretend otherwise is to preserve a fiction that makes the discovery of the justification of the judgment only all the more problematic.

Cynics reading *Bogoshi* would be tempted to ask whether the outcome would have been the same had we not had a Constitution. By adopting this approach, the court in *Bogoshi* encourages this cynicism, for instead of acknowledging the role of the Constitution in the development of the common law, it pretends that the former is unnecessary, thereby providing no guidelines as to how the law should be developed in harder cases to be decided during the constitutional era.

Perhaps more disturbing is its reliance on Canadian precedent in that the Canadian approach is based on the assumption that 'the Charter represents a restatement of the fundamental values which guide and shape our democratic values and our legal system'.[100] As this work has attempted to embrace the quite obvious point that our law is so inextricably linked to our repressive past, as so eloquently illustrated by the law relating to press freedom in particular and to defamation in general, the 'business as usual approach' to the common law may well not be appropriate; hence the need for a careful examination, as a starting point, of all of our common law to ensure that the cancer of 300 years of racism and sexism has not grown into the body of the law.

That leads to the further inquiry as to the law's compatibility with the Constitution. In his judgment in *Holomisa*, Cameron J observed that 'when the Appellate Division assessed the importance of free speech in relation to defamation, South

---

100 *Church of Scientology (supra)* at 156.

Africa's system of government was one of racial oligarchy. To say this is not to score an inexpensive point. Governmental processes previously neither required nor welcomed the adjuncts of free expression and critical discussion, and our legal system did not treasure at its core a democratic ideal.'[101] *Bogoshi*, for all its correct result, is an unimpressive start by the Supreme Court of Appeal partly because of its attempt to downplay the importance of the Constitution and partly because of its refusal to engage in the methodology of an audit which would provide guidance to all courts as to the manner in which our common law should be approached.[102] To pretend that the legal system, including the common law, was not fundamentally affected by the cancer of apartheid is clearly to suffer from the disease of social amnesia. To advocate an audit of the legal system which is based on the immanence of the common law which, properly discovered, is, by pure happenstance, compatible with the Constitution is to continue to develop a legal system devoid of intellectual integrity.

## CONCLUSION

The final Constitution represents, arguably, the most ambitious municipal constitution to have emerged since World War Two. In particular it seeks to infuse all South African law with the spirit of its fundamental values so that the legal system can promote a society based upon human dignity, freedom and equality. It seeks to cut the present system from the Gordian knot of a *laissez-faire* framework dressed up as a universal truth.

But, for all these promises, the reality is very different. Legal scholarship has followed the old public private divide and the constitutional implications are relegated to a separate section of the argument without any appreciation of the manner in which the Constitution should challenge the very assumptions on which the present system is predicated.

Legal traditions prove to be resilient and when reinforced by structural design

---

101 At 604H.

102 In his judgment, Hefer JA rejected the finding in *Holomisa* that the onus was upon the plaintiff to prove the unreasonableness of the statement which was based upon 'an excessive importance attached to the freedom of expression relating to free and fair political activity' (at 1217H). Hefer JA did not accept that reputation may have to give way to freedom of speech. Therefore he placed the onus on the defendant, thereby adopting a parsimonious approach to freedom of political speech which is directed to the attainment of a deliberative democracy.

they can last a whole lot longer. When the negotiations for a new constitution took place in the early 1990s, it was understandable that a new court should be created to interpret and enforce the Constitution — hence the birth of the Constitutional Court. However, the final Constitution insisted that the justification of power, wheresoever sourced, lay at the centre of its ambitions. Legal apartheid was no more. For this reason it is clearly untenable to have both a highest court for non-constitutional matters, the Supreme Court of Appeal, and an ultimate authority for the Constitution, namely the Constitutional Court.

To date the record reveals that the intellectual and conceptual apartheid between 'law' and the Constitution is still alive. Obviously, a merging of the two courts will not be an immediate panacea. But as the courts rise to the new challenge, they will force the academics to come into the constitutional era, a development which the works reviewed in this chapter reveal has hardly happened.

# CONCLUSION

'We, the people of South Africa,
Recognise the injustices of our past;
Honour those who suffered for justice and freedom in our land; ...
We therefore, through our freely elected representatives, adopt this
Constitution as the supreme law of the Republic so as to —

Heal the divisions of the past and establish a society based on democratic values,
social justice and fundamental human rights; ...'

## NEW ALPHABET

If you say A you must say B
A is always against apartheid
B is colour-blind

I want to write you brother but you're further
than the last century than a motherland
than a poem or document

If you say A you must say B
A is always against apartheid
B is colour-blind

so many guides leave me in the lurch
from so many sides I more or less try
to approach you — the more garments I cast off
how colder around me further how further you seem to be

If you say A you must say B
A is always against apartheid
B is colour-blind

My eyes can't get enough of these drowsy thorn trees
between red-grass and plovers my thread-thin legs
my garden smudged with roses — only for my
children I lay down my life.

here I learn to write — I cannot do otherwise[1]

---

1  Antjie Krog *Lady Anne*.

This work has been concerned with an enquiry into the interpretative challenges posed by the constitutional era which commenced in 1994. In its judgment given in the first case heard before it, the Constitutional Court said this about its work:

> '... we are concerned with the interpretation of the Constitution, and not the interpretation of ordinary legislation. A constitution is no ordinary statute. It determines how the country is to be governed and how legislation is to be enacted. It defines the powers of the different organs of state ... as well as the fundamental rights of every person which must be respected in exercising such powers.'[2]

The court has also warned that '[i]f the language used by the lawgiver is ignored in favour of a general resort to "values", the result is not interpretation but divination'.[3] The court has also laid down some substantive markers. Thus in *S v Shabalala* it observed that the Constitution

> 'retains from the past only what is defensible and represents a radical and decisive break from that part of the past which is unacceptable. It constitutes a decisive break from the culture of apartheid and racism to a constitutionally protected culture of openness and democracy and universal human rights for all South Africans of all ages, classes and colours ... the relevant provisions of the Constitution must therefore be interpreted so as to give effect to the purposes sought to be advanced by their enactment.'[4]

What are we to make of these dicta and how should lawyers deal with a text that is directed towards a radical break from the past? Kentridge AJ in *Zuma's* case is concerned that judges do not lose focus in their zeal to parse the text with a transformative lens and dispense with the need to engage with the words of the text. In that he is clearly correct. The words of the text represent the constraint, but within this constraint a number of possibilities for analysis arise. Clearly the analysis developed in this book is one that does not pretend to be value-neutral. Indeed, this work has sought to insist that engagement with the text is not simply a problem of access to the nearest available dictionary. Legal texts use language — even textualists should find that an acceptable proposition. But language is not a neutral medium and how much more so is this the case when locutionary and illocutionary

---

2    *S v Makwanyane* 1995 (3) SA 391 (CC) at para 15, *per* Chaskalson P.

3    *Per* Kentridge AJ in *S v Zuma* 1995 (2) SA 642 (CC) at para 20.

4    1996 (1) SA 725 (CC) at para 26.

elements are so linked as they must be in the language employed by law. For this reason the nature of a legal text and the interpretation of it cannot be unhinged from a moral and political contest.[5]

From this it is understandable why legal judgement becomes so contested but creative an excercise. As Derrida reminds us:

> 'for a decision to be just and responsible, it must, in its proper moment if there is one, be both regulated and without regulation; it must conserve the law and also destroy it or suspend it enough to have reinvented in each case, rejustify it, at least reinvent it in the reaffirmation and the new and free confirmation of its principle'.[6]

In other words, the process of constitutional interpretation is about engagement with a set of prefigured principles possessed by the interpreter. According to Derrida, the inscription of an idea (in this case a legal development) requires a level of force; the more powerful the animating idea, the less force is required. However, any development in law will require some measure of force. Within the context of this argument, I am less concerned with questions which concern post-modernist linguistic theorists and more about the inevitability of value-centred Constitutional jurisprudence. Denied or admitted, the jurisprudential output of the Constitutional Court (and the High Court) involves such a process. My objective, however, has been to examine the words of the directions that this engagement has taken since the introduction of the Constitution.

One clearly defined direction which has been adopted by both Kentridge AJ and Ackermann J is to position the Constitution within the context of a minimal state and a clearly defined zone of autonomy.[7] At the risk of crudity through brevity, one can say that this approach sees the freedom guaranteed in the Constitution as the prevention of individual action through the intervention of some external force. It is this assumption which animates the conclusion that private power and constitutionalism have no common cause and that a constitution exists to ring-fence state interference, and that motivates an unqualified embrace of negative liberty.

---

5   I employ the concepts of J L Austin *How To Do Things With Words* (1965). I am truly indebted to Johan van der Walt and Derek van der Merwe, who reminded me of the importance of Austin to legal theory (H L Hart knew a bit about the influences which were important in shaping legal theory). See 1998 *Acta Juridica* at viiff.

6   Jacques Derrida 'The Mystical Foundation of Law' 1990 *Cardozo Law Review* 945 at 961.

7   See, in particular, Kentridge AJ in *Du Plessis v De Klerk* 1996 (3) SA 850 (CC) and Ackermann J in *Du Plessis'* case as well as in *Ferreira v Levin NO; Vryenhoek v Powell NO* 1996 (1) SA 984 (CC).

But, as I have argued, the key to the societal image that our Constitution embraces is that a post-apartheid society cannot be constructed if individual liberty without equality and dignity remains the sole concern. The Preamble makes that clear. Apartheid, which is this Constitution's Other, forced millions to live in conditions of dependence on the authority of a racist state and the discretionary power of large private bodies. Conditions of dependence constrain freedom and therefore such conditions require societal attention if each individual is to be able to claim freedom.

In short, the debate between Ackermann J's understanding of liberty and that which has been advocated turns on a political view of society. As Quentin Skinner has written in response to one of Berlin's *Four Essays on Liberty*:

> *'Berlin takes himself to be pursuing the purely neutral task of showing what a philosophical analysis of our concepts requires us to say about the essence of liberty. But it is striking ... that his analysis follows exactly the same path as the classical liberal theorists had earlier followed in their efforts to discredit the neo-roman theory of free states.'*[8]

It is this very same argument that fuels my reservations at Denise Meyerson's most thoughtful application of the work of Rawls to the challenges facing South African constitutionalism.[9] At the heart of the original position, and indeed the overlapping consensus, is a fundamental assumption that the fact of excluding knowledge of one's class, intelligence, wealth and gender is sufficient to allow a person a real understanding of what it means to be part of a disadvantaged group. But this assumption is open to major doubt. A person's perspective on life is deeply shaped by class, race, gender, sexual orientation. Thus, as Fredman observes:

> *'It is impossible to reach a full understanding of the concerns of those in positions of disadvantage simply by positing a position of ignorance. This can only genuinely be achieved by incorporating members of such groups into the decision-making process.'*[10]

---

8   Quentin Skinner *Liberty before Liberalism* (1998). This section of this conclusion has been heavily influenced by Skinner's excavation of the earlier foundations of liberty before Hobbes placed a rival concept on the agenda.

9   *Rights Unlimited* (1997).

10  Sandra Fredman *Women and the Law* (1998) at 24. There are, of course, a number of additional objections that can be raised against Rawls. In particular the stark individual premise from which the theory commences means that it is the life of the citizen rather than citizenship of a community or the community that is the heart of the enterprise. This raises questions about whether the commitment of justice to citizens in the public sphere is worth systematically less to those who are prepolitically disadvantaged: Nicola Lacey *Unspeakable Subjects* (1998) at 58.

It is precisely this conflation of difference that allows for the construction of a theory which suggests the discovery of an uncontested process and conclusion of reason and which supports a view that, while the new state 'may never limit our rights in the name of intractably disputed beliefs, or beliefs to which reasonable citizens are not obliged to accord any weight', it is possible to arrive at a neutral approach to the application of the limitation inquiry mandated by s 36(1) of the Constitution.[11] But this conclusion is unsustainable precisely because the reason being employed to sustain it needs to ignore the fundamental differences sourced in the differing concerns referred to earlier. Meyerson's own argument suggests equivocation: at one point, when referring to the need for a principled limitation jurisprudence, she writes of the requirement that any limitation of a right be justified in terms to which all reasonable people would accord some force.[12] That is hardly a startling claim; nor is it a basis for a neutral approach. To understand another viewpoint is not to make of it something which is neutral.

Constitutional contest takes place against the relief of justified but differing perspectives. Hence, while I accord Meyerson's conclusion more force than that of Ackermann J in that Rawls is more in keeping with the constitutional vision as I see it than is Ackermann J's application of Berlin, I would still conclude that the former vision, if implemented, would, on balance, be an unreasonable approach.

If one were to source an argument in 'Oxford' theory, Raz might well prove a better bet. In writing of constitutional rights, he says that fundamental liberal rights deserve special protection and recognition because they express values that should form a part of morally worthy political cultures.[13] This statement becomes more significant when it is read in conjunction with his conclusion that liberalism espouses a conception of the good life which emphasizes the existence of a public culture and the provision of public goods and services in order to promote the realization of autonomy.[14] In short, the state is not neutral between conceptions

---

11  Meyerson *Rights Unlimited* (1997) at 171.

12  Meyerson at 168.

13  Joseph Raz *The Morality of Freedom* (1986) at 262.

14  Raz Chs 5 and 14. At 410ff Raz provides a most illuminating analysis of the relationship between freedom and autonomy. He argues that a person is autonomous when she pursues the good as she perceives it. In short, 'autonomy means that a good life is a life which is a free creation' (at 412). Viewed within the context of value pluralism, this envisages a multiplicity of valuable options from which to choose. A society committed to dignity, freedom and equality must protect and promote the conditions for the attainment of all these options. In such a society the idea that there is one outcome of the application of reason, even in the form of an overlapping consensus, is highly questionable.

of good. Neutrality, whether dressed up as the nightwatchman state or as the reason of individuals that combines to produce the neutral state policy, is illusory, whether it be located in political theory or constitutional law.

If the quest for neutrality,[15] even in the modest manner set out by Meyerson, fails, is any constitutional enterprise possible? I have tried to show that there is such a possibility. It exists in the acknowledgement of contest rather than in the pretence of moral universalism or in the attempt at closure of deliberation. It is to be found in a culture which insists that each interpretation is subject to a requirement of justification and to the analysis and critique by all sections of the population. It is the submission of the determination of key normative questions which go to the heart of society to the possibility of deliberation that sustains the constitutional enterprise rather than the straitjacketing of all these questions into a prescribed rule of reason.[16]

It is the attempt to seek the holy grail of neutrality that drives the recourse to ordinary language theory, and it is for these reasons that I have differed with Fagan's recourse to that theory.[17] If there is an animating theme behind both my resistance of closure and the Constitution, it is the conviction in the value of deliberation as the animating foundation for sustainable democracy. In this context it is perhaps helpful to refer to the work of Amartya Sen, which reveals the importance of deliberation. Sen has shown that freedom of speech may be the precondition for having many of the social and economic rights in our Constitution that are animated by the principle of equality. As he writes 'no substantial famine has ever occurred in any country with a democratic form of government and a relatively free press[18] ... political freedom in the form of

---

15  Meyerson (at xxvii) suggests that it is possible to find standards which are legally authoritative because they make the most moral sense and that their discovery avoids the trap of 'undue subjectivity' in the interpretative process.

16  See, in general, Frank Michaelman 'Do Human Rights need Democratic Legitimation?' (unpublished paper, December 1996); Jurgen Habermas *Between Facts and Norms* (1997) at 60ff.

17  My analysis should not be construed as an 'anything goes' view of adjudication. It is, however, a recognition of (in)determinacy in which judges will be required to justify their decisions. Instead of the old war cry 'the word compelled me to this conclusion', the reader of the judgment will be able to make an assessment of judicial responsibility which gave rise to the judgment. As Alan Hutchinson ('A Postmodern's Hart' (1995) 58 *Modern Law Review* 798 at 814) has said, 'sceptical judges understand that their institutional duty is best fulfilled by taking stands on particular rules and being accountable for those choices.'

18  Amartyn Sen 'Work and Rights' (paper presented to the International Labour Conference, 15 June 1999) at 16.

democratic arrangements help to safeguard economic freedom … and the freedom to survive'.

But if constitutional lawyers should recognize the opposite end of the interpretive spectrum, this requires some clear articulation of an animating vision by the courts. It is in this area that my critique of equality should be located. As Kriegler J said in *The President of the Republic of South Africa v Hugo*:[19]

> '[T]he South African Constitution is primarily and emphatically an egalitarian constitution … in the light of our particular history, and our vision for the future, a constitution was written with equality at its centre. Equality is our Constitution's focus and its organising principle.'

If this proposition held true of the interim Constitution, it is an even more accurate reflection on the final Constitution. Apart from all the references to equality that appeared in the former text and a strong equality provision in s 9, s 7(2) imposes clear obligations upon the state, namely that the state must respect, protect, promote and fulfil the rights in the Bill of Rights. In short, the 1996 Constitution sets up a model in which the state is enjoined to do more than ring-fence activity within which individuals have quiet space. It is required to make an active contribution to the creation of a society in which all can pursue their rights without the burdens of dependency that characterized apartheid society.[20]

Viewed within this context, the task of equality jurisprudence is not to ignore difference or to pretend its non-existence, but rather to structure relations of equality between South Africans within a clear context of different forms of

---

19  1997 (4) SA 1 (CC) at para 74.

20  Jennifer Nedelsky ('Reconceiving Rights as Relationships' (unpublished paper 1992) at 10) makes an observation that is of significance to the South African context, namely:'… human interactions to be governed are not seen primarily in terms of the clashing of rights and interests, but in terms of the way patterns of relationship can develop and sustain both an enriching collective life and the scope for genuine individual autonomy. The whole conception of the relation between the individual and the collective shifts; we recognise that the collective is a source of autonomy as well as a threat to it.' See also Raz (at 415): '[G]overnments should promote the moral quality of the life of those whose lives and actions they can affect.' To the question of whether the government should interfere only on the narrow basis of prevention of harm, Raz suggests a reinterpretation of the harm principle 'according to which it is a principle about the proper way to enforce morality … the principle is derivable from a morality which regards personal autonomy as an essential ingredient of the good life, and regards the principle of autonomy , which imposes duties on people to secure for all the conditions of autonomy, as one of the most important moral principles'.

inequality.[21] For this reason, Sachs J captures much of the concept within the Constitution when he writes:

> '*Equality is not to be regarded as being based on a neutral and given state of affairs from which all departures must be justified. Rather equality is envisaged as something to be achieved through the dismantling of structures and practices which unfairly obstruct or unduly attenuate its enjoyment.*'[22]

But this statement of approach has not been carried through into the content of the judgments examined in this book. By conflating dignity and equality the court has given equality a decidedly individualistic spin. The consequence of this approach is well illustrated in the judgment of O'Regan J in *Harksen*,[23] who relies less on dignity and more upon disadvantage as a guiding principle to ground her analysis in an examination of the position of the group against whom discrimination was directed — in this case married women. Unlike the majority judgment in *Harksen*, which follows the individualistic approach using dignity as the key signpost, O'Regan J comes far closer to an understanding of the structures of discrimination which prevent the existence of transformed relations structured on the basis of equality.[24]

A further and perhaps even more disappointing aspect of the court's approach to equality to date is its failure to give any content to s 9(1),[25] the general guarantee of equality before the law and equal protection before the law. At best, equality has become an anti-discrimination clause; at worst, it is a subset of dignity. We await a comprehensive vision of equality that seeks to ground equality jurisprudence within the transformist vision of the Constitution as set out in this work.[26]

---

21  Nedelsky at 26.

22  *The City Council of Pretoria v Walker* 1998 (2) SA 363 (CC) at para 109.

23  *Harksen v Lane NO* 1998 (1) SA 300 (CC).

24  In developing this critique I have been influenced by the perceptive analysis of equality jurisprudence by Cathi Albertyn and Beth Goldblatt 'Facing the Challenge of Transformation. Difficulties in the Development of an Indigenous Jurisprudence of Equality' (1998) 2 *SAJHR* 248. The authors correctly observe that 'the right to equality is in danger of being defined by the value of dignity rather than the value of equality. The enquiry tends toward a concern with individual personality issues rather than an understanding of systematic issues and social relationships' (at 258).

25  Section 8(1) of the interim Constitution.

26  As Albertyn and Goldblatt note, the conflation of difference and disadvantage serves to de-emphasize structural discrimination and therefore leads the court away from a more transformative reading of the equality right' (at 259).

This analysis of equality leads to the broader question of the effect of the Constitution upon South African jurisprudence in general. In order to examine this question, I first looked at the issue of the application of the Bill of Rights by means of an analysis of s 8 of the 1996 Constitution. Thereafter, I examined a text which, in my view, represents mainstream legal thinking in South African academic life and which is particularly pertinent to the question explored in this book because it was written during the constitutional era.[27]

The South African Constitution rejects the simple dichotomy of state versus individual upon which classical individualist conceptions of the Constitution have been based. As Graber and Teubner have noted recently,

> *'apart from individual spheres of action, there are spheres of social autonomy that need constitutional rights protection against the colonizing tendencies of state politics and that cannot be reduced to mere annexes or derivations of individual autonomy'.*[28]

The Constitution also demanded a change of legal methodology. As noted in this work, the courts have struggled to move out of the dominant approach which has so straitjacketed legal imagination over such a long period.

On occasion these legal techniques raise doubts about the possibility of building a jurisprudence that promotes a deliberative democracy. Illustrative of this possibility is the recent decision of the majority of the Constitutional Court in *The New National Party of South Africa v The Government of the Republic of South Africa & others.*[29] Yacoob J, on behalf of the majority, held that 'courts do not

---

27  For the sake of fairness I should point out that *Southern Cross* was written prior to the conclusion of an agreement on Chapter 2 of the 1996 Constitution and hence the more restrictive application clause of the 1993 Constitution prevailed. However, s 35(3) of the interim Constitution and the possibility of a more generous interpretation of the application clause affords little defence against the constitutionally directed attack against *Southern Cross.*

28  Christoph Beat Grabner and Gunther Teubner 'Art and Money: Constitutional Rights in the Private Sphere?' (1998) 18 *Oxford Journal of Legal Studies* 60 at 66. The authors argue, with reference to the Italian court protecting the film-maker from having his film cut by commercial breaks on TV without his consent, that freedom of art is not primarily related to the unfolding of the artist's idiosyncratic personality, but to the social construction of alternative realities, to the discovery of counterworlds to everyday communication, to the creation of an imaginary world through artistic artefact' (at 67). It is interesting to compare this clause with s 16(1) of the final Constitution, which guarantees freedom of artistic creativity. Viewing this provision within the lens of Grabner and Teubner's argument, it provides another indication of a constitution which is intent on promoting a climate where communication is fostered and closure is frowned upon.

29  1999 (3) SA 191 (CC)

review provisions of Acts of Parliament on the grounds that they are unreasonable. They will do so only if they are satisfied that the legislation is not rationally connected to a legitimate government purpose. In such circumstances review is competent because the legislation is arbitrary.'[30]

For Yacoob J reasonableness is relevant only at the limitation stage. So far there is nothing problematic with this approach. Reasonableness would play a part in the limitation inquiry if it were established that the scheme, while rational, has the effect of infringing a key right, such as the right to vote.

Once the problem of reasonableness is safely relegated to the limitation inquiry to ensure that the issue never goes so far, to the problem that the requirement to vote includes the possession of a new identity document and that evidence existed of departmental inability to provide such documents to all prospective voters, the majority had a complete answer. The time to test the knowledge of Parliament as to whether the department had the capacity to process applications and provide all who were entitled to vote with the relevant document was at the time of the passing of the legislation. As the necessary assurances were obtained from the department, there was no reason to disbelieve there was no justification for holding that irrationality prevailed.

The lone minority judgment of O'Regan J reveals the similarity in approach between this judgment and those in the rather darker days when the trust of the executive constrained review activity. Now review extends to Parliament, but the majority judgment reminds us of the effect of judicial trust of power. O'Regan J was clearly aware that if the matter was left to the limitation stage there would be little left to review. Hence she found that when a court dealt with rights possessing broadly equitable defining characteristics such as free and fair elections or the right to a fair trial or the right to fair labour practices, an inquiry into equity at the threshold is permissible.[31]

Accordingly, when a court is dealing with a right that requires some action to become a right, such as a vote that includes a ballot paper, and a ballot station where the vote can be exercised, the court is entitled to enquire into these arrangements to determine whether the right has been denied. When a court deals with a right as foundational to the entire constitutional state as the right to vote,

---

30  At para 24.
31  At para 123.

it is entitled to demand more of Parliament as the custodian of arrangements for the exercise of the vote than that it should not be arbitrary in its decision to pass the legislative arrangements. The proper approach according to O'Regan J, of the right to vote to be reasonable[32] is to require legislative regulation.

The *New National Party* case may prove to be an exception, a pragmatic approach to ensuring that the election actually takes place. Its potential to encourage the kind of deferential treatment when so crucial a right is at stake is, however, to shine an amber light; the Constitution should insist upon power being justified, not uncritically trusted. O'Regan J's minority judgment eloquently reveals the existence of a cogent alternative and hence compounds the anxiety of a deferential jurisprudence when the hard cases come before the court.

There is a related danger to that which has been illustrated in the *New National Party* case. The Constitution was introduced into a lawless society. As the police continue to convince the public that their incompetence knows no limits and the government responds by fierce verbal threat and silent inaction, the law-and-order lobby has been able to sell its irrational wares to the desperate public. ''ang 'em high', 'lock them up and throw away the key', 'no rights for criminals' has become the order of this lobby. Pressure groups want judges to make way for slot machines so that once a particular crime is committed a fixed sentence must be given irrespective of the facts of the case, the offender or victim. Any judgment that seeks to maintain some rationality in the face of societal brutality is rejected, often without even being read.

None of this should be construed as condoning the savagery that has spread to all parts of our society — the apartheid seeds finally being harvested! But if the Constitution is worth preserving, then the courts need to ensure that the criminal element does not succeed where apartheid left off, namely the violent other becomes hegemonic.

Unfortunately, there are signs that the pressure has begun to tell. In *S v Dlamini & others*[33] the Constitutional Court was required to deal with a range of questions relating to the admissibility of bail proceedings at trial, the test in granting bail, particularly in serious cases. Among the questions with which the court was required to deal was whether s 35(1)(*f*) of the Constitution, which provided that every-

---

32  Para 126.

33  Unreported judgment of the Constitutional Court, 3 June 1999.

one who is arrested for allegedly committing an offence has the right ... to be released from detention if the interests of justice permit, subject to reasonable conditions, trumped provisions of the Criminal Procedure Act, particularly s 60(11A) and (11B), which deals with bail in the context of serious offences.

Kriegler J, on behalf of the court, warns that 'one must be careful to ensure that the alarming level of crime is not used to justify extensive and inappropriate invasions of individual rights'.[34]

The court then engages in an examination of bail in other countries, none of which have our precise constitutional wording and yet their courts jealously safeguard the right to bail, on Kriegler J's own analysis;[35] it concludes by way of assertation rather than any detailed reason that s 60 is a reasonable and justifiable limitation upon rights contained in s 35(1)*(f)*. The judgment is a nod in the direction of pragmatism: crime is rife, we need to help the inept police and to do so will require only a little tweak of the Constitution. Whether this is a fair construction of the judgment's subtext or not, it does represent a fair distance from the principles articulated a few years earlier in *Makwanyane's* case, particularly the view that deterrence starts with detection and apprehension, not with the erosion of the Constitution.

The recognition that the Constitution has to deal with a far broader range of power relationships, including conflicts between individuals and social autonomy, compels a profound re-examination not only of traditional public law thinking, but the whole body of private law. Even before the introduction of the Constitution, there was fleeting recognition of the impact of differing social forces on existing conceptions of the law. For example, in a minority judgment in *Bank of Lisbon and South Africa Ltd*,[36] Jansen JA recognized the importance for the development of contract of the movement from freedom of contract to social responsibility.[37]

It has been the argument of this book that the 1996 Constitution propelled these issues into the foreground of the law. It is not sufficient for legal scholars to throw up their hands at the absence of social justice in the main body of our private law, in a gesture of resignation, and then to hope that the legislature might

34  Para 68.

35  Paras 69–77.

36  1988 (3) SA 580 (A).

37  At 613.

cure some of the more obscene abuses of individual power.[38] The Constitution demands the development of a new jurisprudential alphabet.

Concepts of *boni mores*, *bona fides*, wrongfulness, consensus, *dignitas*, ownership and limited rights of ownership[39] will therefore need to be systemicatically examined within the context of the animating visions of the Constitution. My argument is that the judiciary is compelled to engage with a clearly conceived vision of the fundamental vision of our Constitution to audit all existing law in terms of the new standards.

The old practice in which rules are presented in a pristine manner and all forms of balancing and development are ascribed to 'public policy' rarely receives any content or meaning; hence my concern with *Southern Cross*, which I have sought to analyse as a fine example of how easy it is to be bewitched into believing that an old legal tradition is the way of examining law, so that any other form of thinking can be described as that adopted by 'non-lawyers'.

This kind of thinking refuses to acknowledge that South Africa has experienced a legal revolution. This revolution promises movement away from a culture of authority to one of deliberation and therefore of justification. Whether this revolution remains still-born — which in turn will create ever greater discrepancies between the law and the society to be constructed in the image of the Constitution — will depend to some extent on whether lawyers in the country, including those in the academic community, pretend that as the political transition is over, it is back to legal business as usual.

Much of this form of thinking denies the contest of interpretation, which is not particularly surprising, for such an admission would undermine the culture of authority that it wishes to preserve. To defend the position the ordinary language group who adhere to this approach make a carefully designed move. They argue that law's certainty is inextricably dependent upon the clarity of language employed. Deny the idea that language can provide clarity of answer and one undermines the idea of law, namely that law must be certain. Adhere to the position that language is about contested forms of interpretation and one stands accused of indeterminacy; anything then goes as the judge launches out on her own.

---

38  See Zimmermann in *Southern Cross* at 256.

39  In the context of property see the analysis by André van der Walt *The Constitutional Property Clause* (1997), particularly Ch 2.

The argument of this book is that there is no inevitability that a rejection of ordinary language leads to indeterminacy. The argument has been that while the text requires interpretative work — sometimes of an extensive nature and sometimes of almost a cursory quality — it sets a framework for possible outcomes.

It might be argued that the presence of a limitation clause makes interpretative questions of less importance than is the case with the United States where the absence of such a clause means that all the work including issues of limitation have to be performed at the interpretative stage. However, the provision in s 36(1)(a) that the nature of the right is an important question in testing the limiting provision requires an interpretative engagement of the nature of the right within the constitutional schema.

Although I have made use of Derrida on occasion in this work, it would be incorrect to omit from mention the tendency to reject ordinary meaning and then to have recourse to a post-modernist interdeminacy. While deconstruction of a legal text is useful to illustrate the value-laden approach of the advocates of the culture of authority, it can become an excuse for a form of arcane analysis that squeezes politics out of any such enterprise. Recently it would appear that such approaches have become popular in certain quarters in South Africa.[40] As an example, take this model of clarity by De Ville: 'something is always "unnaturally" excluded, which can, when the text is again interpreted, be included, which can, in turn, affect meaning, ie iterability alters.'[41]

The danger with this kind of approach is that it can lead to an absence of any politics, that is, to an indeterminate game around language. As DeVille comments about another contributor, Van der Walt, 'in order to do justice to the other, exposes the violent economic reductions that take place in law and language without himself imposing/constructing new meaning'.[42]

In a scathing attack on post-modernist scholarship, Terry Eagleton has written that 'American students who … could not recognize class struggle if it perched on top of their skateboards … can vicariously fulfill their generously radical impulses by displacing suppression elsewhere … this move leaves them plunged into fashionably post-modern gloom about the monolithic benightedness of their own social orders'.[43]

---

40  See contributions to the 1998 *Acta Juridica* by Johan van der Walt, Danie Goosen and Jacques de Ville.

41  1998 *Acta Juridica* at 116.

42  At 114. See Johan van der Walt's contribution at 61f.

43  Terry Eagleton 'In the Gaudy Supermarket' (1999) 3 *London Review of Books* 3.

It is possible that a similar tendency is beginning to occur in South Africa — typically as the fad begins to wane in other countries. However, it allows for the veneer of radical scholarship without the danger of embarking into the more disputed territory of the political contests about the nature of law. In some ways it becomes a home for positivists of yore who wish to give politics as wide a berth as L C Steyn advocated some 30 years ago. To return to Eagleton, 'deconstruction like much cultural theory (allows) one to speak darkly of subversion while leaving one's politics slightly to the left of Edward Kennedy'.

Perhaps this post-modernist trickle will become a stream within South African law faculties for it offers the same comfort about non-engagement with the degrading reality of law's implementation (as opposed to its promises) as did the positivist model which has been subject to scrutiny in this book. The argument of this work is that the employment of deconstruction should lead to more fruitful enquiry than playing like Derrida.

Needless to say, democracy and human rights are not the exclusive preserve of lawyers and judges, even in terms of their claim to be the custodians of the constitutional enterprise. However, a developing democratic culture can be supported and strengthened by a wider, more inclusivist, less formalistic notion of law, particularly within the context of a state which possesses such dubious administrative efficiency, as is the case with the current South African state.

The history of South African law was that of a formalism that separated law from politics, the 'civilized majesty' of Roman-Dutch law from the 'prelegal' system of African law, the legal 'philosopher kings' from the balance of the population. The constitutional instruments that formed the basis of the new promise point in another direction. It is with this direction that this book has been concerned. Replacing one formalism with another is merely to substitute one culture of authority with another. The transformation of the law requires an acknowledgment that law and politics cannot be so neatly divided, that the old shibboleth about legal science should be returned to the nearest Pandectist and that the law and its direction are contested. In this way the voices not only of legal scientists will be heard and the law may well contribute to the deepening of deliberation and the enhancement of democracy.

CONSTITUTION OF THE REPUBLIC OF SOUTH AFRICA, ACT 108 OF 1996
## CHAPTER 2 — BILL OF RIGHTS (SS 7-39)

## 7   RIGHTS

(1)   This Bill of Rights is a cornerstone of democracy in South Africa. It enshrines the rights of all people in our country and affirms the democratic values of human dignity, equality and freedom.

(2)   The state must respect, protect, promote and fulfil the rights in the Bill of Rights.

(3)   The rights in the Bill of Rights are subject to the limitations contained or referred to in section 36, or elsewhere in the Bill.

## 8   APPLICATION

(1)   The Bill of Rights applies to all law, and binds the legislature, the executive, the judiciary and all organs of state.

(2)   A provision of the Bill of Rights binds a natural or a juristic person if, and to the extent that, it is applicable, taking into account the nature of the right and the nature of any duty imposed by the right.

(3)   When applying a provision of the Bill of Rights to a natural or juristic person in terms of subsection (2), a court—

    *(a)*   in order to give effect to a right in the Bill, must apply, or if necessary develop, the common law to the extent that legislation does not give effect to that right; and

    *(b)*   may develop rules of the common law to limit the right, provided that the limitation is in accordance with section 36 (1).

(4) A juristic person is entitled to the rights in the Bill of Rights to the extent required by the nature of the rights and the nature of that juristic person.

## 9   EQUALITY

(1)   Everyone is equal before the law and has the right to equal protection and benefit of the law.

(2) Equality includes the full and equal enjoyment of all rights and freedoms. To promote the achievement of equality, legislative and other measures designed to protect or advance persons, or categories of persons, disadvantaged by unfair discrimination may be taken.

(3)   The state may not unfairly discriminate directly or indirectly against anyone on one or more grounds, including race, gender, sex, pregnancy, marital status, ethnic

or social origin, colour, sexual orientation, age, disability, religion, conscience, belief, culture, language and birth.

(4) No person may unfairly discriminate directly or indirectly against anyone on one or more grounds in terms of subsection (3). National legislation must be enacted to prevent or prohibit unfair discrimination.

(5) Discrimination on one or more of the grounds listed in subsection (3) is unfair unless it is established that the discrimination is fair.

## 10 HUMAN DIGNITY

Everyone has inherent dignity and the right to have their dignity respected and protected.

## 11 LIFE

Everyone has the right to life.

## 12 FREEDOM AND SECURITY OF THE PERSON.

(1) Everyone has the right to freedom and security of the person, which includes the right—

   (a) not to be deprived of freedom arbitrarily or without just cause;
   (b) not to be detained without trial;
   (c) to be free from all forms of violence from either public or private sources;
   (d) not to be tortured in any way; and
   (e) not to be treated or punished in a cruel, inhuman or degrading way.

(2) Everyone has the right to bodily and psychological integrity, which includes the right—

   (a) to make decisions concerning reproduction;
   (b) to security in and control over their body; and
   (c) not to be subjected to medical or scientific experiments without their informed consent.

## 13 SLAVERY, SERVITUDE AND FORCED LABOUR

No one may be subjected to slavery, servitude or forced labour.

## 14 PRIVACY

Everyone has the right to privacy, which includes the right not to have—

   (a) their person or home searched;
   (b) their property searched;
   (c) their possessions seized; or
   (d) the privacy of their communications infringed.

## 15 FREEDOM OF RELIGION, BELIEF AND OPINION

(1) Everyone has the right to freedom of conscience, religion, thought, belief and opinion.

(2) Religious observances may be conducted at state or state-aided institutions, provided that—

   *(a)* those observances follow rules made by the appropriate public authorities;

   *(b)* they are conducted on an equitable basis; and

   *(c)* attendance at them is free and voluntary.

(3) *(a)* This section does not prevent legislation recognising—

   (i) marriages concluded under any tradition, or a system of religious, personal or family law; or

   (ii) systems of personal and family law under any tradition, or adhered to by persons professing a particular religion.

   *(b)* Recognition in terms of paragraph *(a)* must be consistent with this section and the other provisions of the Constitution.

## 16 FREEDOM OF EXPRESSION

(1) Everyone has the right to freedom of expression, which includes—

   *(a)* freedom of the press and other media;

   *(b)* freedom to receive or impart information or ideas;

   *(c)* freedom of artistic creativity; and

   *(d)* academic freedom and freedom of scientific research.

(2) The right in subsection (1) does not extend to—

   *(a)* propaganda for war;

   *(b)* incitement of imminent violence; or

   *(c)* advocacy of hatred that is based on race, ethnicity, gender or religion, and that constitutes incitement to cause harm.

## 17 ASSEMBLY, DEMONSTRATION PICKET AND PETITION

Everyone has the right, peacefully and unarmed, to assemble, to demonstrate, to picket and to present petitions.

## 18 FREEDOM OF ASSOCIATION

Everyone has the right to freedom of association.

## 19 POLITICAL RIGHTS

(1) Every citizen is free to make political choices, which includes the right—
  (a) to form a political party;
  (b) to participate in the activities of, or recruit members for, a political party; and
  (c) to campaign for a political party or cause.

(2) Every citizen has the right to free, fair and regular elections for any legislative body established in terms of the Constitution.

(3) Every adult citizen has the right—
  (a) to vote in elections for any legislative body established in terms of the Constitution, and to do so in secret; and
  (b) to stand for public office and, if elected, to hold office.

## 20 CITIZENSHIP

No citizen may be deprived of citizenship.

## 21 FREEDOM OF MOVEMENT AND RESIDENCE

(1) Everyone has the right to freedom of movement.

(2) Everyone has the right to leave the Republic.

(3) Every citizen has the right to enter, to remain in and to reside anywhere in, the Republic.

(4) Every citizen has the right to a passport.

## 22 FREEDOM OF TRADE, OCCUPATION AND PROFESSION

Every citizen has the right to choose their trade, occupation or profession freely. The practice of a trade, occupation or profession may be regulated by law.

## 23 LABOUR RELATIONS

(1) Everyone has the right to fair labour practices.

(2) Every worker has the right—
  (a) to form and join a trade union;
  (b) to participate in the activities and programmes of a trade union; and
  (c) to strike.

(3) Every employer has the right—
  (a) to form and join an employers' organisation; and

*(b)* to participate in the activities and programmes of an employers' organisation.

(4) Every trade union and every employers' organisation has the right—
   *(a)* to determine its own administration, programmes and activities;
   *(b)* to organise; and
   *(c)* to form and join a federation.

(5) Every trade union, employers' organisation and employer has the right to engage in collective bargaining. National legislation may be enacted to regulate collective bargaining. To the extent that the legislation may limit a right in this Chapter, the limitation must comply with section 36 (1).

(6) National legislation may recognise union security arrangements contained in collective agreements. To the extent that the legislation may limit a right in this Chapter the limitation must comply with section 36 (1).

## 24 ENVIRONMENT

Everyone has the right—
   *(a)* to an environment that is not harmful to their health or well-being; and
   *(b)* to have the environment protected, for the benefit of present and future generations, through reasonable legislative and other measures that—
      (i) prevent pollution and ecological degradation;
      (ii) promote conservation; and
      (iii) secure ecologically sustainable development and use of natural resources while promoting justifiable economic and social development.

## 25 PROPERTY

(1) No one may be deprived of property except in terms of law of general application, and no law may permit arbitrary deprivation of property.

(2) Property may be expropriated only in terms of law of general application—
   *(a)* for a public purpose or in the public interest; and
   *(b)* subject to compensation, the amount of which and the time and manner of payment of which have either been agreed to by those affected or decided or approved by a court.

(3) The amount of the compensation and the time and manner of payment must be just and equitable, reflecting an equitable balance between the public interest and the interests of those affected, having regard to all relevant circumstances, including—
   *(a)* the current use of the property;
   *(b)* the history of the acquisition and use of the property;

(c)  the market value of the property;

(d)  the extent of direct state investment and subsidy in the acquisition and beneficial capital improvement of the property; and

(e)  the purpose of the expropriation.

(4)  For the purposes of this section—

(a)  the public interest includes the nation's commitment to land reform, and to reforms to bring about equitable access to all South Africa's natural resources; and

(b)  property is not limited to land.

(5)  The state must take reasonable legislative and other measures, within its available resources, to foster conditions which enable citizens to gain access to land on an equitable basis.

(6)  A person or community whose tenure of land is legally insecure as a result of past racially discriminatory laws or practices is entitled, to the extent provided by an Act of Parliament, either to tenure which is legally secure or to comparable redress.

(7)  A person or community dispossessed of property after 19 June 1913 as a result of past racially discriminatory laws or practices is entitled, to the extent provided by an Act of Parliament, either to restitution of that property or to equitable redress.

(8)  No provision of this section may impede the state from taking legislative and other measures to achieve land, water and related reform, in order to redress the results of past racial discrimination, provided that any departure from the provisions of this section is in accordance with the provisions of section 36 (1).

(9)  Parliament must enact the legislation referred to in subsection (6).

## 26  HOUSING

(1)  Everyone has the right to have access to adequate housing.

(2)  The state must take reasonable legislative and other measures, within its available resources, to achieve the progressive realisation of this right.

(3)  No one may be evicted from their home, or have their home demolished, without an order of court made after considering all the relevant circumstances. No legislation may permit arbitrary evictions.

## 27  HEALTH CARE, FOOD, WATER AND SOCIAL SECURITY

(1)  Everyone has the right to have access to—

(a)  health care services, including reproductive health care;

(b) sufficient food and water; and

(c) social security, including, if they are unable to support themselves and their dependents, appropriate social assistance.

(2) The state must take reasonable legislative and other measures, within its available resources, to achieve the progressive realisation of each of these rights.

(3) No one may be refused emergency medical treatment.

## 28 CHILDREN

(1) Every child has the right—
(a) to a name and a nationality from birth;
(b) to family care or parental care, or to appropriate alternative care when removed from the family environment;
(c) to basic nutrition, shelter, basic health care services and social services;
(d) to be protected from maltreatment, neglect, abuse or degradation;
(e) to be protected from exploitative labour practices;
(f) not to be required or permitted to perform work or provide services that—
(i) are inappropriate for a person of that child's age; or
(ii) place at risk the child's well-being, education, physical or mental health or spiritual, moral or social development;
(g) not to be detained except as a measure of last resort, in which case, in addition to the rights a child enjoys under sections 12 and 35, the child may be detained only for the shortest appropriate period of time, and has the right to be—
(i) kept separately from detained persons over the age of 18 years; and
(ii) treated in a manner, and kept in conditions, that take account of the child's age;
(h) to have a legal practitioner assigned to the child by the state, and at state expense, in civil proceedings affecting the child, if substantial injustice would otherwise result; and
(i) not to be used directly in armed conflict, and to be protected in times of armed conflict.

(2) A child's best interests are of paramount importance in every matter concerning the child.

(3) In this section 'child' means a person under the age of 18 years.

## 29 EDUCATION

(1) Everyone has the right—
(a) to a basic education, including adult basic education; and

(b) to further education, which the state, through reasonable measures, must make progressively available and accessible.

(2) Everyone has the right to receive education in the official language or languages of their choice in public educational institutions where that education is reasonably practicable. In order to ensure the effective access to, and implementation of, this right, the state must consider all reasonable educational alternatives, including single medium institutions, taking into account—

(a) equity;

(b) practicability; and

(c) the need to redress the results of past racially discriminatory laws and practices.

(3) Everyone has the right to establish and maintain, at their own expense, independent educational institutions that—

(a) do not discriminate on the basis of race;

(b) are registered with the state; and

(c) maintain standards that are not inferior to standards at comparable public educational institutions.

(4) Subsection (3) does not preclude state subsidies for independent educational institutions.

## 30 Language and culture

Everyone has the right to use the language and to participate in the cultural life of their choice, but no one exercising these rights may do so in a manner inconsistent with any provision of the Bill of Rights.

## 31 Cultural, religious and linguistic communities

(1) Persons belonging to a cultural, religious or linguistic community may not be denied the right, with other members of that community—

(a) to enjoy their culture, practise their religion and use their language; and

(b) to form, join and maintain cultural, religious and linguistic associations and other organs of civil society.

(2) The rights in subsection (1) may not be exercised in a manner inconsistent with any provision of the Bill of Rights.

## 32 Access to information

(1) Everyone has the right of access to—

(a) any information held by the state; and

(b) any information that is held by another person and that is required for the exercise or protection of any rights.

(2) National legislation must be enacted to give effect to this right, and may provide for reasonable measures to alleviate the administrative and financial burden on the state.

## 33 JUST ADMINISTRATIVE ACTION

(1) Everyone has the right to administrative action that is lawful, reasonable and procedurally fair.

(2) Everyone whose rights have been adversely affected by administrative action has the right to be given written reasons.

(3) National legislation must be enacted to give effect to these rights, and must—

    (a) provide for the review of administrative action by a court or, where appropriate, an independent and impartial tribunal;

    (b) impose a duty on the state to give effect to the rights in subsections (1) and (2); and

    (c) promote an efficient administration.

## 34 ACCESS TO COURTS

Everyone has the right to have any dispute that can be resolved by the application of law decided in a fair public hearing before a court or, where appropriate, another independent and impartial tribunal or forum.

## 35 ARRESTED, DETAINED AND ACCUSED PERSONS

(1) Everyone who is arrested for allegedly committing an offence has the right—

    (a) to remain silent;

    (b) to be informed promptly—

        (i) of the right to remain silent; and

        (ii) of the consequences of not remaining silent;

    (c) not to be compelled to make any confession or admission that could be used in evidence against that person;

    (d) to be brought before a court as soon as reasonably possible, but not later than—

        (i) 48 hours after the arrest; or

        (ii) the end of the first court day after the expiry of the 48 hours, if the 48 hours expire outside ordinary court hours or on a day which is not an ordinary court day;

(e)  at the first court appearance after being arrested, to be charged or to be informed of the reason for the detention to continue, or to be released; and

(f)  to be released from detention if the interests of justice permit, subject to reasonable conditions.

(2)  Everyone who is detained, including every sentenced prisoner, has the right—

    (a)  to be informed promptly of the reason for being detained;

    (b)  to choose, and to consult with, a legal practitioner, and to be informed of this right promptly;

    (c)  to have a legal practitioner assigned to the detained person by the state and at state expense, if substantial injustice would otherwise result, and to be informed of this right promptly;

    (d)  to challenge the lawfulness of the detention in person before a court and, if the detention is unlawful, to be released;

    (e)  to conditions of detention that are consistent with human dignity, including at least exercise and the provision, at state expense, of adequate accommodation, nutrition, reading material and medical treatment; and

    (f)  to communicate with, and be visited by, that person's—

        (i)  spouse or partner;

        (ii)  next of kin;

        (iii) chosen religious counsellor; and

        (iv) chosen medical practitioner.

(3)  Every accused person has a right to a fair trial, which includes the right—

    (a)  to be informed of the charge with sufficient detail to answer it;

    (b)  to have adequate time and facilities to prepare a defence;

    (c)  to a public trial before an ordinary court;

    (d)  to have their trial begin and conclude without unreasonable delay;

    (e)  to be present when being tried;

    (f)  to choose, and be represented by, a legal practitioner, and to be informed of this right promptly;

    (g)  to have a legal practitioner assigned to the accused person by the state and at state expense, if substantial injustice would otherwise result, and to be informed of this right promptly;

    (h)  to be presumed innocent, to remain silent, and not to testify during the proceedings;

    (i)  to adduce and challenge evidence;

    (j)  not to be compelled to give self-incriminating evidence;

    (k)  to be tried in a language that the accused person understands or, if that is not practicable, to have the proceedings interpreted in that language;

    (l)  not to be convicted for an act or omission that was not an offence under either national or international law at the time it was committed or omitted;

*(m)* not to be tried for an offence in respect of an act or omission for which that person has previously been either acquitted or convicted;

*(n)* to the benefit of the least severe of the prescribed punishments if the prescribed punishment for the offence has been changed between the time that the offence was committed and the time of sentencing; and

*(o)* of appeal to, or review by, a higher court.

(4) Whenever this section requires information to be given to a person, that information must be given in a language that the person understands.

(5) Evidence obtained in a manner that violates any right in the Bill of Rights must be excluded if the admission of that evidence would render the trial unfair or otherwise be detrimental to the administration of justice.

## 36 LIMITATION OF RIGHTS

(1) The rights in the Bill of Rights may be limited only in terms of law of general application to the extent that the limitation is reasonable and justifiable in an open and democratic society based on human dignity, equality and freedom, taking into account all relevant factors, including—

*(a)* the nature of the right;

*(b)* the importance of the purpose of the limitation;

*(c)* the nature and extent of the limitation;

*(d)* the relation between the limitation and its purpose; and

*(e)* less restrictive means to achieve the purpose.

(2) Except as provided in subsection (1) or in any other provision of the Constitution, no law may limit any right entrenched in the Bill of Rights.

## 37 STATES OF EMERGENCY

(1) A state of emergency may be declared only in terms of an Act of Parliament, and only when—

*(a)* the life of the nation is threatened by war, invasion, general insurrection, disorder, natural disaster or other public emergency; and

*(b)* the declaration is necessary to restore peace and order.

(2) A declaration of a state of emergency, and any legislation enacted or other action taken in consequence of that declaration, may be effective only—

*(a)* prospectively; and

*(b)* for no more than 21 days from the date of the declaration, unless the National Assembly resolves to extend the declaration. The Assembly may extend a declaration of a state of emergency for no more than three months at a time. The first extension of the state of emergency must be by a resolution adopted

with a supporting vote of a majority of the members of the Assembly. Any subsequent extension must be by a resolution adopted with a supporting vote of at least 60 per cent of the members of the Assembly. A resolution in terms of this paragraph may be adopted only following a public debate in the Assembly.

(3) Any competent court may decide on the validity of—

   *(a)* a declaration of a state of emergency;

   *(b)* any extension of a declaration of a state of emergency; or

   *(c)* any legislation enacted, or other action taken, in consequence of a declaration of a state of emergency.

(4) Any legislation enacted in consequence of a declaration of a state of emergency may derogate from the Bill of Rights only to the extent that—

   *(a)* the derogation is strictly required by the emergency; and

   *(b)* the legislation—

       (i) is consistent with the Republic's obligations under international law applicable to states of emergency;

       (ii) conforms to subsection (5); and

       (iii) is published in the national Government Gazette as soon as reasonably possible after being enacted.

(5) No Act of Parliament that authorises a declaration of a state of emergency, and no legislation enacted or other action taken in consequence of a declaration, may permit or authorise—

   *(a)* indemnifying the state, or any person, in respect of any unlawful act;

   *(b)* any derogation from this section; or

   *(c)* any derogation from a section mentioned in column 1 of the Table of Non-Derogable Rights, to the extent indicated opposite that section in column 3 of the Table.

## TABLE OF NON-DEROGABLE RIGHTS

| 1 | 2 | 3 |
|---|---|---|
| **Section number** | **Section title** | **Extent to which the right is non-derogable** |
| 9 | Equality | With respect to unfair discrimination solely on the grounds of race, colour, ethnic or social origin, sex, religion or language |
| 10 | Human dignity | Entirely |
| 11 | Life | Entirely |
| 12 | Freedom and security of the person | With respect to subsections (1) *(d)* and *(e)* and 2 *(c)* |
| 13 | Slavery, servitude and forced labour | With respect to slavery and servitude |
| 28 | Children | With respect to:<br>— subsection (1) *(d)* and *(e)*;<br>— the rights in subparagraphs (i) and (ii) of subsection (1) (g); and<br>— subsection (1) (i) in respect of children of 15 years and younger. |
| 35 | Arrested, detained and accused persons | With respect to:<br>— subsections (1) *(a)*, *(b)* and *(c)* and (2) *(d)*;<br>— the rights in paragraphs *(a)* to *(o)* of subsection (3), excluding paragraph *(d)*;<br>— subsection (4); and<br>— subsection (5) with respect to the exclusion of evidence if the admission of that evidence would render the trial unfair. |

(6) Whenever anyone is detained without trial in consequence of a derogation of rights resulting from a declaration of a state of emergency, the following conditions must be observed:

*(a)* An adult family member or friend of the detainee must be contacted as soon as reasonably possible, and informed that the person has been detained.

*(b)* A notice must be published in the national Government Gazette within five days of the person being detained, stating the detainee's name and place of detention and referring to the emergency measure in terms of which that person has been detained.

*(c)* The detainee must be allowed to choose, and be visited at any reasonable time by, a medical practitioner.

*(d)* The detainee must be allowed to choose, and be visited at any reasonable time by, a legal representative.

   *(e)* A court must review the detention as soon as reasonably possible, but no later than 10 days after the date the person was detained, and the court must release the detainee unless it is necessary to continue the detention to restore peace and order.

   *(f)* A detainee who is not released in terms of a review under paragraph *(e)*, or who is not released in terms of a review under this paragraph, may apply to a court for a further review of the detention at any time after 10 days have passed since the previous review, and the court must release the detainee unless it is still necessary to continue the detention to restore peace and order.

   *(g)* The detainee must be allowed to appear in person before any court considering the detention, to be represented by a legal practitioner at those hearings, and to make representations against continued detention.

   *(h)* The state must present written reasons to the court to justify the continued detention of the detainee, and must give a copy of those reasons to the detainee at least two days before the court reviews the detention.

(7) If a court releases a detainee, that person may not be detained again on the same grounds unless the state first shows a court good cause for re-detaining that person.

(8)  Subsections (6) and (7) do not apply to persons who are not South African citizens and who are detained in consequence of an international armed conflict. Instead, the state must comply with the standards binding on the Republic under international humanitarian law in respect of the detention of such persons.

## 38  ENFORCEMENT OF RIGHTS

Anyone listed in this section has the right to approach a competent court, alleging that a right in the Bill of Rights has been infringed or threatened, and the court may grant appropriate relief, including a declaration of rights. The persons who may approach a court are—

   *(a)* anyone acting in their own interest;

   *(b)* anyone acting on behalf of another person who cannot act in their own name;

   *(c)* anyone acting as a member of, or in the interest of, a group or class of persons;

   *(d)* anyone acting in the public interest; and

   *(e)* an association acting in the interest of its members.

## 39 INTERPRETATION OF BILL OF RIGHTS

(1) When interpreting the Bill of Rights, a court, tribunal or forum—

    *(a)* must promote the values that underlie an open and democratic society based on human dignity, equality and freedom;

    *(b)* must consider international law; and

    *(c)* may consider foreign law.

(2) When interpreting any legislation, and when developing the common law or customary law, every court, tribunal or forum must promote the spirit, purport and objects of the Bill of Rights.

(3) The Bill of Rights does not deny the existence of any other rights or freedoms that are recognised or conferred by common law, customary law or legislation, to the extent that they are consistent with the Bill.

# INDEX

INDEX

INDEX